AF690557

THE THEORY OF SELF-DETERMINATION

When can a group legitimately form its own state? Under international law, some groups can but others cannot. But the standard is unclear, and traditional legal analysis has failed to elucidate it. In *The Theory of Self-Determination*, leading scholars chart new territory in our theoretical conception of self-determination. Drawing from diverse scholarship in international law, philosophy, and political science, they attempt to move beyond the prevailing nationalist conceptions of group definition. At issue are such universal questions as: When does a group qualify as a "people"? Does history matter? Or is it a question of ethnic status? Are these matters properly solved by popular vote?

Anchored in modern analytical political philosophy but with implications for a wide range of scholarship, this volume will prove essential for scholars and practitioners of international law, global justice, and international relations.

Fernando R. Tesón is the Tobias Simon Eminent Scholar and a professor of law at the Florida State University College of Law. A renowned scholar of political philosophy and international law, he is the author of *Justice at a Distance: Extending Global Freedom* (with Loren Lomasky, Cambridge, 2015) and *Humanitarian Intervention: An Inquiry into Law and Morality* (3rd ed., 2005), among many others. A native of Argentina, he is a founding member of the blog *Bleeding Heart Libertarians*.

ASIL Studies in International Legal Theory

Series Editors

Mark Agrast, ASIL
Mortimer Sellers, University of Baltimore

Editorial Board

Samantha Besson, Université de Fribourg
Allen Buchanan, Duke University
David Kennedy, Harvard University
Jan Klabbers, University of Helsinki
David Luban, Georgetown University
Larry May, Vanderbilt University
Mary Ellen O'Connell, University of Notre Dame
Onuma Yasuaki, Meiji University
Helen Stacy, Stanford University
John Tasioulas, University College London
Fernando Tesón, Florida State University

The purpose of the ASIL Studies in International Legal Theory series is to clarify and improve the theoretical foundations of international law. Too often the progressive development and implementation of international law has foundered on confusion about first principles. This series raises the level of public and scholarly discussion about the structure and purposes of the world legal order and how best to achieve global justice through law.

This series grows out of the International Legal Theory project of the American Society of International Law. The ASIL Studies in International Legal Theory series deepens this conversation by publishing scholarly monographs and edited volumes of essays considering subjects in international legal theory.

Books in the series

The Theory of Self-Determination
Fernando Tesón
Negotiating State and Non-State Law: Global and Local Legal Pluralism
Michael A. Helfand
Normative Pluralism and International Law: Exploring Global Governance
Jan Klabbers and Touko Piipaerinen
Jus Post Bellum and Transitional Justice
Larry May and Elizabeth Edenberg
The Future of International Law: Global Government
Joel P. Trachtman
Morality, Jus Post Bellum, and International Law
Edited by Larry May and Andrew T. Forcehimes
Parochialism, Cosmopolitanism, and the Foundations of International Law,
Edited by Mortimer Sellers

Global Justice and International Economic Law: Opportunities and Prospects
Edited by Chios Carmody, Frank J. Garcia, and John Linarelli
The Role of Ethics in International Law
Edited by Donald Earl Childress III
The New Global Law
Rafael Domingo
Customary International Law: A New Theory with Practical Applications Brian D. Lepard
International Criminal Law and Philosophy
Edited by Larry May and Zachary Hoskins

The Theory of Self-Determination

Edited by

FERNANDO R. TESÓN

CAMBRIDGE
UNIVERSITY PRESS

CAMBRIDGE
UNIVERSITY PRESS

University Printing House, Cambridge CB2 8BS, United Kingdom

Cambridge University Press is part of the University of Cambridge.

It furthers the University's mission by disseminating knowledge in the pursuit of education, learning and research at the highest international levels of excellence.

www.cambridge.org
Information on this title: www.cambridge.org/9781107119130

© Cambridge University Press 2016

This publication is in copyright. Subject to statutory exception and to the provisions of relevant collective licensing agreements, no reproduction of any part may take place without the written permission of Cambridge University Press.

First published 2016

A catalogue record for this publication is available from the British Library

Library of Congress Cataloguing in Publication data
Names: Tesón, Fernando R., 1950– editor.
Title: The theory of self-determination / edited by Fernando R. Tesón.
Description: New York : Cambridge University Press, 2016. | Series: Asil studies in international legal theory | Includes bibliographical references and index.
Identifiers: LCCN 2015034761 | ISBN 9781107119130 (Hardback)
Subjects: LCSH: Self-determination, National | BISAC: LAW / International.
Classification: LCC KZ1269 .T54 2016 | DDC 341.26–dc23 LC record available at http://lccn.loc.gov/2015034761

ISBN 978-1-107-11913-0 Hardback

Cambridge University Press has no responsibility for the persistence or accuracy of URLs for external or third-party internet websites referred to in this publication, and does not guarantee that any content on such websites is, or will remain, accurate or appropriate.

Contents

List of contributors *page* ix

Introduction: The Conundrum of Self-Determination 1
Fernando R. Tesón

1 **Self-Determination and Moral Variation** 13
Bas van der Vossen

2 **The Case for National Self-Determination** 32
Christopher W. Morris

3 **The Right to Self-Determination: Earned, Not Inherent** 45
Frédéric Mégret

4 **The Right to Exist and the Right to Resist** 70
Jens David Ohlin

5 **Self-Determination in Three Movements** 94
Patrick Macklem

6 **Self-Determination for National Minorities** 120
Alan Patten

7 **Self-Determination, Dissent, and the Problem of Population Transfers** 145
Matthew Lister

8 **Civil Disobedience, Dirty Hands, and Secession** 166
Michael Blake

9 **"Mars for the Martians"?: On the Obsolescence of Self-Determination** 184
John R. Morss

10 **The Evolution of Self-Determination of Peoples in International Law** 201
Elizabeth Rodríguez-Santiago

Index 241

Contributors

Michael Blake is Professor of Philosophy and Public Affairs, and Director of the Program on Values in Society, at the University of Washington. He writes on international justice and the ethics of immigration. His most recent book is *Debating Brain Drain: May Governments Restrict Emigration?* (Oxford University Press, 2014), written with Gillian Brock.

Matthew Lister is a lecturer in department of Legal Studies and Business Ethics at the Wharton School of Business, University of Pennsylvania. He earned his PhD in Philosophy and his JD at the University of Pennsylvania. He has taught at Penn Law, Villanova Law School, and the University of Denver Law School, and has been a law clerk at the U.S. Court of International Trade and the Third Circuit Court of Appeals. He writes on immigration, international law, and legal and political philosophy, among other topics.

Patrick Macklem is the William C. Graham Professor of Law at the University of Toronto Faculty of Law. He holds law degrees from Harvard and Toronto, and an undergraduate degree in political science and philosophy from McGill. He served as Law Clerk for Chief Justice Brian Dickson of the Supreme Court of Canada. He is a recurring visiting professor at Central European University. He has been a visiting scholar at Stanford Law School, UCLA School of Law and Harvard Law School, and a Fulbright New Century Scholar. In 2006–2007, he was a Senior Global Research Fellow at the Center for Human Rights and Global Justice at NYU School of Law. In 2007–2008, he was a Member of the Institute for Advanced Study in Princeton, New Jersey. He is the author of *The Sovereignty of Human Rights* (Oxford University Press, 2015) and *Indigenous Difference and the Constitution of Canada* (University of Toronto Press, 2001), and co-editor of *From Recognition to Reconciliation* (University of Toronto Press, 2015), *Canadian Constitutional Law* (Paul Emond, 2010), *Labour and Employment Law* (Queen's IRC Press,

2004), *The Security of Freedom: Essays on Canada's Anti-terrorism Bill* (2001), and has published numerous articles on international human rights law, constitutional law, indigenous peoples, ethnic and cultural minorities, and labor law and policy. He is a Fellow of the Royal Society of Canada.

Frédéric Mégret, PhD, is an associate professor at the Faculty of Law, McGill University. He also holds the Canada Research Chair in the Law of Human Rights and Legal Pluralism and is affiliated with the McGill Centre of the same name. He holds an LLB from King's College London, a DEA from the Université de Paris I, and a PhD from the Graduate Institute of International Studies (Geneva), as well as a diploma from Sciences Po Paris. His work focuses on some of the theoretical dimensions of international law, international criminal justice, international human rights law, and the laws of war.

Christopher W. Morris is Professor of Philosophy and Chair of Department at the University of Maryland. He is a member of the executive board of the Center for Ethics and the Rule of Law, University of Pennsylvania Law School. His interests in political and legal philosophy range over topics concerning state legitimacy and sovereignty, nationalism, imperialism, and premodern forms of political organization. He is the author of *An Essay on the Modern State* (Cambridge University Press, 1998) and recently published an ethics textbook, *Questions of Life and Death: Readings in Practical Ethics* (Oxford University Press, 2011).

John R. Morss was born in London and educated at the Universities of Sheffield, Edinburgh, and Otago. He has held posts in the Universities of Ulster and Otago, and Deakin University, Victoria (Australia). He is a member of the Executive Committee of the Legal Theory Interest Group of the American Society for International Law and of the Coordinating Committee of the European Society for International Law Interest Group on International Legal Theory. He has been Visiting Fellow at the European University Institute, Florence, and at the Lauterpacht Centre for International Law, University of Cambridge. His most recent book is *International Law as the Law of Collectives: Toward a Law of People* (Ashgate, 2013).

Jens David Ohlin is Professor of Law at Cornell Law School. He specializes in international law and all aspects of criminal law, including domestic, comparative, and international criminal law. Ohlin's research also focuses on the laws of war, in particular the impact of new technology on the regulation of warfare, including remotely piloted drones and the strategy of targeted killings, cyberwarfare, and the role of nonstate actors in armed conflicts. In the area of international criminal law, Professor Ohlin concentrates on the application of traditional criminal law theory by international tribunals. He earned a PhD in philosophy and a JD from Columbia University.

Alan Patten teaches political theory at Princeton University. He is the author of *Equal Recognition: The Moral Foundations of Minority Rights* (Princeton University Press, 2014) and *Hegel's Idea of Freedom* (Oxford University Press, 1999). He is the editor of the journal *Philosophy & Public Affairs*.

Elizabeth Rodríguez-Santiago is Assistant Research Professor at the Universidad del Este in Puerto Rico where she conducts her research on international law, specially on self-determination of peoples in colonial and noncolonial contexts and on legal issues relating the Puerto Rican status. She also teaches International Law at the Centro de Estudios Avanzados de Puerto Rico y el Caribe in Old San Juan. In 2012 she received her doctorate in Public International Law from Sorbonne Law School in Paris after defending her dissertation on the subject of self-determination of peoples. Prior to this, and after finishing her BA in Economics at the University of Puerto Rico, she completed the degrees of DEUG, License and Maîtrise (JD equivalent) in French Law, as well as a Diplôme d'Etudes Approfondies (LLM equivalent) in International Economic Law at Sorbonne Law School.

Fernando R. Tesón is the Tobias Simon Eminent Scholar and a professor of law at the Florida State University College of Law. A renowned scholar of political philosophy and international law, he is the author of *Justice at a Distance: Extending Global Freedom* (with Loren Lomasky, Cambridge University Press, 2015) and *Humanitarian Intervention: An Inquiry into Law and Morality* (3rd ed., 2005), among many others. A native of Argentina, he is a founding member of the blog Bleeding Heart Libertarians.

Bas van der Vossen is Assistant Professor in Philosophy at the University of North Carolina Greensboro. His research interests are in political and legal philosophy. His work has appeared in the *Journal of Political Philosophy*, *Law and Philosophy*, *Social Philosophy & Policy*, and the *Oxford Journal of Legal Studies*, among other places.

Introduction

The Conundrum of Self-Determination

FERNANDO R. TESÓN

As I write these lines, Ukraine is beset by turmoil. Ample majorities in Ukraine's Russian-speaking provinces of Crimea, Donetsk, and Luhansk have voted to leave Ukraine and join Russia. Russia welcomed Crimea (the fate of the other two provinces is uncertain), but the annexation was condemned by virtually everyone else.[1] This rejection is largely inconsequential, however. Not only will the world eventually accept the annexation of Crimea, but also, as I write, it watches impotent while Russian troops cross the Ukrainian border.[2] The questions for academics are: Did Crimea have a *right* to secede from Ukraine and join Russia? Was majority vote the appropriate way to implement this right? If Crimea has this right, could California vote by referendum to join Mexico or become independent? What is the nature and basis of the right of collective self-determination (whether or not its exercise leads to secession)? Who has this right and under what circumstances? And what are the consequences for the group and for outsiders?

This volume begins to answer these vexing matters. It has convened international law scholars, philosophers, and political theorists. The purpose of the volume is to present salient aspects of self-determination from the perspectives of law, philosophy, and history.

No other area of international law is more indeterminate, incoherent, and unprincipled than the law of self-determination. When international law (or any legal system, for that matter) establishes a right, it must specify with

[1] For an account of the events, see Alan Yuhas, "Ukraine Crisis: An Essential Guide to Everything That's Happened so Far," *The Guardian*, April 13, 2013, at www.theguardian.com/world/2014/apr/11/ukraine-russia-crimea-sanctions-us-eu-guide-explainer.

[2] Annie Gowen and Karoun Demirjian, "Ukraine Says Russian Forces Cross Border in Tanks, Armored Vehicles," *Washington Post*, Aug. 25, 2014, at www.washingtonpost.com/world/europe/ukraine-says-russian-forces-cross-border-in-tanks-armored-vehicles/2014/08/25/8cb7d1d4-2c3f-11e4-994d-202962a9150c_story.html.

a reasonable degree of certainty three things, if the right aspires to be operational. It must identify the *holder* of the right, it must identify the *content* of the right, and it must specify the correlative *duties* of insiders and outsiders to the group in question.

International law, as it stands at present, is deficient on the three fronts. Let us start with the pertinent international documents. The common Article 1 to the United Nations human rights covenants reads:

> 1. All peoples have the right of self-determination. By virtue of that right they freely determine their political status and freely pursue their economic, social and cultural development.
>
> 2. All peoples may, for their own ends, freely dispose of their natural wealth and resources without prejudice to any obligations arising out of international economic co-operation, based upon the principle of mutual benefit, and international law. In no case may a people be deprived of its own means of subsistence.[3]

The trouble starts in the very first sentence: "all peoples have the right of self-determination." This means that not every population has this right; only "peoples" do. So when is a group a people? It would seem that a people is a bonified group of some sort.[4] For example, arguably the state of Florida is not a people, so it does not have the collective right to vote itself out of the United States. In fact, when the Southern states attempted to secede, the United States federal government prevented it by the sword. But Scotland apparently has such right. Why? Is it because the United Kingdom does not care? What if the British Parliament vetoes Scotland's secession? Or is it because the Scots, unlike the Floridians, are a "people" in the relevant sense? Does international law give the Scots a remedy against the United Kingdom's veto?

International practice has offered two distinct accounts of this issue. The first is an ostensive *historical* definition: "peoples" are *only* the indigenous populations that inhabited the territories in Asia, Africa, and elsewhere that were colonized by Western European powers in the fifteenth through the nineteenth centuries.[5] Uganda, Algeria, India, Mexico, Nigeria, Cameroon,

[3] Article 1, United Nations Covenant on Civil and Political Rights, 1966.

[4] Thus in the *Western Sahara* opinion the International Court of Justice explained why sometimes populations were not consulted in a territory's change of status: "Those instances were based ... on the consideration that a certain population did not constitute a "people" entitled to self-determination." (Western Sahara opinion, 1975, para 59.)

[5] In none of its opinions on self-determination did the Court depart from the restrictive view that only former colonies (and a few territories assimilated to colonies) had the right to self-determination. See, e.g., *Legal Consequence for States of the Continued Presence of South*

for example, are "peoples" in this specific historical sense. These territories were all conquered by Europeans and, under the law of decolonization, their populations have a collective right – the right of self-determination – to terminate the colonial relationship and (usually) become independent. This definition of self-determination, developed during the Cold War, was music to the ears of the Soviet Union, because the territories that the Soviets had conquered, such as the Baltic States, Ukraine, and others, were not (for unclear reasons) colonies in the historical sense. Therefore, the Soviets argued, these populations did not have the right to self-determination. For anyone thinking properly, this argument would not pass the laugh test. However, most governments and lawyers supported the view, not because they thought it was particularly principled, but because they feared that recognizing a broad right to secede would bring chaos. Confining the right of self-determination to the European colonies not only allowed the Soviets to cover for their aggressions: it also allowed other states, including the newly independent colonies who had fiercely supported self-determination for *them*, to prevent, often by force, attempts at secession by their own provinces.[6]

Yet, as I indicated, it does not take much to see how unprincipled this position is. Why did only *some* unjustly conquered populations have the right to break the chains of domination and not others? If India had the right to break away from unjust British domination, so Estonia had the right to break away from unjust Soviet domination. Eventually, the deserved collapse of the Berlin Wall brought with it the equally deserved collapse of this view. Suddenly, all these territories that supposedly did not have the right of self-determination nonetheless exercised that right and became independent. Lawyers, as is their wont, had to readjust to these realities. Gradually, the view that only former European colonies had the right of self-determination gave way to a new view that preserved the idea that a "people" was a bonified kind of population but did not confine it to historical colonies.

This is the *nationalist* view of self-determination. The populations that qualify as peoples are now defined by some kind of *ethnic status*. The separatists in Ukraine, for example, think that a *language* is a defining factor: unlike the rest of Ukrainians, they speak Russian. They appeal, moreover, to a mysterious Russian *ethnicity* as the distinctive factor – this, in territories where

Africa in Namibia (South West Africa) Notwithstanding Security Council Resolution 276 (*Namibia* opinion), International Court of Justice, June 21, 1971, paragraph 52.

6 For a lengthy study on the Soviet position, see Karen Christine Knop, *The Soviet Position on the Right to Self-determination as Applied to Nations Within Existing States* (New York: Columbia University Press, 1990)

the different races have intermingled for thousands of years. A few years before, the South Ossetian and South Akazian separatists in Georgia put forth similar ethnic arguments, this time with a racist overtone: they tried to show that while they were closest to the Russian race, the Georgians were ethnically linked to some other race. Another popular incarnation of ethnic status is *religion*. For Kosovars, being Muslim was the decisive factor in their argument for independence from Serbia. Here, too, religious differences were not enough to set them apart, so Kosovars added for good measure the interesting fact that they, unlike the Serbs, are ethnic Albanians. So being Muslim and Albanian is enough justification for a group to secede from the parent state and take the territory away.

The nationalist conception enjoys considerable support in diplomatic practice and crops up in a variety of diplomatic and judicial pronouncements, although that practice is not uniform. Among philosophers, variations of the nationalist view have been defended by David Miller and by Joseph Raz and Avit Margalit. Miller's view is closest to the more traditional nationalist conception. He claims that a nation, defined by a variety of traits, is the proper holder of the right of self-determination. For Miller, national identity is an important source of personal identity, and nations thus circumscribed have valid reasons to be self-determining.[7] Raz and Margalit have a milder nationalist view: to them, only "comprehensive cultures" have the right to national self-determination.[8] The idea is that living in a comprehensive culture is essential for the well-being of individuals, and providing self-government is a particularly strong way to affirm that comprehensive culture. They offer a few conditions, including the requirement that groups may not be oppressive and must respect the rights of women and minorities. (Why not everyone's rights?)[9]

The nationalist position, however, is plagued by a number of difficulties. The most glaring concerns the status of those members of the population who do not share the ethnic trait in question (race, religion, language, culture). If ethnic status is the foundation of the state, as the nationalist position would have it, then these persons are not, in a moral sense, citizens of the state. They can be legal citizens, of course, but if the reasons that justify X's being a state are ethnic reasons, someone who does not possess the ethnic trait fails to share

7 See David Miller, *On Nationality* (Oxford University Press, 1995)

8 See Avishai Margalit and Joseph Raz, "National Self-Determination," *The Journal of Philosophy* 87 (1990): 439–61.

9 Margaret Moore can be included among supporters of the nationalist view. See Margaret Moore, *A Political Theory of Territory* (Oxford University Press, 2015).

in the reasons that make her a member of X. She is not a member of the "people," since peoplehood is defined by a trait she does not possess. These are the worries, in the United States, that people justifiably raise every time someone proclaims that the United States is a "Christian nation." These statements disrespect Americans who are not Christian. One idea behind the nationalist view of self-determination is a supposed right to be governed by "someone like me." This approach is dangerous because it easily leads to exclusion, discrimination, and ultimately ethnic conflict.[10]

Given these and other difficulties, recent approaches to self-determination have steered away from nationalism. Cara Nine, for example, has suggested that collective entities (including but not limited to states) are the proper holders of the right of self-determination. These collective entities must satisfy some nonethnic conditions, such as sharing a sense of justice.[11] Others have argued that the right of self-determination is always *remedial*: a group has the right of self-determination just in case it has been wronged by the parent state is some way.[12] Finally, some authors have pursued an *individualist* account of self-determination, according to which any analysis of the right of self-determination must be translated without loss of meaning to an analysis of the rights and interests of individuals.[13] These new lines of argument are, to my judgment, philosophically superior to the nationalist view, but, as indicated, the latter is widely accepted in the messy arena of international politics.[14] One reason, I suspect, is that nationalist themes have a stirring appeal moored to romantic notions of popular sovereignty and the desire to shake off foreign domination – real or imaginary.

10 See Fernando R. Tesón, A *Philosophy of International Law* (Boulder, CO: Westview Press, 1998), chapter 5.

11 Cara Nine, *Global Justice and Territory* (Oxford University Press, 2012), 45–50.

12 The concept was introduced by Allen Buchanan in his seminal work on secession. See especially his article "Secession" in the Stanford Encyclopedia of Philosophy, at http://plato.stanford.edu/entries/secession/ (2013). Recently the World Court mentioned remedial secession without addressing it. International Court of Justice, *Accordance with International Law of the Unilateral Declaration of Independence in Respect of Kosovo*, Advisory Opinion, July 22, 2010, paragraph 82.

13 See A. John Simmons, "On the Territorial Rights of States," *Philosophical Issues: Social, Political, and Legal Philosophy*, 11 (2001): 300–26; Hillel Steiner, "Territorial Justice," in Simon Caney, David George, and Peter Jones, eds., *National Rights, International Obligations* (Boulder, CO: Westview Press, 1996); and Fernando R. Tesón, "The Mystery of Territory," forthcoming in *Social Philosophy and Policy*.

14 Christopher Wellman defends a broad, but still collective, right to secede. See Christopher Heath Wellman, A *Theory of Secession: The Case for Political Self-Determination* (New York: Cambridge University Press, 2005). In my view, this approach is superior to the nationalist view as well.

What is the content of the right of self-determination? According to the applicable texts, peoples "freely determine their political status and freely pursue their economic, social, and cultural development." This merits several comments. First, the description uses the adverb "freely" in a curious sense. Here "freely" does not mean "with due regard to individual freedom." Nor does it mean "democratically." The right of peoples to freely determine their economic, social, and cultural development means that that the relevant groups are entitled to do this without *foreign* direction. This is not individual freedom; it is collective freedom, the freedom of a collective from domination by another collective. Second, the meaning of the freedom of a people to pursue its "economic, social, and cultural development" is uncertain. International law and morality place boundaries on the permissible forms of political organization. For example, one would expect that groups may not pursue a development that includes violation of human rights, subjugation of women, or the sheer impoverishment of the population. Alas, this is exactly what has happened in many of these pursuits. The principle of self-determination simply forbids foreigners to *dictate* to a "people" how it should conduct its affairs. If the people conduct those affairs contrary to international law or morality, then this is a separate question. This is the way in which the issue has been understood in international practice. That Idi Amin committed atrocities in Uganda does not mean that it is justified to reinstate British sovereignty over Uganda.

Third, the phrase "political status" means *international* political status. The idea is that the "people" alone can decide whether it should remain with the parent state, join another state, or seek independence. (Recall that the population has to be a "people," whatever that means. Not every province, community, entity, or political group has these options.) Several international documents have specified adult popular suffrage as the proper procedure for the people to express these preferences.[15] However, again, this does not mean that voters have the right to elect their rulers. The right of self-determination is *not* a right to democratic governance (whether international law recognizes this right is a separate question). But this requirement of popular vote is murky. A particularly disconcerting example of a "people's" pronouncement

[15] For example, in 1991 the United Nations Security Council voted to create a Mission for the Referendum in Western Sahara. See UN SEC Res 690, April 29, 1991. But in the Crimea case, the United Nations General Assembly declared the Crimean referendum invalid. See www.asil.org/blogs/general-assembly-adopts-resolution-declaring-crimea-referendum-invalid-march-27-2014. The General Assembly, however, has no legislative or other binding powers. A similar measure brought up in the UN Security council was vetoed by Russia. See www.nytimes.com/2014/03/16/world/europe/russia-vetoes-un-resolution-on-crimea.html?_r=0.

was the recent declaration of independence by the Serbian province of Kosovo. The International Court of Justice, confronting the question, opined that nothing in international law prohibits a declaration of independence. For the Court this had no bearing on the question of secession. In other words, people may declare whatever they want, but this will not have any legal effect on the status of territory one way or the other, because the principles that govern mere declarations differ from the principles that govern secession. For the Court, a group can declare itself independent, or declare itself anything else for that matter, but this will have no legal effect, whether or not it does so by referendum. Referenda are not the same as declarations of independence by some constitutional convention, but the same reasoning might apply: for example, under the Court's reasoning the recent referenda in the Ukrainian provinces might not suffice to establish the annexation of those provinces to Russia. Is this because these provinces are not "peoples"? No one really knows. Applicable principles, then, fail to distinguish between cases such as Kosovo, on one hand, and Crimea, on the other. Perhaps a clean referendum is a *necessary* condition for a population to become independent, even if it is not a sufficient condition. But even this is uncertain, as the independence or merger secured by many territories at one point or another was not preceded by a popular referendum.[16]

This leads us to another difficulty with the principle of self-determination in international law. This is the inconsistency between the right of self-determination and the right of states to keep their territory intact – the principle of territorial integrity. If Crimea has the right of self-determination and Ukraine has the right of territorial integrity, which one should prevail? The answer in international practice is this: whoever wins in the battlefield, literal or political, has implemented the relevant principle. If the government prevails, then territorial integrity has been vindicated. If the secessionists prevail, then self-determination has been vindicated. International law has long recognized the principle of *effectivité*, according to which political realities, effective political power, and territorial occupancy form the basis of international relations. So it does not really matter if the inhabitants of Crimea or Scotland are or are not "peoples." If Ukraine or the rest of the world does nothing about the annexation to Russia, then Crimea will become legally part of Russia and the principle of self-determination would have been vindicated.

16 The transfer or return of Hong Kong to China, for example, was not preceded by a referendum among the inhabitants of the isle. See Hurst Hannum, *Autonomy, Sovereignty, and Self-Determination: The Accommodation of Conflicting Rights* (Philadelphia: The University of Pennsylvania Press, 1990), 129–50.

If, on the contrary (and improbably), Ukraine prevents Crimea from joining Russia, then the principle of territorial integrity would have been vindicated. Under international law, there is no *ex ante* metaprinciple to decide between the two. If Scotland decides by referendum to secede from the United Kingdom and the United Kingdom does nothing, then Scotland will be legally independent. The same position holds for Kosovo, Quebec, Catalonia, and the rest.[17]

We can now see the profound deficiencies in the standard understanding of self-determination. They are at least three. First, because of the principle of *effectivité*, it is not possible to decide *ex ante* if a specific group has a right of self-determination. It can only be decided in the battlefield or in the corridors of politics. Most lawyers (with specious arguments, in my view) affirmed prior to 1990 that Estonia did not have the right of self-determination. When the Soviet Union collapsed, suddenly the Estonians became a self-determining unit. But suppose Estonia and the Soviet Union had appeared before an impartial court *prior* to the Soviet collapse and asked the court's opinion on whether Estonia had the *right* of self-determination. If that court followed international practice, it would have been forced to say: "I don't know. Why don't you fight it out and we'll see?" In my judgment, this is not law but antilaw, where might makes right. A right that can only be implemented by a war between the right-claimant and the right-denier is not a right in any meaningful sense of the word.

Second, the right of self-determination, despite the stirring rhetoric of its advocates, is profoundly illiberal. It is not a right *against* a state but a right *to* a state. It is unconcerned with the legal and moral rights of individuals but is concerned with asserting a new sphere of political power – often more oppressive than the one left behind. It masks the ambitions of political entrepreneurs who claim to represent the "people" regardless of whether or not they have been properly elected, and regardless of the views of minorities and individuals who do *not* want to secede or be autonomous. This might not be a widespread view, but I do not think the preferences of Scots who do not want independence from the United Kingdom are worth nothing. Even in the successful and largely beneficial cases of self-determination, such as the

[17] In the *Kosovo* opinion the Court wrote that states have a right to territorial integrity *only* against other states, not against their own constituent parts. *Kosovo* opinion, paragraph 80. This would mean that in 1861 the United States breached international law when it tried to keep the Union together. This is another startling statement in an opinion that is silly in many regards. One may or may not like states, one may or may not like secessions, but it is well established that, absent persecution, genocide, and similar atrocities, a sovereign state has the authority to oppose dismemberment of its territory.

American Revolution, it is often hard to see the *ex ante* moral justification to secede, other than the fact that the revolutionaries ultimately conquered their independence on the ground.

But the tension between self-determination and liberal principles runs deeper. The idea that collective entities have the right to determine themselves is so rooted in the political imagination and in international law that it may sound farfetched to deny it. Yet, if the right of self-determination means the right of some to forcibly enroll others in their projects, then it should be subject to a more searching philosophical scrutiny that has received so far. In particular, the right of self-determination is vulnerable to a classical-liberal challenge. Let me explain.

Many people think that just as individual autonomy is a value, so group autonomy is a value; just as persons pursue individual projects, so groups pursue collective projects; just as persons seek the private good, so groups seek the collective good. But this analogy does not hold in a straightforward way. Surely groups can have value for their members. Groups can facilitate the achievement of goals that cannot be achieved individually. But this value of groups holds *as long as they are voluntary*. Groups are importantly disanalogous to individuals. An individual has a mind that makes plans and weighs options, alternatives, values, and goals. She may err, of course, but her error will be the result of her considered judgment about how she desires to pursue her personal project, how to lead her life in her own terms. Groups, on the contrary, do not have minds. They are collections of individuals where some cooperate but others dominate, exploit, and prey on others. When an individual forms a life plan she acts freely (with the usual caveats and exceptions). When a ruler devises a plan for society he coercively enrolls others in his projects, whether his projects are shared by many or few.

Classical liberals do not dispute the claim that it is *possible* to say that groups have ends, interests, or projects that are not conceptually reducible to individual ends, interests, or projects.[18] But it does not follow that the group leaders can *coercively* impose those ends on the dissenters within the group. This is quite obvious in the cases of nondemocratic governance, but is also often true where majority rules. Most of the time an individual is the best judge of her interest and welfare; conversely, most of the time group rulers are *not* the best judges of the interests of its members. This means that *nonvoluntary* collective self-determination, that is, a collectively *coerced* decision about the political status, or the cultural identity, or the economic system of a group, is morally

[18] See Phillip Pettit and Christian List, *Group Agency* (Oxford: Oxford University Press, 2011).

suspect. The realization of human ends, including those that can be realized collectively, should in the last analysis be the result of voluntary interaction among free individuals. On the classical liberal view, there are no nonconsensual goods for collectives, nations, or tribes (over and above the goods of persons who comprise the collectivity) that group leaders can permissibly enforce. The classical liberal claim, then, is normative, not conceptual: the only morally valuable projects are (1) individual projects and (2) voluntary group projects. Even if we can meaningfully speak of a group project, group leaders cannot permissibly impose that project on dissenters (with the usual caveats and exceptions). In my judgment, self-determination advocates have yet to meet this challenge.

The third congenital problem is that self-determination advocates often conceal the fact that their real aim is to appropriate territory.[19] The self-determination rhetoric emphasizes religion, race, shared history, past wrongs, and similar factors to support their claims. In reality, a self-determination claim is a claim to exercise control over the land and resources over which the "people" sit. When the Crimeans assert their purported right to join Russia, what they really mean is to take away the land and resources of Crimea and hand them to Russia. When the Quebecois insist that they deserve to break away from Canada because they are a "distinct" society with their own language and culture, what they really mean is that they, and not Canada, "own" the territory of Quebec. Because of the nationalist rhetoric the territorial dispute between the irredentist "peoples" and their parent states gets invariably obfuscated.

Having rejected, then, the nationalist–ethnic rationale for self-determination, I suggest two kinds of reasons that may reasonably support a self-determination claim. The first is political injustice. As I pointed out, writers and courts have dubbed this *remedial* secession. When the parent state unjustly persecutes the inhabitants of a province or similar territory, it may be that breaking ties is the only remedy available to the latter. Contrary to prevailing rhetoric, such persecution need not be based on race, religion, or language. It may be just political persecution, or other forms of serious harm that the central authorities inflict on the inhabitants of the territory. When this occurs, I think the right of self-determination should be broadly recognized. If the inhabitants of a territorial subunit of Cambodia could have claimed the right of self-determination as the only available remedy against the massive crimes of the Khmer Rouge in 1975–77, I believe such claim should have

[19] See Lea Brilmayer, "Secession and Self-Determination: A Territorial Interpretation," *Yale Journal of International Law*, 16 (1991): 177–202.

recognized and the secession encouraged, regardless of ethnicity (perpetrators and victims had the same ethnicity), religion, history, or territorial title. Even if it could be argued that Cambodia and not the subunit "owned" the relevant territory, territorial sovereignty collapses when the sovereign renders itself guilty of crimes of this magnitude.

The second reasonable claim is *territorial* injustice. When the territorial sovereign is a usurper that has forcibly imposed its governance in a territory, then the inhabitants of that territory have the right to restore the original sovereign. This is so, I suggest, even if the usurper is otherwise reasonably well behaved. This right to restore the lawful territorial sovereignty needs considerable elaboration. To begin with, it requires an account of territorial title. As I already mentioned, the literature on this topic is still in its infancy and it is quite inconclusive. What makes the United States and not the state of Florida the territorial sovereign over the territory of Florida? Quebec? Catalonia? And so on. Moreover, a new state created for the purpose of restoring the original sovereign must itself be morally justified. It must respect human rights, for example. Now obvious as this requirement seems, it leads to startling consequences. For example, many states issued from the decolonization movement were illegitimate, for the simple reason that their leaders, after shaking off the unjust colonial yoke, created oppressive states of their own. The logic that rejects foreign oppression but accepts oppression by one's own is hardly defensible. Consider the future Palestinian state, which virtually everyone supports these days. Suppose that the Palestinians have a right to self-determination and also territorial title over the land of the future state. Still, I would think they are not entitled to create an oppressive state. Such state must be morally legitimate: it must respect human rights, be democratic, and so forth. We can see, then, that the plausible rationales for self-determination that emerge once one rejects the nationalist view are themselves quite tentative and problematic.

The essays collected in this interdisciplinary volume tackle these questions and many more. The first half is devoted to foundational issues, the second, to self-determination in context. The division is somewhat arbitrary, however, as this volume is about the theory of self-determination, so all the essays address in one form or another foundational questions.

The first half of the book collects essays that deal head on with the conundrum I have presented. Relying on research on group agency, Bas van der Vossen (Chapter 1) proposes a plausible concept of collective self-determination and concludes that no actual state satisfies it. Christopher Morris (Chapter 2) suggests that nationalist ideas have been unfairly singled out for derision, in view of the fact that individualist foundations of the state (such as consent) do not seem terribly plausible either. Frédéric Mégret (Chapter 3) strives to reconcile international practice with moral ideals by suggesting that the right of self-determination must be a reward for attractive traits of groups. The right, thus, is not inherent: some groups may wield it; other may not. In different ways, Jens David Ohlin (Chapter 4) and Patrick Mecklem (Chapter 5) aim at reconstructing the right of self-determination in international law. For Ohlin, the current emphasis on nations and peoples (as opposed to states) can be explained by central ideas in political theory, such as the natural right to resist unjust governance and the right of self-defense. Patrick Macklem analyzes the history of the principle and suggests that three different movements have converged toward one goal: to mitigate the twin injustices of power distribution in the world and bad governance within states.

In the second half of the book, the authors weave the foundational concepts into various issues of law and diplomacy. Alan Patten (Chapter 6) proposes a moderate version of the much-derided nationalist conception of self-determination applicable to national minorities, one that attempts to immunize it against the liberal criticisms summarized in this introduction. Matthew Lister (Chapter 7) applies the idea of self-determination to the neglected but topical problem of population transfers, and suggests that this issue must be part of any plausible theory of secession. Using the recent *Kosovo* opinion as a springboard, Michael Blake (Chapter 8) suggests that the usual list of reasons given to justify secession may be unduly restrictive. In particular, Blake thinks that the right of a group to announce that it wishes to secede may be compatible with the right of the parent state to resist the attempted secession. Two chapters focused on international law complete the volume. John Morss (Chapter 9) argues, from a cosmopolitan perspective, that the concept of self-determination has outlived its usefulness and must be modified or replaced. Elizabeth Rodríguez-Santiago (Chapter 10) traces the history of the principle to conclude that the best reading of the principle of self-determination is treating it as a remedial measure.

The principle of self-determination in international law exhibits a curious duality. On one hand, courts and governments proclaim it as one of the pillars of the international community. On the other hand, analysts disclose its serious conceptual and practical difficulties. My hope is that the theoretical inquiries in this volume may at least begin to answer vexing questions about the principle's continuing endurance or, conversely, its impending demise.

1

Self-Determination and Moral Variation*

BAS VAN DER VOSSEN

Self-determination plays a central role in debates about international morality and law. One important argument invokes the value of self-determination in order to show that rules of international morality and law should be modest or limited in content. The basic idea is clear enough. Self-determination seems to involve a kind of social process by which different groups, including political states, can develop their own distinctive shared moral codes. And so there can be legitimate moral variation between political societies. Because self-determination is valuable, the argument goes, acceptable international norms should allow for this variation, at least within certain limits. Self-determination thus constrains the demands of global justice and, consequently, international law.[1]

* Thanks to Fernando Tesón, David Lefkowitz, and David Shoemaker for very helpful constructive comments on earlier versions of this paper.

1 David Miller asks rhetorically: "If political communities are in general to be self-governing in matters of economic and social policy and so forth, what scope is left for cosmopolitan principles of justice that seek to treat people equally regardless of which community they belong to?" See David Miller, "Defending Political Autonomy: A Discussion of Charles Beitz," *Review of International Studies* 31 (2005): 381–88, p. 388. Miller has developed this thought in detail in various places. See, e.g., David Miller, *On Nationality* (Oxford University Press, 1995), ch. 4; and David Miller, *National Responsibility and Global Justice* (Oxford University Press, 2007). For related arguments, see Michael Walzer, "The Moral Standing of States: A Response to Four Critics," *Philosophy & Public Affairs* 9 (1980): 209–29; or Chris Armstrong, "National Self-Determination, Global Equality and Moral Arbitrariness," *Journal of Political Philosophy* 18 (2010): 313–34.

An often overlooked example of this view, I believe, is John Rawls, *The Law of Peoples: With "The Idea of Public Reason Revisited"* (Harvard University Press, 2001). There are two striking points to Rawls's view. First, in contrast to his earlier argument that states are legitimate only if they are liberal (see John Rawls, *Political Liberalism* (Columbia University Press, 1993), p. 137), *The Law of Peoples* ascribes this status to both liberal and nonliberal but "decent" societies. That is, both liberal and merely decent societies are full members of international

We can state this argument in the following (enthymematic) form:

(1) States can have a right to self-determination.
(2) Self-determination allows for moral variation between different communities.
(3) Therefore, to respect state self-determination, international moral norms should be limited.

The relevance of this argument goes beyond the point that international principles of justice should be more modest than domestic ones. The claim that states have a right to self-determination is among the most commonly accepted principles of international ethical and legal thought. And state self-determination is often thought to be important precisely because it allows for moral variation between societies.[2] Self-determining states are thought to enjoy a kind of moral status – one that calls for respect, noninterference, independence, democracy, and even a right to curb immigration.[3]

society, have rights of political independence (pp. 37ff), and their citizens are obligated to obey the law (pp. 65–66). Second, Rawls denied that his preferred principles of distributive justice applied internationally. The kinds of inequality Rawls thought unbearable between citizens of liberal society he accepted between different societies.

Both points are part of Rawls's attempt to recognize the value of self-determination. First, while decent societies are not liberal, Rawls insists that their political institutions contain a system of "consultation." This is supposed to ensure that people's voices and interests will be among the main inputs of political decision making. The view that arises is that the good of self-determination is part universal, part local. What is universal is that a society must be organized around "its common good idea of justice" (pp. 65–68). But this requirement can be fulfilled in different local ways, including but not limited to the liberal way. This, Rawls suggests, preserves "significant room for the idea of a people's self-determination" (p. 61, see also p. 111). Moreover, second, Rawls announces that the good of self-determination is his reason for endorsing limited redistributive principles internationally (p. 85).

2 Many argue, for example, that self-determination matters because it allows for distinct national cultures that provide a background for people to develop meaningful characters and make meaningful decisions about how to live. See Miller, *On Nationality*; Armstrong, "National Self-Determination, Global Equality and Moral Arbitrariness"; Will Kymlicka, "Territorial Boundaries: A Liberal Egalitarian Perspective," in David Miller and Sohail Hashmi (eds.), *Boundaries and Justice: Diverse Ethical Perspectives*, (Princeton University Press, 2001), pp. 249–75; and Margaret Moore, "Cosmopolitanism and Political Communities," *Social Theory and Practice* 32 (2006): 627–58.

3 For examples of such arguments, see Daniel Philpott, "In Defense of Self-Determination," *Ethics* 105 (1995): 352–385; Margaret Moore (ed.), *National Self-determination and Secession* (Oxford University Press, 2003); Michael Walzer, *Just And Unjust Wars: A Moral Argument with Historical Illustrations*, 4th ed. (Basic Books, 2006); Michael Walzer, "The Moral Standing of States"; Christopher H. Wellman, *A Theory of Secession* (Cambridge University Press, 2005); Andrew Altman and Christopher H. Wellman, *A Liberal Theory of International Justice*, reprint (Oxford University Press, 2011).

Yet despite its prominence and potential implications, it is difficult to find any precise accounts of what exactly is involved in self-determination, why it matters, or how it might lead to legitimate moral variation. That is, while many seem confident in their assertions about what is required to *respect* self-determination, few seem confident to assert what self-determination really *is*. This poses a problem because many of the former assertions are disputed, and some, including the earlier argument, are highly controversial. But without a real grip on what self-determination is, we lack the means to settle questions about what we have to do to respect it.

The purpose of this essay is to move away from this state of affairs. It offers an account of why self-determination can lead to genuine moral variation, and it asks whether political states can indeed be self-determining in this sense.

1. DESIDERATA FOR A THEORY OF SELF-DETERMINATION

Formulating an account of the nature of self-determination is no easy task. Some of its contours are clear enough: the idea of self-determination is closely related to the idea of autonomy, and self-determining communities are often described as self-governing. Beyond that, it is notoriously difficult to explicate the idea in any clear and convincing way.

A satisfying theory of self-determination should occupy the space between two commitments that are seemingly in tension. The first of these is that self-determination can happen only when people live and act, in some robust sense, together. Its locus is the group or community, not just the individual or even the sum of individuals that make up the group. As Christopher Wellman puts it, self-determination is "something that can be exercised by a collective *as a whole* rather than individually by persons in a group."[4] Self-determination is, importantly, a *collective* value.[5]

The second commitment expresses *moral individualism*. This demands that an account of self-determination avoid excessive romanticism, or even mysticism, about the state or political society. Such romanticism occurs when one views society or the state as a moral entity in and of itself, with a kind of moral status that is independent of, and maybe even more important than, the true ultimate locus of moral value: the individual. To satisfy the demands of moral

[4] See Wellman, *A Theory of Secession*, p. 41 (emphasis in original).

[5] See Altman and Wellman, *A Liberal Theory of International Justice*. See also Walzer, "The Moral Standing of States," and Walzer, *Just and Unjust Wars*.

individualism, one's account of self-determination and its value must ultimately be based on observations about individuals and their value.[6]

The difficulty of developing a satisfying theory of self-determination thus lies in explaining how truly collective social processes can lead to legitimate moral variation between societies, in a way that does not posit groups or states as independent entities of moral value. More precisely, we can formulate the following three (again, seemingly conflicting) desiderata for a theory of self-determination. Such an account must explain how:

(a) Self-determining groups can develop different moral codes.
(b) These codes can be different from, and not simply reducible to, the moral beliefs of their individual members.
(c) Groups, societies, and states are not fundamentally morally valuable, but derive whatever value they have from their individual members.

Many available approaches to self-determination fail to adequately incorporate all of these desiderata. A purely institutionalist theory, for example, might suggest that the value of self-determination lies in people living under political institutions they have created themselves.[7] But this leaves unexplained why self-determination might bring about legitimate moral variation between societies. After all, it seems perfectly consistent with such a view to maintain that each of those states should implement exactly the same norms. International and domestic norms might thus be the same. The idea of self-determination thus cannot be fully understood by merely focusing on the creation of independent political institutions.

A purely individualist theory, by contrast, might see group self-determination as simply the sum of individuals choosing to live together.[8] In such a view, the outcomes of self-determination would be a collection of individual choices. But how can that explanation capture self-determination's collective nature? Self-determination, we said, is something that essentially occurs at the level of the group, not just among several separate individuals. The collective nature of self-determination disappears from sight if we simply reduce it to individual choice.[9]

6 See the careful discussion in Wellman, *A Theory of Secession*, ch. 3.

7 For a possible example of such a view, see Wellman, *A Theory of Secession*. Wellman suggests (p. 57) that violations of self-determination are wrongful because they disrespect the collective achievement of people to create their own state.

8 See, e.g., Philpott, "In Defense of Self-Determination."

9 Hegel's theory of the state might be an example of a view that fails commitment (c). Hegel wrote: "The state is the actuality of the ethical idea. It is ethical mind *qua* the substantial will manifest and revealed to itself, knowing and thinking itself." And: "The state is absolutely

In what follows, I offer a theory of self-determination that aims to incorporate each of these three commitments. Drawing on recent findings by Christian List and Philip Pettit about group agency and judgment aggregation,[10] I will describe how groups can come to have moral codes that are at the same time based on, yet separate from, the moral views of their individual members. I will then explain why the development of such group moral codes can be valuable. Finally, I will ask whether these processes can take place within political states. Here, my conclusions will be skeptical. While self-determination can lead to genuine moral variation, the requisite processes do not take place within states.

2. THE POSSIBILITY OF COLLECTIVE SELF-DETERMINATION

A moral code is a set of propositions about morality that is endorsed by its holder.[11] A group moral code, if such a thing is possible, thus consists of the set of beliefs about morality that is shared by a group. The theory of self-determination I will develop holds that when different individuals together form a group, their several beliefs about morality (their several moral codes) can combine into a new and separate moral code. This new moral code will be held by the group as such, and will not be readily reducible to the beliefs of its members. As a result, this theory can explain how self-determination can lead to genuine moral variation between groups. After all, different groups, being constituted of different members, can produce different moral codes. However, because the group's code is ultimately based on, or the product of, the moral codes of its individual members, this theory still satisfies the demands of moral individualism.

rational inasmuch as it is the actuality of the substantial will which it possesses in the particular self-consciousness once that consciousness has been raised to consciousness of its universality. This substantial unity is an absolute unmoved end in itself, in which freedom comes into its supreme right. On the other hand this final end has supreme right against the individual, whose supreme duty is to be a member of the state." See G.W.F. Hegel, *The Philosophy of Right: The Philosophy of History*, trans. T.M. Knox (Oxford University Press, 1967), pp. 155–56. See also the discussion in Fernando Tesón, *Humanitarian Intervention: An Inquiry into Law and Morality*, 3rd ed. (Transnational, 2005), pp. 62ff.

10 The argument that follows relies on the argument presented in Christian List and Philip Pettit, *Group Agency: The Possibility, Design, and Status of Corporate Agents* (Oxford University Press, 2011). In a way, what follows can be seen as the extension of List and Pettit's findings about group agency to the realm of group self-determination. The title of the next section pays homage to the title of the first part of their book.

11 No doubt this is to simplify considerably. The intuitive notion of a moral code may well include more than merely propositions, such as attitudes, affects, and so on. I set these complications aside for the sake of argument.

To see how this is possible, we need to consider on what grounds we might ascribe beliefs about moral propositions to groups. To stay true to the individualism we have endorsed, such group beliefs must be ultimately explainable in terms of the beliefs of individual members. There are numerous ways of doing this, but let us here focus on the most obvious one: a simple majoritarian rule. A group, we might then say, has a certain belief if the majority of its members has that belief.

Of course this way of understanding group beliefs seems to ignore the aforementioned claim b. That is, it seems to understand group beliefs as straightforwardly reducible to those of its members. But this appearance is deceiving. For, under certain conditions, there simply is no way of understanding group beliefs as aggregated individual beliefs. More precisely, it is not possible to arrive at a consistent set of group beliefs in this way. Even more precisely, if moral beliefs have basic logical connections, and a group's moral code is going to satisfy minimal requirements of consistency between those beliefs, then it can be necessary for the group to endorse certain propositions that are not held by the majority of its members.

It will be easier to see this by looking at an example.[12] Consider a group's beliefs about distributive justice. Let us assume that there is no single morally correct system of distributive justice but that, within certain limits, a variety of different regimes are acceptable. Among these figure regimes that enforce strongly egalitarian distributions as well as regimes that allow markets to be the primary determinant of holdings. Let us further suppose that the individual members of the group base their views about distributive justice on their views concerning two other issues – to put it slightly differently, they treat their views about distributive justice as conclusions based on these premises. These are: (i) that the point of a society's economic system is to enhance economic productivity and (ii) that tampering with people's property rights through redistributive policies will significantly reduce productivity.[13]

[12] The example here is a variation on a problem that can arise in legal contexts, first presented in Lewis A. Kornhauser and Lawrence G. Sager, "Unpacking the Court," *Yale Law Journal* 96 (1986): 82–117. List and Pettit discuss similar cases, which they call "discursive dilemmas."

[13] Two points of clarification. First, as should be obvious, nothing for the present argument turns on this particular example. The assumptions in the text are only chosen for ease of exposition. If you strongly disagree with these points, you are free to insert your own favored issue. Second, and equally obvious, the example given here significantly understates the complexity involved. The propositions (i) and (ii) are really not simple, but are complex propositions, on each of the constituent parts of which people might take diverging views. This complexity bolsters the following result as well as its implications. That is, the more complex the issues involved, the stronger the case for the possibility of self-determination. See also List and Pettit, *Group Agency*, p. 77.

TABLE 1.1 *Group Beliefs on Distributive Justice*

	Property to enhance productivity	Redistribution reduces productivity	Market outcomes should determine holdings
P1	Yes	No	No
P2	No	Yes	No
P3	Yes	Yes	Yes
—	—	—	—
G	Yes	Yes	No

Finally, suppose that there are certain basic logical connections between the conclusion about distributive justice and these two issues such that a consistent person must favor the market as the primary determinant of people's holdings if he or she assents to both (i) and (ii). Table 1.1 lists the views on these issues of a three-person group. The views of each individual, as well as the views of the group based on the views of the majority, are listed in the table.

Note that each of the individuals has internally consistent beliefs about distributive justice. None of the persons endorses both premises of the argument without also endorsing the conclusion. However, the aggregate views of the group are inconsistent in just this way. For while the majority of the group believes both that the point of property systems is to enhance economic productivity and that redistributive policies interfere with this, the majority of the group also believes that a strongly egalitarian distribution ought to be enforced. Thus, *ex hypothesi*, the group's moral views are internally inconsistent even though none of its members' are.

The result here, of course, is not a product of the particular issue concerning distributive justice. It can occur with any set of beliefs that have modest logical connections. Less obviously, the result is also not a feature of the majoritarian method of aggregating individual beliefs. As List and Pettit have shown, given a number of plausible conditions, this problem can arise for *any* method of aggregation (participatory, hierarchical, majoritarian, supermajoritarian) – with the only exceptions being unattractive methods such as dictatorships.[14]

For obvious reasons, a group's moral code should be internally consistent. If the group is at the same time committed to premises that imply a conclusion

[14] See Christian List and Philip Pettit, "Aggregating Sets of Judgments: An Impossibility Result," *Economics and Philosophy* 18 (2002): 89–110. The result here is an extension of Arrow's famous impossibility theorem.

and the denial of that conclusion, it will not be able to come to any determinate views. Proponents of the conclusion will be able, and quite reasonably so, to point to the group's views about the premises. Opponents of the conclusion will be able, and quite reasonably so, to point to the group's view about the conclusion. Thus, without an internally consistent group moral code, the group will lack the ability to arrive at determinate answers for certain cases – such as the case of distributive justice.[15]

This raises some difficult questions. Groups face a choice between basing their views on the majority's views concerning the premises or the majority's views concerning the conclusion of a certain issue. It is a substantive moral issue which of the two will be the correct way to go, and this question lies beyond the focus of this essay. But the very fact that there is such a choice to be made shows something important for our purposes. For, whichever way we go, it will be true that certain propositions need to be recognized as genuine elements of a group's moral code even though they are not directly reducible to the views of its members. If the group adopts the majority's views on the conclusion, then it will commit itself to beliefs about the premises that are contrary to the majority's views. If it adopts the majority's views on the premises, this will come at the price of ignoring the majority's views on the conclusion. In either case, the group will have adopted a view that is (directly) contrary to its views on one issue, even though it is (indirectly) based on its members' views about another issue. That is, in either case, the group will have a view that is genuinely formed at the group level.

Note just how far-reaching this result is. For one, the beliefs of a group's members turn out to be both unnecessary and insufficient for particular group beliefs. In this way, the group can achieve views that are, in a sense, autonomous or self-standing. A group as a whole might endorse something even though each of its members does not endorse it. In fact, the group might endorse something that each of its members opposes.[16]

[15] List and Pettit claim that this kind of consistency is a condition of group agency. Some people have challenged this thought. See, e.g., Robert Sugden, "Must Group Agents Be Rational? List and Pettit's Theory of Judgement Aggregation and Group Agency," *Economics and Philosophy* 28 (2012): 265–73, p. 269. But even if Sugden's challenge succeeds against the theory of group *agency*, the account of group *self-determination* I am offering here survives. For my account relies on the very plausible assumption that *morality* should be consistent.

[16] This, in turn, seems to violate certain other intuitive ideas about how rational groups should behave, such as that they allow Pareto-superior moves. See Robert Sugden, "Team Preferences," *Economics and Philosophy* 16 (2000): 175–204, p. 188. For a different kind of argument, see Margaret Gilbert, *A Theory of Political Obligation* (Oxford University Press, 2008), p. 137.

Let us call group norms that arise in this way *emergent* group norms.[17] The processes by which emergent group norms arise, I propose, are processes of group self-determination. Self-determination, then, can indeed lead to genuine moral variation between groups.

This account helps explain both the "self" and the "determination" of self-determination. It is "determination" because groups, as such, can produce their own moral codes. And it is determination by the "self" because these processes occur on the basis of members' moral codes. This account therefore satisfies all three claims (a)–(c) identified in the previous section. It demonstrates (a) how genuine moral variation between self-determining groups is possible, (b) why this variation is not simply variation between the views of groups' individual members, yet (c) it does so by invoking only facts about its individual members (and no mysterious or magical group entities or values).

3. THE VALUE OF GROUP SELF-DETERMINATION

With this basic description of how self-determination works in place, we can now turn to the question of its value. What, if anything, is the importance of these processes such that their results command the kind of respect that self-determination is usually thought to command?

The answer to this question is not obvious. It will not do, for example, to simply state that it matters for people to live on shared or mutually agreed terms, and that those terms require group membership. One might think this, say, if one thought of self-determination as a simple extension of the autonomous choices of individual members, or based on something like Rousseau's idea of a general will. Such approaches typically regard a group's moral code as something that its individual members are rationally committed to endorse – either because they actively endorsed it (through voting, say) or because the group outcome represents their views in a relevant way.

But while it may well be true that there is value in living on mutually agreed terms, this cannot explain the value (if any) of group self-determination. For group self-determination can actually be in tension with living on mutually agreed terms. After all, as we have seen, self-determining groups can produce emergent moral codes that contain elements that their members individually reject. In such a case, living on the terms that are the outcome of self-determination means living on terms that one rejects.

[17] In technical terms, the group's beliefs *supervene* on the beliefs of its members. Roughly, A supervenes on B if, and only if, necessarily, the facts about A cannot change without some accompanying change in the facts about B. For discussion, see List and Pettit, *Group Agency*, p. 65.

The real question, then, is how group self-determination might have value for the reason that it enables emergent group norms that are relatively independent of individual beliefs and norms, not in spite of it. One such source of value is that group self-determination offers a particularly attractive way for individuals who would otherwise have intractable moral disagreement to interact and cooperate. Consider different people who disagree on a certain issue, such as the correct interpretation of distributive justice. There are a number of ways in which they might interact with one another. One way would be to deliberate and discuss the issue. Often, people come to certain conclusions on the basis of faulty reasoning, and deliberation might help people to identify their mistakes, thereby removing the source of the disagreement. Another way is to sideline the issue. Sometimes we can "compartmentalize" issues and allow different people to act on their different views of how things ought to be. Freedom of religion might be a case in point, which enables theists and atheists to live together without having to settle on a shared view about the existence of God or the importance of religion.

But these options cannot resolve all cases of disagreement. For one, as the example of group inconsistencies in Table 1.1 showed, even those who reason in internally consistent ways can nevertheless end up with collectively inconsistent beliefs. And not all moral issues can be compartmentalized in the way that religious freedom achieves. Sometimes people need to coordinate on a single outcome, and perhaps distributive justice is one such case.

In these cases of disagreement, norms that emerge as a result of group self-determination can help solve the problem. That is, members of the same group, whose individual moral outlooks are incompatible on issues where compatibility is required, can use the group's emergent norm as a salient point of convergence for their actions. Consider again the case illustrated in Table 1.1. The three persons involved there deeply disagree about not only the requirements of distributive justice itself, but also about the merits of the premises that support their respective views about this. The process of group self-determination offers them a way of overcoming their disagreement: they can use the group's emergent view as a point on which they can converge.[18]

This feature of self-determination is attractive for a number of reasons. First, the process is reliable. Because none of the views of individual members are necessary or sufficient for the group's norms, it turns out that even people with very complex and intricately different individual moral views can combine to

[18] Recall: this emergent view can be either the conclusion of the argument or one of the premises. The point here is neutral between the two.

bring about a relatively simple and clear moral code at the group level.[19] Second, and more obviously, it allows people to resolve what might otherwise become a conflict. Members of groups who take emergent norms as devices for coordinating their actions can thus live together peacefully.

Emergent norms are particularly well suited for this purpose because they are not, as we have seen, readily reducible to any of the personal views of the disagreeing parties. This allows them to have a kind of impartial character – something different than one of the parties insisting that his or her view is correct after all. Yet, because they are indirectly (and, given certain methods of aggregation, potentially symmetrically) based on the views of the parties involved, they are not simply imposed on them either. These group codes are still importantly connected to the views of their members. In fact, group norms and individual views are not static. Group norms and individual views can interact. When a group adopts a certain position, this can lead individual members to reconsider their own views on the matter. Thus, processes of self-determination will likely involve repeated adjustments of individual views to group norms, and vice versa. This tightens the connection between emergent group moral norms and the views of the group's members.[20]

It can make sense, then, for people to value the processes by which emergent norms come about. And it can make sense to insist that others respect these norms. The reason is the same: the process of group self-determination provides people who would otherwise face real problems of disagreement with the possibility of living together on terms that are logically and morally consistent as well as self-imposed in the sense that they are the result of their own views.

Before moving on, two points are worth stressing. First, the fact that self-determination can be valuable does not undo the need for independent moral standards that determine what emergent norms are acceptable. It may be tempting here to suggest that we should evaluate the acceptability of a group's emergent norms in terms of the underlying norms of its members. But this will not do. For even though the group's norms are the product of its members' views, the two are importantly separate. It is in principle possible for a group to develop a problematic collective code even if all its members' views are acceptable, as well as for people who each have deeply unjust views to develop a morally acceptable code as a group. If we are to continue to distinguish

[19] Cf. List and Pettit, *Group Agency*, p. 77.

[20] Note that this bolsters the idea of self-determination itself. For when there is this kind of back-and-forth relation between group and individual beliefs, it becomes even more difficult to reduce the group's moral code to its members' respective views.

between morally acceptable and unacceptable group norms, then, we need to appeal to something other than the views of group members. We need independent moral norms to make this judgment. It follows that morality and justice cannot be constituted by processes of self-determination.

Second, the coordination made possible by group self-determination is different from other ways in which disagreeing people can manage to cooperate. Self-determination cannot be equated, for example, to coordination by rational but disagreeing persons on the basis of conventions. Such conventions can allow people to cooperate when they prefer to act on the same terms – even if this means they cannot act on their individually preferred option. In such scenarios, if a convention exists that identifies an option as the one on which to coordinate, it can become the best option for each person to act in that way.

An example of this is the kind of convention that often arises in subway tunnels. If everyone in the tunnel is walking on the right-hand side, and assuming they do not want to bump into people all the time, this gives all people entering the tunnel a reason to walk on the right-hand side as well. By walking on the right side, they all can get to where they are going, and that is ultimately what they care about the most. This is true even if only some of them like this way of doing things, while others think it would be better if everyone were walking on the left. Thus, the convention can help people with varying preferences coordinate their actions.

Such conventional coordination is a common and important social phenomenon. Yet there are fundamental ways in which it differs from cooperation on the basis of emergent group norms. For example, conventional cooperation is successful because each of the parties involved sees coordinating action as in their self-interest. Such cooperation thus cannot survive the absence of a shared preference for coordination. When people disagree about whether it is preferable to act in a coordinated way, conventional cooperation breaks down. The same is not true for emergent group norms. These can survive even disagreement about whether to coordinate in a given case.[21]

Another difference is the ways in which conventional norms and emergent group norms come about. Conventions can arise between persons who are perfect strangers, and not members of a group in any meaningful way, such as people entering a subway tunnel. All that is needed is that they share a preference for coordinating their actions in certain ways. By contrast,

[21] Obviously, the absence of agreement to cooperate will cause significant practical problems even in cases of self-determination. The point here, however, is different: emergent group norms can exist independently of agreement or preference to coordinate, while conventions cannot. This suffices to demonstrate the difference between the two.

emergent group norms can only arise in what I have called self-determining groups. They require a kind of aggregation procedure and can only provide reasons for compliance to their members.

4. SELF-DETERMINATION IN POLITICAL STATES

Recall the argument with which we started:

(1) States can have a right to self-determination.
(2) Self-determination allows for moral variation between different communities.
(3) Therefore, to respect state self-determination, international moral norms should be limited.

The account of self-determination here vindicates the second premise of this argument: self-determination can give rise to moral variation through emergent group norms. What about the first premise? Can these processes take place within political states? The answer to this question depends on whether the conditions of membership in self-determining groups allow for states to be among them. This section argues that, contrary to what is commonly thought, states cannot satisfy those conditions.

The question of the membership conditions in self-determining groups matters not just because it allows us to see whether states can be truly self-determining groups. It also matters because such membership might mean that one be *bound* to follow the group's emergent norms. Some philosophers think, for example, that it is a general feature of group membership that one becomes obligated to follow the group's collective rules or plans.[22] This raises the stakes of our discussion considerably. For while we have so far been focusing on the opportunities that group self-determination brings, the possibility of emergent group norms being binding provides some potential threats as well. If mere membership in a group can make one bound by the emergent group norms, then self-determination can also significantly limit the liberty one would otherwise enjoy.

Another reason this question matters is that changes in a group's membership can affect its emergent moral code. Since the composition of members' views determines the group's views, currently present members will have a stake in who else becomes a member of their group. Given a certain membership profile, the group's moral code might resemble more closely a code that

[22] See, e.g., Gilbert, *A Theory of Political Obligation*.

fits with one's interests, beliefs, or preferences. This raises a number of questions. Groups can be created, and their membership can be influenced and molded in several ways. Some of these are more agreeable than others, and so the possibility of self-determination may incentivize bad behavior. Similarly, one might raise questions about the morality of immigration. If states are self-determining groups, does this mean they get to control who joins them through restricting immigration?[23]

For these reasons as well as others, it cannot be true that just any set or collection of persons will qualify as a self-determining group. And of course that is clearly right. For example, there is in some sense a group that contains all people living within a mile of the Mason-Dixon Line. But it is highly implausible that this group is capable of self-determination or generating obligations. The reason is clear: the condition of membership in this group refers to the morally arbitrary or meaningless fact of mere geographical location. And groups with membership conditions that refer to only morally arbitrary or meaningless facts cannot have the kind of moral characteristics I have attributed to self-determination.[24]

It is easy to identify certain sufficient conditions for membership in morally relevant groups. Most plausibly, genuine consent can suffice. Consider, for example, a group such as a union, the members of which each agree to join the group. As such, they can all become bound by the union's decisions regarding controversial matters, such as the acceptable terms of labor contracts, including decisions that do not reflect their own evaluation of the matter at hand. In general, genuine consent can change one's moral status. And it can clearly generate the kind of membership that can come with obligation.

There are also plausible examples of groups (including those that might be characterized by obligations) that do not require consent. Consider, for example, a group of neighbors whose houses are all painted a certain color. Suppose the neighbors chose to live in the neighborhood because they like color-coordinated houses. And suppose it is commonly known among them that the houses are supposed to remain that color. Under those conditions, it may be that the neighbors form a kind of group, and perhaps even that they are, as members of the group, obligated not to change the color of their homes.

[23] Some theorists think that this fact about self-determination can justify coercive immigration restrictions for states. For the argument that such views fail *even if*, contrary to the point here, states can be genuinely self-determining, see Bas van der Vossen, "Immigration and Self-Determination," *Politics, Philosophy and Economics* 14 (2014): 270–290.

[24] For a similar point, see A. John Simmons, "External Justifications and Institutional Roles," *Journal of Philosophy* 93 (1996): 28–36.

One of the more permissive accounts of group membership, in the sense of accepting weak conditions for membership, is Margaret Gilbert's "plural subject" theory. According to Gilbert, groups (and group obligations) are the result of people undertaking "joint commitments" to act together as a group. Such joint commitments are the result of certain kinds of behavior on the part of the people who will become the members of the group. These kinds of behavior express their mutual readiness to become jointly committed in ways that are common knowledge among the would-be members. This is the source of the group's existence and its accompanying obligations because it involves a commitment of the will on the part of its members.[25]

Let us call theories that require this kind of involvement of the will for group membership in self-determining (or obligating) groups *soft-voluntarist* theories. We can call them voluntarist because they insist that the morally relevant properties in virtue of which people are members of groups make essential reference to their wills. But we can call them soft-voluntarist because they will recognize as sufficient undertakings of the will that fall short of consent or other clear outward signs of acceptance usually associated with voluntary undertakings. (Insisting on these would be a sign of hard-voluntarism.) Soft-voluntarism is plausible as a necessary condition for membership in at least certain groups. It rules out cases like that of the people living close to the Mason-Dixon Line. But it rules in cases like that of the color-coordinating neighbors.

We cannot here settle the debate over whether soft-voluntarist conditions, like Gilbert's idea of joint commitment,[26] can also be sufficient for membership in groups and for the accompanying obligations. The important question for our purposes, instead, is whether those views, if true, would support the first premise of the earlier argument. If people can become jointly committed by being members of a neighborhood, do they also become jointly committed by being members, citizens, or subjects of the state? That is, when people live together as citizens in a state, might they thereby become members of self-determining groups in the way required for them to become obligated to comply with the state's emergent norms?[27]

25 See Gilbert, *A Theory of Political Obligation*, pp. 128, 135, 138, 144, 166, and 271.

26 For other examples, see Raimo Tuomela, *The Importance of Us: A Philosophical Study of Basic Social Notions* (Stanford University Press, 1995). Tuomela writes: "A central thesis to be defended is that the performance of a joint action, X . . . requires that the participants have explicitly or implicitly agreed to perform action X" (p. 73). Or see Robert Sugden, "Team Preferences," pp. 184, and 192ff who defends "taking oneself to be a member" as a condition for membership.

27 Gilbert might think so, as she argues that membership in a state can generate obligations. See Gilbert, *A Theory of Political Obligation*, parts II and III.

There are two reasons why this thought ought to be resisted. The first has to do with the normative significance of baseline, or normal, behavior. One cannot become jointly committed merely by remaining where one is, going about one's ordinary life. Undertaking new obligations requires some sort of personal engagement, uptake, or indication. This is an implication of the voluntarism that soft-voluntarist theories accept. Thus, even if others take their going about their normal daily lives to indicate their readiness to become obligated, and even if this is publicly known, that fact alone cannot suffice to render one's normal daily life obligating.

To see this, consider the following example. Suppose Donna lives in a neighborhood populated by extremely virtuous people. At some point, Donna's neighbors start a campaign for organ donation. They post signs saying things like "This neighborhood donates kidneys!" and "We all donate!" The significance of these signs is common knowledge among the neighbors and they take themselves to be obligated to donate their kidneys. But suppose that Donna does not want to donate a kidney, and also does not want to leave the neighborhood. If Donna chooses to remain where she lives, she plainly does not thereby still become obligated to donate her kidney. Her merely staying where she was, living her normal life, cannot suffice for this.

If this is right, then mere citizenship in a state is not sufficient to become a member in the sense required here. After all, most people become citizens of their states in much the same way as Donna became part of the organ-donating neighborhood. They are citizens by birth, ascription, or the decisions of their ancestors. For most, citizenship requires no personal engagement, uptake, or indication whatsoever. Indeed, actions that might normally constitute the relevant signals (getting government-issued identification, for example) are in many countries necessary simply in order to live a normal life. But if such actions are not sufficient to render Donna obligated to follow her group's norms about organ donation, then it seems similarly true that they are not sufficient to render citizens obligated to follow their state's emergent group norms. They are simply part of the ordinary baseline of behavior.

The second reason for doubting that states are actually self-determining units is slightly different: the appropriate conditions for *taking* people to be obligated are sensitive to the comprehensiveness and impactfulness of the obligations in question. This is due to the uncertainties and possible confusions that typically accompany the conditions of membership, and especially the type of "soft" conditions that are involved in proposals such as Gilbert's idea of joint commitment. A lot can be unclear here: the nature and extent of the joint commitments around which a group is organized, the actions that constitute their acceptance, what people already count as its members, and so on. These are all matters of interpretation and, as such, are often surrounded by ambiguities, uncertainties, and indeterminacies. That is, while it might be common knowledge that certain behaviors are obligating, the details about the behaviors, the obligations, and the group might all be less than fully clear.

So even if people in such situations do become obligated in some particular way, it is not true that others can be justified in holding them to be bound, unless there is some reassurance that they were committing themselves in just that way. This is especially true if the obligations in question are onerous and far-reaching in nature. As a general rule, the more comprehensive or impactful the implications of group membership, the more demanding we should be of the conditions for membership. For groups the impact of which is relatively minor, such as the color-coordinating neighbors, "soft" actions, such as moving into the neighborhood, might suffice. But for groups the impact of which is far-reaching, clearer and "harder" conditions are plainly required.

To see this, consider a slightly different example. Suppose Donna comes across a march of people who are campaigning for more organ donations. They hold signs saying things like "On our way to donate kidneys! Will you?" And "Come donate kidneys with us!" Suppose that Donna cares about organ donation, sees the march in progress, and decides to walk along. When the march arrives at a hospital, its participants start preparations to have their kidneys removed for donation. Can the hospital's physician take the fact that Donna was part of the march to be sufficient for removing her kidney? Clearly, the answer is no. Given what is at stake, the mere decision to join in the march, even though it satisfies Gilbert's conditions of joint commitment, cannot be enough. For others to take Donna to be obligated to donate her kidney, more than just this is required. Donna would have to do something like sign a consent form.

If this is correct, then the prospects for the thesis that citizenship is sufficient for taking membership in the state as a self-determining group are also dim. States are among the most comprehensive and impactful groups. They are coercive institutions that require and enforce the obedience of their subjects. They use their powers to legislate on a wide variety of social, economic, cultural, and personal matters. And the possibility of self-determination occurring at the state level further increases their impactfulness by attaching a binding emergent moral code to membership. Given that the argument we are inspecting here concerns how to treat people globally, any demand that we water down the rights and freedoms of individuals in the international realm in the name of self-determination again needs some "harder" forms of assurance. We should expect, then, that for present purposes the conditions of membership in the state *qua* self-determining group be more like agreeing to a kidney transplant than like moving into a neighborhood.

Note that this is not to reassert the consent theory of political obligation or state legitimacy. According to that theory, people are subject to the state's authority if and only if they voluntarily give their consent.[28] But we have not been focusing on state authority as such. Instead, our question has been whether membership in a group can imply that one is bound to follow the group's emergent norms. And when this kind of membership becomes as pervasive as being subject to state authority, consent, or something close to it, seems required. This leaves open the possibility that state authority is immune to this argument about group membership. Perhaps state authority is special in ways that group membership is not. And it leaves open the possibility that membership in less impactful and comprehensive states can result from the satisfaction of softer conditions.

Either way, then, the upshot is that for all practical purposes we cannot accept that being identified as a citizen or subject by the governments that rule us is sufficient for membership in a self-determining state. Absent the requisite undertakings, engagements, or indications on the part of all individual persons who live there, the mere fact of such identification by the state is as brute and morally impotent a fact as living close to the Mason-Dixon Line. Genuine state self-determination thus is a mirage.

This seems the correct result. If being considered a citizen were sufficient for membership in a self-determining group, then some seriously counterintuitive implications would follow. It would render incoherent, for example, claims made by secessionist movements on the grounds of self-determination. These, we would be forced to say, are simply mistaken because, by their current state's identification as citizens, the people seeking secession already qualify as full members of a genuinely self-determining group. It would therefore not even be possible for their right to self-determination to be denied. Calls for secession would thus be obviously mistaken in the face of state self-determination. This is implausible.

The account proposed here of course also implies that secessionist groups cannot establish self-determining states, but the reasoning is importantly different. For the account does allow groups as such to be self-determining. It only rules out that the state they want to establish – which will identify members and nonmembers of the group as citizens on grounds of residence or birth and coercively govern them – will be. But this is a general result. And so

[28] The classic discussion remains A. John Simmons, *Moral Principles and Political Obligations* (Princeton, 1979).

the implausible implication is avoided. Secessionist states lack a right to self-determination for the same reason as larger states do.[29]

Note that this argument cannot be challenged by claiming that membership in a self-determining group requires only the acceptance, consent, or agreement of that group's majority. For in order to identify the majority of a group we first need to know who counts as its members. We cannot say that 51 people's votes constitutes a majority without knowing that the group has no more than 100 members, and who those members are. But that is precisely the question we are addressing here. We are asking about the boundaries of group membership, who does, and who does not, count as a member in the first place. Important though majority rule might be, this is one problem it cannot solve.

5. CONCLUSION

The argument with which we started this essay thus turns out to be unsound. Self-determination can give rise to moral variation, but political states are not the sites of the requisite processes. Insofar as the demands of global justice go, then, defenders of modest or minimalist international moral standards should look elsewhere for support.

[29] States can approximate self-determination to greater or lesser extents. Many of the things normally associated with the idea of self-determination move a state closer to this ideal, including secession. By seceding, a group would create a state the citizenship of which is closer to membership in the self-determining group. Similarly, democratic politics and deliberation might move states closer to true self-determination. These are aggregation procedures that translate individual beliefs and preferences into group codes. State sovereignty protects a society against the kind of outside interference that would override a group's ability to arrive at its own emergent norms (i.e., norms that are the product of the beliefs of its members).

2

The Case for National Self-Determination[1]

CHRISTOPHER W. MORRIS

> When in the Course of human events, it becomes necessary for one people to dissolve the political bands which have connected them with another, and to assume among the powers of the earth, the separate and equal station to which the Laws of Nature and of Nature's God entitle them. . . .
>
> Thomas Jefferson, Declaration of Independence (1776)

> Aux armes, citoyens,
> Formez vos bataillons!
> Marchons, marchons!
> Qu'un sang impur
> Abreuve nos sillons!
> Claude Joseph Rouget de Lisle (1792)

How good is the case for national self-determination? Nationalist and associated cultural forces are as present today in the world as they ever were. What to think about the case in favor of national self-determination?

"Self-determination" is not a clear term, and its meaning differs applied to individuals and to collectivities. I won't say much about these unclarities, but the ambiguity of the predicate "national" needs be resolved. The national self-determination that is at issue here is that of nations and peoples, not that of states. I am asking what to think about the case in favor of self-determination for nations or peoples.

My aim is limited. What generally to think about the case for national self-determination? I do not plan, in this short essay, to address all of the difficult questions about the self-determination of a nation or people, only to ask very

[1] I am grateful to discussants for comments on a presentation at the meeting of the International Legal Theory Interest Group of the American Society of International Law, 9 November 2012, Washington, D.C. A referee offered helpful comments for which I am also grateful.

generally what to think about the case for its self-determination. Our assessment of the strength of the case for something depends first on what that something is and how controversial it is. It also depends on the standards of evaluation: good in what respects, compared to what? We shall consider both of these aspects of our question. I shall argue that the case for national self-determination is "pretty good", certainly better than it is widely thought to be in many academic settings, especially American. A large part of my project is to present the case for national self-determination in a comparative setting, noting how much or how little different arguments for attributing a certain status to states achieve. My position will be controversial, as I find the case for self-determination "pretty good"; it will also disappoint many nationalists, as I do not think the case establishes as much as they might like. I present my argument in a very compact form; many details will be familiar to most readers of this volume, and I am most concerned with evaluating the case for national self-determination comparatively, as I have said.

1. NATIONAL SELF-DETERMINATION

How should we understand "national self-determination"? There was a time when it was thought by many that not only do all national groups have a right to a state of their own, but that every state should be a "nation-state", the state of (with) its own nation. And today some even go so far as to *define* nationalism as the view "which holds that the political and national unit should be congruent".[2] The latter claim, that state and nation should be congruent, is quite implausible, and I challenge it elsewhere.[3] And the former claim, that every national group has a right to a state of its own ("the separate and equal station to which the Laws of Nature and of Nature's God entitle them"), is also implausible. It is overreaching; there are far too many national groups – even linguistic groups – for them to have states of their own.[4]

[2] Ernest Gellner, *Nations and Nationalism* (Ithaca, NY: Cornell University Press, 1983), p. 1. See also Elie Kedourie, *Nationalism*, 4th ed. (Oxford: Blackwell, 1993 [1960]), p. 1 ("Nationalism ... holds that the only legitimate type of government is national self-determination"), and Yael Tamir, *Liberal Nationalism* (Princeton, NJ: Princeton University Press, 1993), p. 124 ("Modern states have, therefore, chosen to adopt national self-determination as their justifying principle, even when their members do not constitute a nation").

[3] See Christopher W. Morris, *An Essay on the Modern State* (Cambridge: Cambridge University Press, 1998), ch. 8.

[4] "On any reasonable calculation, the ... number of potential nations is probably much, *much* larger than that of possible viable states.... [N]ot all nationalisms can be satisfied, at any rate at the same time.... [V]ery many of the potential nations of this world live, or until recently have lived, not in compact territorial units but intermixed with each other in complex

Sometimes the fact that a group is a national group is a central part of the case for "national self-determination", that is, for significant political independence and quite possibly a state. Given that almost all of the landmass of the globe is now the territory of a state, greater political independence for a national group will often consist of increased autonomy within a federal system (e.g., Québec in Canada) or within a regional political union such as the EU (e.g., Cataluña or the Basque Country). In an empire, increased autonomy or political independence short of independent statehood can often be accommodated (e.g., Canada, Hong Kong). The more controversial forms of increased self-determination are the institution of a new state, normally by secession. A lot of our attention will be on this case, as it is the more controversial one.

I shall affirm that a strong case can be made for national self-determination, albeit highly constrained. This case is based on the social unity of the group, on cultural bonds between the members. The groups in question will typically be peoples or nations. They are what Avishai Margalit and Joseph Raz have dubbed "encompassing groups".[5] A number of political thinkers have in the last few decades made a case for national self-determination.[6] I shall focus in detail on Margalit and Raz's case as I think it is strong as well as instructive. Margalit and Raz defend the thesis that there is a limited moral right to self-determination, and this right belongs to certain groups. The right is that to national self-determination: "the right to determine whether a certain territory shall become, or remain, a separate state (and possibly whether it should enjoy autonomy within a larger state)". This right of self-determination, they argue, is not ultimate but is "grounded in the wider value of self-government", which is itself only instrumentally justified.

The structure of their argument is rather complex. They ask first: What groups might have such a right? Their answer is "encompassing groups". What is the value of political independence for such groups? Basically, membership in such groups is important for individual well-being; the

patterns. It follows that a territorial political unit can only become ethnically homogeneous, in such cases, if it either kills, or expels, or assimilates all non-nationals". Gellner, *Nations and Nationalism*, p. 2.

5 Margalit and Raz, "National Self-Determination", *Journal of Philosophy* LXXXVII, 9 (September 1990), pp. 440–41.

6 See, for instance, Tamir, *Liberal Nationalism*, and David Miller, *On Nationality* (Oxford: Oxford University Press, 1995). Tamir is critical of the approach taken by Margalit and Raz; see her "The Right to National Self-Determination", *Social Research* 58, 3 (Fall 1991), pp. 565–90. The revival of interests in nationalism among political thinkers in the English-speaking world is due in no small part to the writing of Charles Taylor and before him, Isaiah Berlin. For the latter, see "Nationalism: Past Neglect and Present Power", in *Against the Current: Essays in the History of Ideas* (New York: Penguin, 1979).

prosperity of the group is important to the well-being of members; and sometimes, being an independent sovereign state is helpful or even crucial to a group's prosperity. What is the case for attributing a *right* to such groups? Simply that it is often best to give the individuals concerned the power (e.g., a right) to determine what to do.

The right is conditional. Its exercise should be by "overwhelming majority"; it must be exercised for right reasons, namely, "to secure conditions necessary for the prosperity and self-respect of the group"; the group must respect the basic rights of (all) inhabitants of its territory, and measures must be taken to prevent or minimize damage to the interests of others.[7] I shall emphasize the importance of these conditions at the end of the essay; they may be significant constraints.

One of the most interesting parts of their argument is the first step, the determination of the group that possesses this right. They agree that "It is far from clear that peoples or nations rather than tribes, ethnic groups, linguistic, religious, or geographical groups are the relevant reference groups". Their strategy in determining the relevant group is to rely on their understanding of the benefits of self-government; the relevant groups are those whose characteristics are such that they stand to benefit from self-government. These turn out to be "encompassing groups", with six defining characteristics:

1. "The group has a common character and a common culture that encompass many, varied and important aspects of life. ... [The groups] have pervasive cultures, and their identity is determined at least in part by their culture".
2. "[P]eople growing up among members of the group will acquire the group culture, will be marked by its character".
3. "Membership in the group is, in part, a matter of mutual recognition. Typically, one belongs to such groups if, among the other conditions, one is recognized by other members of the group as belonging to it".
4. Membership is important "for one's self-identification". These are "groups, membership of which has a high social profile, that is, groups, membership of which is one of the primary facts by which people are identified, and which form expectations as to what they are like".
5. "Membership is a matter of belonging, not of achievement. ... Qualification for membership is usually determined by nonvoluntary criteria. One cannot choose to belong. One belongs because of who one is. One can come to belong to such groups, but only by changing, for example

7 Margalit and Raz, "National Self-Determination", pp. 458–60.

by adopting their culture, changing one's tastes and habits accordingly – a very slow process indeed".

6. "The groups concerned are not face-to-face groups.... They are anonymous groups where mutual recognition is secured by the possession of general characteristics".

Virtually everyone belongs to some such group, Margalit and Raz claim; they add that membership need not be exclusive.[8]

Encompassing groups are important in part because of the ways they shape the goals and relationships of individuals. Given the relation between people and culture, the prosperity of the latter is important for the well-being of the individual. Specifically, "individual dignity and self-respect require that the groups, membership of which contributes to one's sense of identity, be generally respected and not be made a subject of ridicule, hatred, discrimination, or persecution".[9]

Margalit and Raz reject the thesis that self-government has ultimate or inherent value. "There is nothing wrong with multi-national states, in which members of the different communities compete in the political arena for public resources for their communities".[10] The case for a right to self-determination, then, must be instrumental: "Sometimes the prosperity of the group and its self-respect are aided by, sometimes they may be impossible to secure without, the group's enjoying political sovereignty over its own affairs. Sovereignty enables the group to conduct is own affairs in a way conducive to its own prosperity.... It depends on historical conditions".[11]

All these considerations, Margalit and Raz claim, amount to is a case for self-government. They do not by themselves establish a *right* to self-determination. This right, I noted earlier, is "the right to determine whether a certain territory shall become, or remain, a separate state (and possibly whether it should enjoy autonomy within a larger state)". That is, this right is a "right to determine that a territory be self-governing, regardless of whether the case for self-government, based on its benefits, is established or not".[12] The

8 Margalit and Raz, "National Self-Determination", pp. 443–47. Some of these groups "are rather like national groups, e.g., tribes or ethnic groups. Others are very different. Some religious groups meet our criteria, as do social classes, and some racial groups. Not all religious or racial groups did develop rich and pervasive cultures. But some did and those qualify" (p. 447).

9 Margalit and Raz, "National Self-Determination", p. 449.

10 Margalit and Raz, "National Self-Determination", p. 453. See also Raz, "Multiculturalism".

11 Margalit and Raz, "National Self-Determination", p. 450.

12 "In other words, the right to self-determination answers the question 'who is to decide?', not 'what is the best decision?' ... [If a group] has the right to decide, its decision is binding even if

case for this right derives from "the value of a collective good", "the value of membership in encompassing groups":

> It rests on an appreciation of the great importance that membership in and identification with encompassing groups has in the life of individuals, and the importance of the prosperity and self-respect of such groups to the well-being of their members. That importance makes it reasonable to let the encompassing group that forms a substantial majority in a territory have the right to determine whether that territory shall form an independent state in order to protect the culture and self-respect of the group, provided that the new state is likely to respect the fundamental interests of its inhabitants, and provided that measures are adopted to prevent its creation from gravely damaging the just interests of other countries.[13]

I mentioned earlier the qualifications of this right. Given the conditions on the exercise of the right, it is not clear that it will justify statehood for many encompassing groups, at least in present conditions. The right is highly constrained. And Margalit and Raz are not proposing national self-determination as the ground for the state generally. National independence is warranted when other arrangements fail.[14] It has long been recognized that establishing a state for each or most national groups is unrealistic.

It is important to understand the basis for national self-determination on the view we are considering; Margalit and Raz's case is dependent on the contributions of forms of political organization to people's well-being. The argument they make can be supplemented. Suppose that we think of a society as "a cooperative venture for mutual advantage", to deploy Rawls's expression[15]; that is, we think that societies ought to be cooperative ventures of this kind. Then features that

it is wrong, even if the case for self-government is not made". Margalit and Raz, "National Self-Determination", p. 454. Note that this feature of the right (or of rights in general) does not rule out its being "conditional on its being exercised for the right reasons, i.e., to secure conditions necessary for the prosperity and self-respect of the group" (p. 459).

13 Margalit and Raz, "National Self-Determination", pp. 456–57. "In our world, encompassing groups that do not enjoy self-government are not infrequently persecuted, despised, or neglected. Given the importance of their prosperity and self-respect to the well-being of their members, it seems reasonable to entrust their members with the right to determine whether the groups should be self-governing".

14 It is important to study Margalit and Raz's defense of a group right to self-determination alongside the latter's piece on multiculturalism, "Multiculturalism: A Liberal Perspective", reprinted in his *Ethics in the Public Domain: Essays in the Morality of Law and Politics* (Oxford: Clarendon Press, 1995), pp. 170–92. Some have read this essay as a retreat from the unpopular conclusions of the self-determination paper, but it is not. Raz's view is that liberal multiculturalism is the best policy for our societies; separation and independence is only for those who fail to live together (personal correspondence).

15 John Rawls, *A Theory of Justice* (Cambridge, MA: Harvard University Press, 1971), p. 4.

sustain and facilitate mutually beneficial cooperation will be rationalized thereby. Consider the rule of law and its importance for cooperation of different kinds among large groups of individuals. For instance, law provides assurance that others will not defect from mutually beneficial arrangements. Trust also facilitates cooperation. Now social identity and associated sentiments of solidarity also facilitate cooperation by providing assurance, by reinforcing trust, and in many other ways. Insofar as bonds of nationality and culture help to reinforce trust and to provide assurance, they facilitate cooperation among member of the relevant group(s) and this fact strengthens the national consideration.

In addition, increased solidarity and trust increase stability and efficiency. As a consequence, they may reduce the need for the enforcement of law. This is of some importance. The illiberal tendencies of most nationalist movements have long been noted. But the ways in which nationalist sentiments and values may make possible a reduction in the coercive activities of states and especially their use of force have not been sufficiently appreciated.

I tentatively conclude that the case for national self-determination is "pretty good": national identity can be a strong consideration favoring significant political independence and quite possibly independent statehood for national groups. This is Claim 1. The constraints on national self-determination are important and not to be ignored. But my principal concern is with evaluating the strength of the case for. To this end I need now to examine how this case fares comparatively, that is, compared to other cases for political independence and statehood.[16]

2. STATEHOOD

I have said that the case for national self-determination is "pretty good". I am being deliberately imprecise for now. I want to ask, "pretty good, compared to what"? In order to focus on what is most controversial, let me assume, less controversially, that the case for a special status for national groups in a federal state is solid (though defeasible). What is most controversial is the case for independent statehood, and it is to this that we turn our attention.

Suppose then that national self-determination can be a strong consideration favoring independent statehood. There are many other considerations that

[16] I note that I am agnostic about whether the case for national self-determination supports a claim-right or only a liberty. Margalit and Raz are explicit about supporting the former, a (claim-)right to national self-determination: "the right to determine whether a certain territory shall become, or remain, a separate state (and possibly whether it should enjoy autonomy within a larger state)". But we shall not pursue this question.

also support statehood. The question, then, is what is so special about national self-determination? It may seem to be one among many considerations favoring statehood. For instance, consider that states do many important and useful things. Most anarchists deny it, but suppose it to be true, even if states also do many useless or harmful things. A state's performance of certain functions or tasks (e.g., providing security for its subjects, a number of important public or collective goods) seems to be a consideration in favor of it. For many, how well a state does with regard to the tasks given to it determines what we should think of it. To the extent a state does well in performing these tasks, that is a consideration in its favor.

Jefferson famously assigned to government the task of securing certain rights and noted that governments "deriv[e] their just powers from the consent of the governed". The consent of the government is often thought to be a consideration in favor of a state. Lockeans and many others hold that consent here must be actual, a dated event. If I cannot remember consenting and there is no evidence I ever did, then we have reason to be sceptical of claims that I have. Consent must be an event, observable to others. By contrast, hypothetical consent need not be observed or noticed, much less an event. There are many accounts of the importance of hypothetical consent for the justification of a state. But hypothetical consent is not genuine consent, and consequently it is a different consideration than "consent of the governed".[17]

Both hypothetical and actual consent are often confused with consensus.[18] Normally they should be distinguished. The subjects of a state may believe that their state is just or competent, and even that it merits their support, even though they have not consented. The absence of such a consensus, some think, may lead to a crisis of legitimacy. Certainly the support a government has depends considerably on opinion.

There seem to be several different types of considerations favoring states: the performance of useful tasks and services, actual consent, hypothetical consent, and consensus or agreement (in belief). I have not presented a complete taxonomy – Hegel's view of the state is not easily fit into these

[17] "It is therefore, on opinion only that government is founded; and this maxim extends to the most despotic and most military governments, as well as to the most free and most popular". David Hume, "Of the First Principles of Government", in *Essays, Moral, Political, and Literary*, Eugene F. Miller, ed. (Indianapolis, IN: Liberty Fund, [1742] 1987), pp. 32–37.

[18] Ernest Renan's famous essay on the nature of nations is a good example of confusion about these and other distinctions. "L'existence d'une nation est (pardonnez-moi cette métaphore) un plebiscite de tous les jours". ("The existence of a nation (forgive me this metaphor) is a daily plebiscite", tr. mine). Ernest Renan, *Qu'est-ce qu'une nation?* (Paris: Pierre Bordas, 1991 [1882]), p. 41.

familiar types. The considerations highlighted by each view are importantly different. The important point for our discussion is that there seem to be several kinds of considerations, most of which may support statehood. This is my Claim 2.

In one respect Claim 2 diminishes the significance of Claim 1; there are *many* considerations in favor of political independence or statehood. What is special about one of them? We need to know about their relative strength. I have intentionally been talking imprecisely of considerations in favor of something; we know from other contexts that considerations vary tremendously in strength, some so insignificant that they are not worth considering. There is little consensus in the literature on the comparative value of these considerations – more will be said about this presently.

The suggestion is that national self-determination is a consideration in support of statehood, and we have noted that there are others, mentioning the main contenders. A supporting consideration can of course be quite weak or, more to the point, in other ways insufficient to ground certain claims. For instance, my wish to repay a large debt or to buy an expensive present for someone may be a consideration in favor of robbing a bank, but this consideration does not give me the right to the money I take. Similarly, certain facts – for instance, the existence of a consensus or hypothetical consent – may be considerations in favor of political independence. But it is not clear they establish the requisite rights. In fact, they do not; none of the traditional stories show what they are supposed to show. My Claim 3 is that the considerations mentioned, including national self-determination, do not establish what they are meant to show; they do not establish that a particular (nation-)state is legitimate in particular sense.

To say that a particular state is legitimate or that a particular group of people is entitled to form a new (legitimate) state is to attribute a certain status to it, according it "the separate and equal station" to which it is entitled according to Jefferson. Legitimacy is a status that gives the holder a right to exist and to rule. The latter is usually interpreted as the power to make, adjudicate, and enforce laws and also the power to make agreements and form alliances with other states and entities. In addition, one of the distinguishing features of modern states is a claim to *exclusivity* of rule: the state has the right to rule its territory, and no one else does. States claim *sovereignty*: they are the ultimate source of political authority within their realm.[19]

[19] For details see my *Essay on the Modern State*, ch. 2.

The right to rule will now be our focus. The classical interpretation of the state's right to rule would have it entail certain correlative obligations. Those subject to the law (e.g., citizens, residents) are obligated to support it in various ways (e.g., military service, taxes, loyalty) and not to undermine the state in various ways (e.g., insurrection, revolution). More importantly, subjects are obligated to obey the law; that is, to obey each and every (genuine) law that applies to them, on each and every occasion that is applies. This obligation is meant to be not just a consideration that subjects are to use to determine what they are to do but a consideration that settles what they are to do. The fact that a valid law requires one to do something is meant to be a reason to do it, a reason which overrules other considerations and settles what one is to do.[20] Such a reason *preempts* other considerations; it is meant to be a preemptive reason. The fact that the law requires me to refrain from robbing the bank or to obey the traffic signs is supposed to be a preemptive reason for me to do so. Many laws will be supported by a number of considerations, but all are supposed to share one property, namely their authority. The story I am sketching here is familiar; Raz is the best contemporary expositor and defender of this view. A version of the account is to be found in Hobbes' view of law as command, where "Command is, where a man saith, *Doe this*, or *Doe not this*, without expecting other reason than the Will of him that sayes it".[21]

There is considerable scepticism about this classical view of the right to rule. It is not likely the case that the subjects of legitimate states have an obligation (and reasons) to obey every law that applies to them. It is easy to think of circumstances in which complying with many laws would not be a good use of one's time; a familiar example is coming to a full stop at a stop sign in the desert. While we may have obligations to obey in such cases, it is unlikely that we will have preemptive reasons; one may have a reason to come to a full stop but not a preemptive one.[22]

The problem here is the universal quantifier or, rather, quantifiers: *all* (valid) laws, *all* subjects. It is difficult to see how a claim this strong could be established, even where it is true that most people have reasons most of the time to obey most laws. I cannot defend this position here; it is now widely but certainly not universally accepted. The second source of the difficulty

[20] A reason can settle what is to be done while being defeasible, that is, overrideable by another reason. For instance, a promise to meet someone can settle what I am to do today even though certain events (e.g., illness) might have overridden it.

[21] Hobbes, *Leviathan*, ed. R. Tuck (Cambridge: Cambridge University Press, [1651] 1996), ch. 25.

[22] For the argument, see Raz, *The Morality of Freedom* (Oxford: Clarendon Press, 1986), chs. 3–4. See also my *Essay on the Modern State*.

concerns restricting the set of those obligated to the subjects of the state, that is, the citizens and residents. The problem here is "the particularity requirement" on accounts of the obligation to obey the state: such accounts must show that subjects of the law are obligated to obey the laws of *their* state and not necessarily those of other states.[23] Modern states rule *territorially*; that is, their laws apply in the first instance to agents who find themselves in the state's territory. This means that all subjects and no nonsubjects are supposed to have obligations to obey. Suppose, for instance, that we think that the state's services are considerations for its status. Then might not some Canadians, protected as they are by American national defense, be obligated to obey American law?[24]

The subjects – *all* the subjects – of a classically legitimate state have obligations and preemptive reasons to obey the valid laws that apply to them. Accordingly it has proved very hard to show that any existing state is classically legitimate, that is, to show that all citizens and virtually no noncitizens have obligations to obey the state. We can, however, consider a weaker set of standards for legitimacy. To summarize, if a state is legitimate, it has a right to exist and a right to rule. In a classical legitimate state, in addition to an obligation (and a preemptive reason) not to undermine the state and to support it in various ways, subjects have an obligation to obey the law – that is, an obligation to obey every valid law that applies to them. What I will call weak legitimacy imposes mainly an obligation on subjects not to undermine the state and to support in certain ways. So, if a state possesses weak legitimacy, subjects have an obligation (and a preemptive reason) not to undermine the state and to support it in various ways. If it possesses classical legitimacy, subjects also have an obligation (and a preemptive reason) to obey the law. We should note that nonsubjects will in both cases have obligations not to undermine legitimate states and, in certain circumstances, to support it.

[23] See A. John Simmons, *Moral Principles and Political Obligations* (Princeton, NJ: Princeton University Press, 1979) and *Justification and Legitimacy: Essays on Rights and Obligations* (Cambridge: Cambridge University Press, 2001); Leslie Green, *The Authority of the State* (Oxford: Clarendon Press, 1988).

[24] In addition to the particularity problem, there is controversy about the specifically territorial basis of the authority of the modern state. See my *Essay on the Modern State*, chs. 2, 8, and elsewhere. Margalit and Raz address this matter in passing: "The right is over a territory. This simply reflects the territorial organization of our political world. The requirement that the group be a substantial majority of the territory stems from further considerations aimed at balancing the interest in self-government against the interests of nonmembers" (p. 458). I am indebted to Matthew Lister for some helpful comments on this question, which I am not addressing here.

Interestingly, the obligations of subjects and nonsubjects toward a weakly legitimate state may be similar.[25]

My first claim, deliberately imprecise, was that "the case for national self-determination is 'pretty good': national identity can be a strong consideration favoring significant political independence and quite possibly independent statehood for national groups". I then argued that there are many considerations favoring statehood but that none of these considerations are likely to support the classical legitimacy of a state. So the "pretty good" consideration does not yield that which it aims to establish. But we have reason to abandon the goal of securing classical legitimacy for a state; no state seems to achieve it, and it is not clear it is needed. Some states are or seem to be weakly legitimate; they provide law and order, some important public goods, and the like, and thereby merit our support. There may also be a consensus that these states are worth supporting, a large number of subjects (genuinely) consented, and the like.

The question now is whether national self-determination supports the weak legitimacy of a state. Weak legitimacy comes in degrees, so the answer is likely to be affirmative if national self-determination facilitates the state's performance of its appropriate functions, if it increases the consensus or consent supporting the state, and the like. I have argued in effect that national self-determination can do these things. In addition – my supplementary argument – the nationalist sentiments and values of subjects can strengthen the trust and consensus of members of a polity and facilitate cooperation. This may have the effect of lessening the coercion and possibly the force needed for governance. Insofar as a state is more stable and less reliant on coercion and force, the stronger the case may be for supporting it.

As I have stressed, there is little agreement about the relative weight of the considerations favoring states. That is, there is disagreement between the partisans of the different traditions I have mentioned. There is greater agreement that most of these are genuine considerations in favor of states, that is, in support of what I have called their weak legitimacy. But there is little consensus about the relative strength of the different ones. We cannot easily conclude that national self-determination is as strong, say, as consensus or hypothetical consent. But I think we can say that the case for national self-determination seems "pretty good".

[25] For a more detailed explication of my views about legitimacy, see my "State Legitimacy and Social Order", in *Political Legitimization without Morality*, Jörg Kühnelt, ed. (Heidelberg: Springer, 2008), pp. 15–32. This essay corrects some of the claims I make about legitimacy in my *Essay on the Modern State*, where I do not clearly distinguish legitimacy from justication.

As I said at the outset, my argument will disappoint many nationalists. The conclusion I reach is not very strong. I think that nationalist considerations have been given short shrift, especially in American settings,[26] and I wish to give them their due. But I need also to note some of the limitations of national self-determination. While I have mentioned the conditions that national self-determination cases must meet, I have not dwelt on the familiar excesses of nationalist movement. A violation of these conditions undermines the case for statehood. Some of the excesses are nuisances – for instance, parts of the French language law in Québec. But others are damning; ethnic cleansing and mass murder (e.g., Srebrenica) obviously undermine any case for national self-determination. The language and metaphors found in some of the more innocent nationalisms should give us pause. If the blood of our enemies is impure ("un sang impur"), we may be more inclined to think of them as inferiors.[27] Nationalism, especially that associated with mass movements, can be worrisome, to understate the matter.

There is much to be said about nationalism and the case for national self-determination, but there is also much to worry about. I do not wish to downplay the latter. The case for national self-determination is "pretty good" but limited. The worries about nationalism are not diminished by acknowledging what may be said in its favor. I have been concerned here only with the latter.

[26] It is quite interesting to note that in contemporary Anglo-American political theory, much of the writing in any way sympathetic to nationalism is by British philosophers (e.g., Berlin, D. Miller), Canadians (e.g., Kymlicka, Norman, C. Taylor), Israelis (e.g., Margalit, Raz, Tamir), and Americans with strong ties to Israel (e.g., Walzer).

[27] Some of the lines of the French national anthem are awkward to sing. For the ethnic nationalism in Jefferson's Declaration, see my essay, "Peoples, Nations, and the Unity of Societies", in *Cultural Identity and the Nation-State,* Carol C. Gould and Pasquale Pasquino, eds. (Lanham, MD: Rowman & Littlefield, 2001), pp. 19–29.

3

The Right to Self-Determination

Earned, Not Inherent

FRÉDÉRIC MÉGRET

This chapter is dedicated to the notion that self-determination is not an inherent right but a right that is earned. It seeks to depart from a tradition of international legal thinking on self-determination that is strong on the recognition of the principle but weak on its characterizations, particularly as a result of a romanticization of the concept of "peoples." International legal thinking on the idea of self-determination has arguably been marked by a constant decay since the principle was first mooted in international law after the First World War. The chapter tries to rescue the principle from this decay by opening it up to moral scrutiny and forging a concept of self-determination that is less based on identifying peoples in the abstract than on identifying the conditions under which a people renders itself worthy of the recognition of self-determination that it claims for itself.

A few preliminary words on definitions and methods are in order here. First, self-determination will be understood as incorporating the search for all kinds of political arrangements that further the ability of groups to govern themselves, including the search for autonomy or federalization within existing states. In other words, self-determination is a much broader notion than secession, particularly unilateral secession, which has been the focus of much debate.[1] Even as a territorial quest it may seek less than secession (e.g., territorial autonomy), and it need in fact not be a specifically territorial quest in the first place (e.g., some form of self-governance or regulation occurring on a personal rather than territorial basis).[2] Indeed it seems that

[1] In that respect, although I take Brilmayer's point about secession being mostly a territorial issue, I do not agree that the same need be true of self-determination more broadly. See Lea Brilmayer, "Secession and Self-Determination: A Territorial Interpretation," *Yale Journal of International Law* 16, no. 1 (1991): 177–202.

[2] Frédéric Mégret, "Is There Ever a 'Right to One's Own Law?' An Exploration of Possible Rights Foundations for Legal Pluralism," *Israel Law Review* 45, no. 1 (2012): 3–34.

the twenty-first century has never been more ripe for forms of collective self-governance that shun territory altogether, so that the traditional focus on secession as the be-all and end-all of self-determination theory, historically and politically important as that question has been, may lead to significant distortions of what is at stake. In fact, some of the difficulties that the international law of self-determination has occasionally gotten itself into are linked to its inability to think of self-determination in all but territorial terms, which typically triggers powerful prudential counterreactions from international lawyers. Emphasizing the possibility of alternative nonsecessionist options for self-determination is often the reasonable endpoint conclusion of some of the finer treatments of the issue. By the same token, the chapter does propose to take the possibility of secession and its place within any overall theory of self-determination seriously, even as it resists treating it as the paradigmatic example of the issue. Secession rightly holds a particularly interesting place within all theories of self-determination because of the way it radicalizes its stakes and because of the way as, henceforth, the exception it helps define the rule. In focusing on "peoples" the hope is to come up with theoretical insights that are applicable to both so-called "external" and "internal" self-determination.[3]

Second, what follows is in the tradition of the moral critique of the law, specifically of the moral critique of the international legal tradition. Taking self-determination seriously as a moral issue means that its possibility or impossibility must ultimately be based on considerations of justice or rights. The theory of self-determination, in particular, has deep links with democratic theory. It is difficult, as a result, to conceive of a theory of self-determination that would not anchor itself within a horizon of rights and democracy without in the end devouring itself or simply condoning the worst excesses. This chapter, however, does not seek to develop a fully fledged theory of self-determination based on first principles. Rather, it seeks to develop a theory of self-determination that could be anchored within existing international legal principles, even as it might depart from some of the current limitations associated with international law. The goal is thus the relatively modest one of seeking to develop the best possible moral theory of international law's existing recognition of the right. This exercise is close to Allen Buchanan's treatment of the question "as a matter of international institution morality, including a morally defensible system of international law,"[4] except perhaps that the argument seeks to be more embedded in existing legal structures.

3 A similar starting point is evident in Daniel Philpott, "In Defense of Self-Determination," *Ethics* 105, no. 2 (1995): 352–385.

4 Allen Buchanan, "Theories of Secession," *Philosophy & Public Affairs* 26, no. 1 (1997): 31–32.

Third, within moral theory, the chapter is interested in the possibility of a *principled* international legal justification of self-determination.[5] It treats with circumspection, therefore, purely prudential or pragmatic arguments about why international law ought to allow or limit self-determination, or the claim that such arguments have a monopoly on international ethics. The point is not to disqualify these arguments – indeed they may be perfectly valid in some circumstances – but to better identify them as second-order arguments for a certain position, rather than the first-order arguments they sometimes try to pass themselves as. Moreover, the chapter will try to argue, contra Allen Buchanan's influential view that an ideal theory of self-determination cannot be reconciled with an understanding of its international institutional implications because it necessarily creates "perverse incentives,"[6] that the two can in fact be reconciled. A theory of self-determination based on primary (rather than just remedial) rights can be defended without representing a descent into chaos. In other words, it will be argued that a principled justification of self-determination – notably one focused on who can exercise it, when, and how as questions going to its fundamental justifiability – already includes inbuilt breaks to the tendency of the principle to otherwise prompt a seemingly endless stream of claims.

There are at present roughly three categories of theories of thinking about self-determination. The first focuses on who is "a people" for the purposes of self-determination; the second focuses on the just means that a people ought to use to achieve self-determination; and the third looks at what type of self-determination (i.e., internal or external) may be sought on the basis of the political circumstances experienced by a people. This chapter seeks to bridge the gap between these theories by arguing that who is a people for the purposes of international law and what a people ought to do to achieve what sort of self-determination are intimately related questions. It argues, in fact, that a people worthy of self-determination emerges from the experience of and struggle for self-determination. Instead of the idea of a people existing in isolation and separately from international society, it emphasizes the extent

5 A good analogy for what I am interested in is the work that has been going on in the last decade on the justification of the laws of war. For examples in the laws of war context, see Jeff McMahan, "The Ethics of Killing in War," *Ethics* 114, no. 4 (2004): 693–733; Jeff McMahan, "The Morality of War and the Law of War," in *Just and Unjust Warriors: The Moral and Legal Status of Soldiers*, eds. David Rodin and Henry Shue (Oxford: Oxford University Press, 2008), 19–43.

6 Buchanan, "Theories of Secession," 32 (see n. 7).

to which peoples construct themselves dialogically and politically, and the degree to which international law's primary task should be to identify peoples that have earned their right to self-determination in the process of claiming it.

The chapter begins with a brief overview of the positive international law of self-determination and the relatively pitiful state in which it finds itself as a principle of international legal ordering (Section 1). At the heart of the ambiguity of the concept of self-determination is the difficulty of defining the "self" of the principle. I argue that we need to return to the centrality of what constitutes "a people," but that there are no "peoples" in the absolute from which a right to self-determination would unproblematically flow, only peoples who decide to constitute themselves as such through their aspiration to self-determine (Section 2). In an effort to move beyond the circularity of that definition, the chapter then suggests a turn to a vision of self-determination as a right that is earned rather than inherent. It outlines a number of ways in which a people might behave that should incline the international community to recognize their right to self-determination (Section 3). The chapter leads to the sketch of theory of self-determination that may ultimately not be noticeably more open than existing theories and remains quite cautious, yet helps us move beyond certain unhelpful simplifications (Section 4).

1. A BRIEF OVERVIEW AND CRITIQUE OF THE POSITIVE INTERNATIONAL LAW OF SELF-DETERMINATION

Let us begin with a very concise account of the right to self-determination as a legal right in the twentieth century because so much hinges on what self-determination has effectively become historically. It is important to note that the view that there is a right to self-determination in international law is very much a legal claim both in the weak (there is a "right") and in the strong sense (self-determination is *amenable* to the law rather than being, say, a prior political condition of the law's possibility). International law's attitude to self-determination has oscillated in the last century between the temptation of encouraging group aspirations to forms of political and territorial power and a recoiling at the possible consequences for international order and stability. The fate of self-determination in international law began with the term being loosely tossed around at Versailles, based on Woodrow Wilson's vision for Europe "that every people has a right to choose the sovereignty under which they shall live."[7] In this context, the right was clearly linked to certain subjects, identified as "peoples," as something derivative of an underlying reality.

It soon emerged, however, that the principle's utility in that context had little to do with anything more than the dismantling of the old European and Ottoman empires. Self-determination had its winners (Poland, arguably) and its many losers, perhaps all the more so that they took its promise seriously. The United States's own engagement with the principle had been a very ambiguous one from the Civil War to the colonization of the Philippines. The Bosheviks sought to put Wilson before his contradictions by arguing for self-determination for all peoples, including those under colonial domination, but to predictably little avail. The principle of national self-determination, it turned out, was less about nationhood than it was about the continuing normalization of the Westphalian order and, in the best of cases, democratic statehood as against amorphous empires (which may well have also suppressed nationalities but which were mostly too unwieldy for everyone else's good, and at any rate corpses on which the Allies fed happily). Influenced in Versailles by his advisor Lansing, Wilson was only too aware that:

> In point of logic, of pure logic, this principle which was good in itself would lead to the complete independence of various small nationalities now forming part of various empires. Pushed to its extreme, the principle would mean the disruption of existing governments, to an indefinable degree.[8]

The principle would again be seized upon after the Second World War, this time as offering a conceptual pathway to decolonization. In that respect, its success was nothing short of startling and its ongoing popularity is no doubt associated with this golden age. Simultaneously, the principle's centrality to the international legal order was increasingly and ritually affirmed. Its importance was ratified by the UN Charter itself, which made it into a goal of the United Nations. Self-determination began being talked about not only as a property of public international law but increasingly as a human right,[9] even as a collective right conditioning the enjoyment of all individual rights. That

7 Presidential Address, President Woodrow Wilson, address delivered at the First Annual Assemblage of the League to Enforce Peace: "American Principles" (May 27, 1916), www.presidency.ucsb.edu/ws/?pid=65391.

8 Allen Lynch, "Woodrow Wilson and the Principle of 'National Self-Determination': A Reconsideration," *Review of International Studies* 28, no. 2 (2002): 425.

9 International Covenant on Civil and Political Rights art. 1, Dec. 16, 1966, S. Treaty Doc. No. 95-20, 6 I.L.M. 368 (1967), 999 U.N.T.S. 171; International Covenant on Economic, Social and Cultural Rights art. 1, Dec. 16, 1966, S. Treaty Doc. No. 95-19, 6 I.L.M. 360 (1967), 993 U.N.T.S. 3.

mix of rationales is nowhere more clear than in resolution 1514 of the UN General Assembly, which emphasized that "the subjection of peoples to alien subjugation, domination and exploitation constitutes a denial of fundamental human rights, is contrary to the Charter of the United Nations and is an impediment to the promotion of world peace and co-operation." The link between self-determination and rights language has increasingly meant that self-determination is considered to be inherent in particular "peoples,"[10] an expression that seems to be used by analogy with the inherent rights and dignity of the human person.

However, the principle was again interpreted in very narrow terms to mean the right of peoples living in particular *outre-mer* colonial dependencies to obtain their sovereignty. It was certainly not understood as an invitation to reconfigure African states, for example. Those who took the principle too literarily, from Katanga to Biafra, learned their lesson painfully. Newly independent states that had emerged on the territory of former colonial dependencies on the basis of a right to self-determination were prompt to deny that right to groups within them, whatever the heterogeneity and minority problems that resulted, based on the awkward sanctification of colonial boundaries (the uti possidetis principle). Thus came about that most significant of results: that the right of self-determination could be used to both promote the emancipation of some and confirm the subjugation of others.

In effect, the right to secession was reduced to an option exercisable only by Third World people colonized by Europeans, and even then one that had to be exercised within the arbitrary territorial limits set by that colonization itself. The theory was thus led to make relatively specious distinctions between different categories of "peoples" that only make sense from a very reductionist view of what self-determination is about. For example, the distinction between colonial dependencies having a right to external self-determination (the so-called salt water test) and a number of irredentist groups in Europe or indigenous groups in the Americas only having such a right in extreme cases

[10] Although the expression is not exactly a term of art in international law, the term "inherent" is tossed liberally into actual claims of and the literature on self-determination. See Markus B. Heyder, "The International Law Commission's Draft Articles on State Responsibility: Draft Article 19 and Native American Self-Determination," *Columbia Journal of Transnational Law* 32, no. 1 (1994): 168, 169, 173, 175; Catherine J. Iorns, "Indigenous Peoples and Self Determination: Challenging State Sovereignty," *Case Western Reserve Journal of International Law* 24, no. 2 (1992): 224, 232, 292, 302–08. On a closely related "inherent right to self-government," see Jennifer E. Dalton, "Aboriginal Self-Determination in Canada: Protections Afforded by the Judiciary and Government," *Canadian Journal of Law and Society* 21, no. 1 (2006): 11–37.

of oppression is, ultimately, hard to defend. All may implicate at a certain level some form of colonialism, or at least of oppression that cannot easily be distinguished from colonialism as it expressed itself as a specific European ideology of domination of non-Western peoples. It is ultimately very hard to justify in principled terms why secession should be granted to certain African people merely because it was initially denied to them in the late nineteenth century from overseas European metropolis, but not to others who were, if not colonized, at least subjugated, repressed and tormented by their more immediate "neighbour" (in Europe or in Africa). French colonization of Africa, for example, may be a more glaring case of suppressing a peoples' right to self-determine, but French Jacobinism's suppression of local identities and aspirations to autonomy is difficult to understand morally as being of an inherently different nature.[11]

Even as the principle was reaching the pinnacle of its solemnity and creating momentous expectations, its scope was thus significantly restricted. Human rights bodies have been largely reluctant to adjudicate on the right of self-determination per se, instead focusing on individual cultural rights. This effectively reduces the right to self-determination to very little, disaggregating its collective dimension into an infinite quantity of individual aspirations to be different that are barely distinguishable from the ordinary exercise of freedom. The death knell to the principle's more ambitious sovereignty and territory-reconfiguring potential was brought by the wars of former Yugoslavia. Although the breakup of Yugoslavia itself was impossible to prevent, it was understood that the breakup should respect the frontiers of the Yugoslav federation the Badinter Commission insisted that there was no right to secede.[12] The attempts by the Bosno-Serbs to carve out a statelet within Bosnia have been vigorously fought over the last two decades by the international community. By the time Quebec asked the Canadian Supreme

[11] Certainly the passage of time and the fact that memories of oppression may have dimmed, consolidating peoples into a single nation, is not itself decisive in cases where certain peoples' sentiment of distinctness is in effect resurrected. Awareness of group identity may be just as strong, if not stronger, among the Quebecers of Canada or the Basques of France and Spain, than it was amongst the Nigerian "people" on the eve of decolonization. Indeed, some classically colonized peoples may to this day not seek secession, so that to claim that they are being denied their right to self-determination if they are not granted an independent state may be disingenuous.

[12] Conference on Yugoslavia, Arbitration Commission Opinion No. 3 (Jan. 11, 1992), 31 ILM 1499 (1992). See also UN General Assembly (GA), Resolution 2625, "Declaration on Principles of International Law concerning Friendly Relations and Cooperation among States in accordance with the Charter of the United Nations," Oct. 24, 1970, www.un.org/en/ga/search/view_doc.asp?symbol=A/RES/2625(XXV).

Court, self-determination was equated, essentially, with a right to self-determine internally, that is, as an entitlement to democracy.[13]

This idea, however, can be faulted for its vacuity. If self-determination is understood merely as an entitlement to liberal democracy, then the concept loses much of its bite because it might as well be called the international right to democratic governance, a right whose separate existence is occasionally, more or less credibly, touted in international law circles.[14] The problem of collapsing the right to self-determination and the right to democracy, moreover, is that it confuses two levels of analysis, the question of the best or fairest regime in the abstract and the question of appropriate political community. It takes for granted that an unproblematic people exist for whom the question of the best possible regime arises in the abstract. This ignores the fact that democracy always raises the question "for whom?" and that we hardly live in a post-historical world in which the question of community has ceased to have significance.

From the ashes of what were once wild and clearly historically misplaced hopes for the congruence between "peoples," political power and territory, have emerged two notions. First, the idea that there might still be room for secessionist claims as a specifically "remedial" right has become a hallmark of political and moral theorizing on the issue,[15] helping to preserve the promise of self-determination's radical potential as a principle of sovereign political organization. In this configuration, peoplehood is no longer the ultimate basis for self-determination, injustice is. This is clearly a step in the right direction, the direction of defining peoples in political rather than organic terms. Yet international law has seemed to remain rather agnostic about whether secession in particular is ever a legitimate part of a right to self-determination. The reception of remedial theories of secession in positive international law, apart from a passing recognition in the Quebec secession reference,[16] has been lukewarm to say the least.

Rather, the international community seems to have settled for a position in which it will recognize the results of a successful secession while not actually

[13] *Reference re: Secession of Quebec*, [1998] 2 S.C.R. 217 (Can.) ("A state whose government represents the whole of the people or peoples resident within its territory, on a basis of equality and without discrimination, and respects the principles of self-determination in its own internal arrangements, is entitled to the protection under international law of its territorial integrity.")

[14] Thomas M. Franck, "The Emerging Right to Democratic Governance," *American Journal of International Law* 86, no. 1 (1992): 46–91.

[15] See Allen Buchanan, "Secession" in *Stanford Encyclopedia of Philosophy*, at http://plato.stanford.edu/entries/secession.

[16] *Reference re: Secession of Quebec*, [1998] 2 S.C.R. 217 (Can.).

recognizing that there is a right to it. In practice, the effectiveness of secession has often acted as a substitute for its fairness, and for every Tibet, Republika Srpska, or Chechnya there is an Eritrea, Bangladesh, Kosovo, or South Sudan. Normatively, this is arguably the worst possible result, an invitation to political adventurism that is not even remotely constrained by normative ambition and ends up merely recognizing what is based on purely pragmatic grounds. A principle that had started as a potentially radical means to restructure the international system, then, is at risk of being turned into a principle to justify the system as it exists at any given time. It is, at best, a mere supplementary defense of a particular political regime – democracy – whose fortune is now linked to the existence of particular peoples. International law ends up with the worst of both worlds: a rigid and conservative system that condones the existing distribution of states and groups within them on the one hand, and that occasionally recognizes some secessions based on the *fait accompli* and the luck of arms on the other. When given an opportunity in concrete circumstances to define the scope of a right to self-determination, notably to secession, the International Court of Justice (ICJ) preferred to largely elude the question, in a telltale sign of how fraught and confused the debate has become.[17]

Moreover, the focus on secession as the decisive issue for self-determination has arguably overshadowed any more fine-grained assessment of the second idea to emerge about self-determination, namely that of an entitlement to some form of recognition, even autonomy for minorities.[18] Although international law is more open that it has ever been to this notion, its success in pressing for such regimes remains limited; and although autonomy is presented as a solution to problems of ethnic fragmentation, the contours of a "right to autonomy" have not been convincingly clarified. Long before the question of remedial secession arises, the question of the right to some form of minority recognition is an issue that remains mired in controversy. This is despite the fact that presumably in order to prevent a situation deteriorating to such a point that remedial secession becomes morally justifiable (if not legally protected), some answer must be given to the question of who is entitled to

[17] For a critique, see Robert L. Howse and Ruti Teitel, "Humanity Bounded and Unbounded: The Regulation of External Self-Determination under International Law," *Law & Ethics of Human Rights* 7, no. 2 (2013): 155.

[18] Marc Weller and Stefan Wolff, "Self-Determination and Autonomy," in *Autonomy, Self-governance and Conflict Resolution: Innovative Approaches to Institutional Design in Divided Societies*, eds. Marc Weller and Stefan Wolff (London: Routledge, 2005); Kristin Henrard, *Devising an Adequate System of Minority Protection: Individual Human Rights, Minority Rights, and the Right to Self-Determination*, vol. 62 (The Hague: Martinus Nijhoff, 2000).

autonomy in the first place. Moreover, remedial secession's very theory (that secession becomes a possibility when a *people* are being oppressed or unfairly denied self-determination) implies that we know what a people are.

Common to the difficulties of assessing the scope of both internal and external self-determination, therefore, are arguably persistent doubts about what constitutes "a people" worthy of recognition as such. An important part of the aspiration to self-determination has always been about the definition of a relevant "peoples" for the purposes of the exercise of power. Secession, even framed as a remedial right, is ultimately a special case of a *peoples'* right to self-determination. The idea that a people who are victim of grave injustice may earn a right to secede unilaterally still begs the question of what constitutes them as a people in the first place. And while a remedial theory of unilateral secession may be defendable, it is implausible that minority protection or recognition should itself be remedial. This is because substate groups legitimately aspire to recognition even in cases where they have not been the victims of massive injustice. Requiring injustice as a condition of secession makes sense because of the hugely disruptive potential of secession. The following two sections thus endeavor to take seriously the notion of "peoples" as the conceptual and normative substratum to any right of external or external self-determination.

2. THE IMPORTANCE OF THE "SELF" IN "SELF-DETERMINATION": WHAT/WHO IS "A PEOPLE"?

The classic basis for being recognized as having a right to self-determination, particularly in international legal discourse, has been that a group is "a people." As the first article of both the international covenants on human rights put it, "all *peoples* have the right to self-determination." In its simplest "human rights" form, this suggests an ontology and a process that are far more straightforward than the reality. While all may agree superficially that such a thing as a right to self-determination exists, the problem is there is very little agreement as to what constitutes, precisely, a people. Indeed, the idea that the problem of who should self-determine can be avoided by relying on an identification of a prior "people" is, I will argue, ultimately misleading, at least unless it is significantly problematized. From a human rights point of view, incidentally, this underlines the distinctness of the right to self-determination in that its subject is forever shrouded in controversy – there is no similar ambiguity (or at least much less of it) when it comes to defining who is a human being.

Part of the problem is that thinking about self-determination has long been too wedded to the romantic notion that there are "peoples" that exist in a certain more or less unproblematic state, and onto which can be grafted the right of self-determination. This idea was dominant in the nineteenth century and continues to influence international legal debates to this day, perhaps unsurprisingly given how indebted international law remains to this earlier era (in that respect, the trajectory of someone like Woodrow Wilson, straddling as it did the nineteenth and twentieth centuries, is particularly interesting). It is typically based on a primordialist or essentialist vision of the nation that sees it as an organic whole preceding its self-reflective and, more importantly, political coming into being. So-called "ascriptive theories of self-determination,"[19] then, would grant self-determination to any people qualifying as such objectively.

There are many problems with such theories. One of them is that some people so identified may not actually be interested in their right to self-determination, or even actually self-determining in any sense of the term (simply because they share ethnic characteristics and a language, e.g., does not mean that they seek to self-direct themselves collectively, or are ready to press claims). Moreover, apart from the fact that the international legal order has *not* been ready to really grant self-determination to all such peoples anyhow (which surely is no trivial detail), the theory has led to the somewhat vacuous search for what might constitute "a people." Is it ethnicity? Is it religion? Is it culture? Is it language? A combination of some or all of the above? The problem is that these things, important for processes of nation building as they may be, do not unproblematically constitute a people. As Yaelle Tamir put it:

> all attempts to single out a particular set of objective features – be it a common history, collective destiny, language, religion, territory, climate, race, ethnicity – as necessary and sufficient for the definition of a nation have ended in failure. Although all these features have been mentioned as characteristic of some nations, no nation will have all of them.[20]

It is important, in this respect, not to confuse slogans and strategies for internal mobilization or external consumption with a fully fledged case for peoplehood or self-determination. The fact that certain characteristics are ordinarily highlighted politically as signaling a people and triggering a right to self-determination is not the same thing as saying that these characteristics always, in and of themselves, exhaust the question of who is a people.

At the very least it seems necessary to inject a subjective element into the definition of a people, along the lines of David Miller's suggestion that

[19] Buchanan, "Theories of Secession," 38 (see n. 7).

[20] Yael Tamir, *Liberal Nationalism* (Princeton, NJ: Princeton University Press, 1995), 65.

"a nationality exists when its members believe that it does."[21] The better view of what constitutes a people/nation has always been, from Ernest Renan ("a daily plebiscite") to Benedict Anderson ("imagined communities"),[22] that they are voluntary – if not always conscious – constructs.[23] In other words, following Ernest Gellner, it is not nations that create nationalism but nationalism that creates nations.[24] Importantly, this is not only the case of nations that self-consciously construct themselves as civic nations. Rather, it is true even of "peoples" that see themselves in essentialist terms but inevitably turn out to be the result of some complex political construction and resource mobilization in favour of crystalizing some form of identity at the expense of others. In saying this, I do not want to deny that many groups have had, over time, relatively constant group identities based on certain characteristics that may be described using the repertory of ethnicity. What I mean is that a "people," at least for the purposes of self-determination under international law, is always the result of a political reinterpretation of these characteristics as founding a particular distinct collective that aspires to self-determine. History, moreover, suggests that this choice is much less evident than it may seem a posteriori, often involving the foregrounding of certain elements at the expense of others, and various forms of political entrepreneurialism.

Of course, the dilemma one runs into is that the subjective belief in peoplehood or nationhood might then be a subjective belief that something objective exists, that arguably cannot exist in that objective sense.[25] However, there is no reason to think that one should be the prisoner of that non sequitur. "Peoplehood" may well be a pure subjective belief in a purely subjective notion: it would be no less real for it. It is the idea of an essence preceding existence, only to then be "discovered" to be fundamentally flawed. The circularity of subjectivism can be overcome if one sees the subjective belief as oriented not toward some spurious underlying "objective" notion of the nation but toward self-determination itself. The subjective belief is not that a group *is* a people in some objective, incontrovertible sense, but that a group aspires to be a people *through self-determination*. Self-determination, therefore, does not as much flow from

[21] David Miller, "In Defence of Nationality," *Journal of Applied Philosophy* 10, no. 1 (1993): 19.

[22] Benedict Anderson, *Imagined Communities: Reflections on the Origin and Spread of Nationalism*, 2nd ed. (London: Verso, 2006).

[23] David George, "National Identity and National Self-Determination," in *National Rights, International Obligations*, Simon Caney, David George, and Peter Jones, eds., (Boulder, CO: Westview Press, 1996), 13–33.

[24] Ernest Gellner, *Nations and Nationalism* (Ithaca, NY: Cornell University Press, 2006).

[25] David Archard, "Nationalism and Political Theory," in *Political Theory in Transition* (London: Routledge, 2000), 158–159.

the existence of a people as it is its founding act. The practice of constituting a group as a people conditions not only the operation of the right, but its very existence in a particular case.

This has considerable implications for the normative theory of self-determination. It means that the existence of a people does not precede their political coming into being. The business of guaranteeing the right to self-determination cannot be first and foremost that of finding peoples so that they can be allowed to engage in a politics of their own. Rather, the concept of what constitutes a people is deeply enmeshed in the actual manifestation of self-determination by particular peoples, and the search for its political recognition.[26] Conversely, a people who do not aspire to some form of self-determination is simply a collection of individuals that may be united by some shared characteristics that an external observer might identify as indicating anthropological groupness but little beyond that. Moving beyond an essentialist concept of peoples both opens up prospects for self-determination and refocuses it on the quest of groups that want to choose themselves as the relevant governance and regulatory unit for at least some purposes. It guards against forms of self-determination "paternalism" based on a careful selection of which "sufficiently 'stable,' 'authentic' or 'sustainable' groups are entitled to it."[27] Self-determination can no longer be seen as merely the privilege of some essentialized peoples existing, for example, in the ethnic sense of the term but is better seen as part of the complex production of identity.

In other words, if ethnocultural projects of self-determination are normalized as merely that – that is, one type of political project among others – then they should have no particular pride of place within normative theories of self-determination. An ethnonatural basis is one possible *political* way of projecting and inventing a destiny of self-determination, and in practice perhaps the most likely. But this does not exhaust the potential of the idea: a project of self-determination could also be one to carve out a state based on civic citizenship within an encompassing state that enforced a strict notion of ethnicity as its

[26] See, in that respect, the very interesting Avner De-Shalit, "National Self-Determination: Political, Not Cultural," *Political Studies* 44, no. 5 (1996): 906–20.

[27] There are many theoretical attempts in that genre, among which one could mention. My sense is these often confuse the fact that some claims for self-determination are more probable and realistic, for an exhaustive argument about which groups ought to see their self-determination recognized. Christopher H. Wellman, "A Defense of Secession and Political Self-Determination," *Philosophy & Public Affairs* 24, no. 2 (1995): 142–71 (groups that are "of sufficient size to perform satisfactorily the functions necessary for a state to legitimize its claim to territory"). Kai Nielsen, "Secession: The Case of Quebec," *Journal of Applied Philosophy* 10, no. 1 (1993): 29–43 (groups that are "plainly predominant in a certain territory").

basis; or it could merely be one based on a group's feeling that their values and political aspirations should ultimately lead them in a different direction than the majority regardless of any strong concept of ethnic identity (this has emerged in the last years as a renewed grounding for Quebec nationalism, one that stresses that, regardless of ethnonational distinctiveness, Quebecers vote in a way that is consistently at odds with the federal majority). It seems indefensible to argue that only cultural or linguistic groups, for example, should benefit from a right to self-determination, just as it is inconceivable that the vocation of the state would be only to serve as a vehicle for the preservation of language or culture.

At the same time, the fundamental politicization of the concept of self-determination entailed by a post-ontological move also fundamentally restricts the possibility for self-determination. The state itself may well be merely a particular political project of "artificial" nationhood rather than a vehicle for some manifest destiny (contrary to what it claims), but peoples claiming self-determination cannot criticize it from some higher, more "authentic" ground. As David Miller put it, "The Canadians and the Spanish have a claim to be self-determining too, and a claim to determine the future of the territory that has historically been identified as Canada or Spain."[28] In fact, those who point out the artificiality of the state cannot escape the criticism that their claim for recognition of a particular identity is also artificial. Both the Canadian and the Spanish, the Quebecer and the Basque self-determination projects are all essentially complex political arguments about what is/what should be the most appropriate distribution of power among communities and should be assessed on these terms.

In a post-romantic age, it should at least be clear that one cannot hope for some speedy resolution of these debates based on a facile opposition between "genuine" ethnocultural claims and "artificial" state ones, where one could be granted priority over the other as a matter of principle. Some senses of civic identity may be just as strong or even stronger than supposedly ancient ethnic identity. An ethnonational basis for self-determination it is not in itself a conclusive claim without the deployment of a range of political arguments as to why it should be a basis for a particular form of self-determination that will inevitably lead to its political problematization. The debate is fundamentally a political one about which people ought to self-determine and to what extent, and it hardly seems susceptible to any intellectual quick fix.

[28] David Miller, "Secession and the Principle of Nationality," *Canadian Journal of Philosophy* 22, no. 1 (1997): 262.

I argue that the weakness of most existing concepts of self-determination, even the more avowedly political ones, is that they are a priori theories that still seek to anchor self-determination in what a people *is* rather than what a people *do* for the purposes of obtaining self-determination. What is missing is an attention to self-determination *as a process*, indeed as an actual political struggle. Here, one may make a useful comparison with individual human rights to highlight what is specific about the right to self-determination. Although this was of course not always the case, the notion of who is a human being is by now fairly evidently settled. One should not have to conquer one's recognition as a human being: human rights simply presume that all humans are indeed human. This means that although an element of struggle is certainly not adverse to human rights promotion, it is certainly not ontologically required, and one ought to have one's rights recognized even if one does nothing to pursue them. By contrast, the right to self-determination of peoples is more ambiguous, since peoplehood is essentially a political product, a process of identity formation that is anything but evident. Peoples are more alone and need to be more self-reliant in pursuing their right to self-determination than individuals in benefiting from their rights. Moreover, individual human rights already presuppose an entity vested with the obligation to grant them in the form of the state, where self-determination is more consciously the attempt to create governance structures that could become the proper repository of the right.

This idea of the right to self-determine flowing from the struggle to self-determine is very similar to the idea of peoplehood flowing from the ability/willingness to self-determine in the first place. It merely pushes the pure political rationale for self-determination a step further. What I am interested in are the conditions under which a people burnish their credentials as a people whose right to self-determination ought to be recognized through something that they do. Of course, simply having "won" one's right to self-determination through force of arms does not in itself justify it. It may attest to a certain fortitude in seeking self-determination, and obviously a certain success in doing so, but might does not create right. This is the moral dead end in which international law currently finds itself.

3. PEOPLES DESERVING OF SELF-DETERMINATION

The political existence of a people aspiring to self-determination, then, is a necessary but not sufficient condition of its recognition. It is necessary because there is obviously no point in recognizing the right to self-determination of a group that does not seek to exercise it; it is insufficient because a group's existence and aspiration to self-determination cannot operate as a solipsistic device to exercise political power "on one's own." Rather, self-determination, whether in its autonomy-seeking or secessionist variant, is always both an inward claim "to be oneself" separately, as it were (an autonomous group, an independent state), *and* an outward claim to be "part of something" that guarantees one's status as a self-determining entity (an existing state, the international community). Self-determination does not just spring from the constituted body of a people but is always a demand for *recognition* in that one cannot exercise forms of collective self-determination in isolation from the world. It is an aspiration to be a self-determining people among self-determining peoples.

In this, I am inspired by Iris Marion Young's work, which explores the potential of self-determination as a relational concept, particularly but not exclusively in relation to indigenous peoples.[29] This view is particularly apt for an analysis of autonomy within states, but can also be applied to the search for independence within the international community: in both cases one seeks a certain closure from the world in the process of openly relying on it. The very idea of a *right* to self-determination suggests that what is sought is a form of communal recognition of one's credentials as a self-determining people (a right), far more than a break from that communal horizon. This, then, is international law's chance: rather than ontological and inherent, the process of self-determination is necessarily relational and dialectic and involves a demand for participation in forms that international law has conceived of. The overall justice of self-determination should thus be evaluated in relation to (i) the particular people seeking self-determination, (ii) the population of the state within which they do so, (iii) potential third parties significantly affected by it, and (iv) the international community.

This is all the more so because every claim to self-determination by one group has the potential to diminish or constrain the exercise of self-determination or the enjoyment of rights by competing groups (the minority within the minority, the existing state's overall population), so that in the great competition of identities and sovereignties not every claim to self-determination can win, and in fact some must lose for any to win. A fortiori in the case of secession, the possibility of amputation of territory and creation of new minorities highlights an irreducible element of give or take; but even in the case of minority arrangements there will be "winners" and "losers." The right to self-determination,

[29] Iris Marion Young, "Two Concepts of Self-Determination," in *Ethnicity, Nationalism, and Minority Rights*, eds. Stephen May, Tariq Modood, and Judith Squires (Cambridge: Cambridge University Press, 2004).

then, is not an absolute prerogative to exist at the expense of all others but a demand to "make space" within existing allocations of power and, as the case may be, territory. It is a demand for a disruption of existing arrangements to one's benefit.[30] This is crucial in terms of conceptualizing the legitimacy of any particular claim.

Thinking of self-determination as a dialogical process, then, allows us to emphasize that what matters most ultimately is *the way* in which self-determination is sought rather than some a priori case for peoplehood or even victimization, not to mention the brute fact of success. In saying this, I do not want to argue that all human groups that are in the political business of claiming self-determination start from the same point. There are some who will have more going for them as a matter of principle, more assets both political and symbolic as well as more arguments to make a claim for self-determination vis-à-vis the particular audiences they seek to convince. A group of ethnically homogeneous islanders with a very strong concept of self who have been brutally colonized by some distant people have a better case a priori than a small group within a state that has historically been treated well, participates in the life of the polity, and may even benefit from existing autonomy arrangements. In fact, as I will go on to argue, this starting point may well have an impact on the sort of steps that need to be taken to establish one's right to self-determination.

But the point is that the distant islanders could lose their claim and the benignly treated territorial minority win theirs as a result of the process of seeking self-determination. Thus regardless of the starting point, self-determination may be won or lost *normatively* (independently of whether self-determination is won or lost actually) based on how that right is sought. The recognition of one's otherwise legitimate aspiration to self-determine is one's to lose if one exercises it in ways that caution against recognition. There is, therefore, no final a priori case for self-determination, only a long road littered with obstacles whose wise navigation is what ultimately determines whether a people is worthy of the particular self-determining arrangements it claims for itself.[31] Presumably the more disruptive the arrangement one seeks, the more exceptional one's degree of desert will have to be. Furthermore, the

[30] Although I disagree with her emphasis on territory, especially in the current era, I take this to have been Brilmayer's central point, namely that the disruptive potential of self-determination – if not in terms of territory at least in terms of power allocation – raises the bar for would-be self-determining groups. Brilmayer, "Secession and Self-Determination" (see n. 1).

[31] When I say "won" or "lost," note that I do not mean this in a permanent way because there should be nothing permanent about whether one ought to be able to claim a right to self-

argument here is not simply one about the legitimacy of the means used in relation to an end that is unproblematically assumed to be valid, as in the classic political ends–means dilemma. Rather, a group can become a people entitled to self-determination by virtue of the means the group has pursued because they have shown in their quest for self-determination that they are worthy of it. There is, in other words, a dynamic and constitutive relation between means and ends.

What, then, are the processes and practices that highlight a group that ought to have its claim to self-determination recognized? A first requirement of the fair search for self-determination might be the ability to articulate one's right to self-determination as a political claim to the exercise of a right rather than as an inherent, God-given, or ethnos-rooted right. One may think that this is pushing the case too far: there might be groups that deeply (even if mistakenly) believe in their right to self-determination as something inherent and unproblematic and whose politics are nonetheless benign and would deserve recognition. Still, I believe that the political maturity manifested by the move beyond some claim to absolute rights is more likely to be followed by the sort of responsible conduct that this chapter argues is a hallmark of the sort of peoples whose right to self-determination ought to be taken seriously. A people that is a good candidate for self-determination, therefore, is a people that is not tempted by some quixotic grandstanding or conceptual shortcut but are imbued with an awareness of self-determination as a complex proposition whose merits in any given case must be argued and conveyed politically and dialogically, the emphasis being on persuasion rather than violence. Their reasons for seeking self-determination may still be bad in terms of justice (e.g., because of lack of sufficient internal following, or because they would make the population of the existing state far worse off), but at least they are being articulated as part of political claims made to others.

A second requirement is that, internally, a self-determination struggle not belie the notion that it is an exercise of freedom by employing means that are in themselves in contradiction with that freedom. Self-determination, needless to say, is not an individual's or a faction's right. It is a *peoples'* right that must therefore be sought collectively because it must eventually be exercised collectively. The idea that one would fight for self-determination in isolation from the group whose interests one purports to represent or, worse, in opposition to it is anathema to the idea of self-determination. Note that this imposes a constraint of inclusion of minorities and opponents within the

determination. I merely mean that a people is temporarily successful in obtaining what it seeks or not.

self-determining group that will probably in and of itself act as a natural break on the more outlandish claims to self-determination – claims that are often all the more outlandish that they are made without the hard work of building political platforms by simply claiming to "speak in the name of." The unproblematized focus on peoples (say, the Basques or the Quebecers) typically falls for the myth that because they are presumptively part of the same peoples, these groups of individuals self-determine collectively and must want the same thing. In fact, groups are typically significantly divided on what political fate they aspire to, and a collective will is often only be extracted through the operation of problematic political assumptions (about who leads, who is the majority, or who expresses the "authentic" peoples' voice). At any rate, an avant-garde cannot be a substitute for the hard exercise of obtaining the assent – even an inchoate one in a case where formal democratic structures do not and cannot exist – of those whose self-determination one claims to bring about.

A third requirement of a fair process of self-determination is that the people claiming the right take seriously what I would call the presumptive validity of existing territorial-population arrangements (typically states but also potentially empires). This is only a presumptive validity and its basis lies elsewhere than the typical argument for order and stability, but it is a minimum recognition of the normative force of what is. Why should the state within which a group exists provide the framework for making claims to self-determination?[32] After all, the aspiring self-determining group might consider that the state is precisely the source of the problem of its being denied its rights. This is fair enough and there would not be much point in playing by the rules, even temporarily, of a genocidal or tyrannical state. However, although in the present argument the presumptive validity of existing people–power–territory arrangements may be relatively low, so is the alternative autonomous or secessionist proposal. At least the existing state delineates a political space, imperfect as it may be, within which claims of discontent can be first aired (a fortiori if the state is democratic) and in which they can be engaged as relational claims ("We want to be independent from *you*" rather than simply "we want to be independent").

Channeling one's claim to self-determination through existing political structures can also help guard against the danger that political and possibly

[32] Note that this does not contradict my earlier argument that there is no reason to *always* respect existing arrangements in and of themselves. What I am saying here is that even though those arrangements may not be in a position to elicit eternal obedience as such, they at least ought to be taken seriously as the appropriate forum to bring one's claim for autonomy or secession.

democratic arrangements will be flippantly undermined by groups whose claim is really nothing but a refusal to play the democratic game altogether, or who evidence a blatant lack of solidarity with the rest of the population (e.g., groups who would secede for example for no other reason than to escape their share of the national debt). In the same way one would think that separation and certainly divorce is first and foremost a matter to be deliberated under the laws that consecrated the marriage in the first place rather than as a matter of unilateral deliberation by one of the spouses, so it should be with any form of political distancing/separation. Finally, it is in confronting the dominant polis with one's claim to self-determination that one provides it with an opportunity to correct what may need to be corrected, and that one engages in a conversation about what ought to be the most just outcome. If the polis agrees, then the problem is solved; if it does not and does so unreasonably, then the lines are drawn and the group seeking autonomy or secession can proceed from that base line.

A fourth requirement of fair self-determination is that it include the utmost concern for those who are not part of the group and who may be impacted by its being recognized autonomy or a right of secession. Autonomy and secession do not only concern the people who seek it: they also crucially affect others who stand to be affected by it including the rest of the state's population and that part of it that may be affected by autonomy/secession. Therefore, an aspiration to self-determination worth recognizing is one in which the people seeking self-determination display a sensitivity to the distributive outcomes of the arrangements they propose, rooted in the same rights that they demand be respected vis-à-vis themselves. These distributive outcomes are evident and result from the way in which no reconfiguration of power (let alone territory) can occur without significantly remodeling the situation of each participant in the previous arrangement. In a context of displacement of the status quo, the onus is on the displacer not only to show how their group would be better off (including members of the group who do not share the desire to change the status quo), but also to show how other peoples would not be worse and even, ideally, be better off (e.g., through a renewed commitment to minority protection within the emerging structure, and certainly through appropriate rights protections).

A secessionist group might, for example, make a plausible political case that the costs to the now-minority within a new secessionist state will be more than offset both by adequate minority arrangements and the general political benefits of secession (a greater ability to affirm a particular political project, a better functioning democracy, fewer tensions, etc.). After all, it may be better for a group to be a minority in a new autonomous or sovereign entity committed to protect its rights than part of a majority (or a minority) in an existing state that is not committed to respecting rights generally (we certainly have no reason to presume that the existing state is always doing a good job of protecting minorities). The important point here is that international law is not committed to particular peoples as such but to the principle of self-determination in general, so that every candidate for self-determination must be in a position to make the case that the arrangements it proposes would make not just its own self-determination more effective, but that of all peoples more vibrant.[33] Moving beyond the zero-sum game view of self-determination (where one group's increasing power to self-determine is seen as a net loss by other groups) is therefore one of the crucial ethical stakes of autonomy or secession.

Fifth, a people that ought to be taken seriously as candidates for self-determination are a people who make the least disruptive demands possible compatible with their goals. This emphasis on "economy of demands" is in line with the previous requirements and, in a sense, flows from them. The idea is that given the costs of obtaining self-determination and the potentially negative incidence on other groups, the changes that one proposes to better take into account a people's right to self-determination should be the least compromising possible of existing ones. Here, the concern is not only or even mostly with the persona of the state as such, but with the part of the population that does not recognize itself in that particular push for self-determination, and might stand to lose from it. Attention to the needs and rights of those who would stand to lose (because an autonomy arrangement endows a minority with rights or privileges that the majority does not have, or because a secession risks losing the country from which the secession operates a major resource), even if the shift can ultimately be justified, manifests a worthwhile attention to the other that denotes political virtue. Even internally within the group seeking self-determination, such a drive should not exact more efforts from the "peoples" than strictly necessary to achieve their goals.

Sixth, I would argue that a legitimate process of self-determination is one that is sensitive to the means it must use to achieve its aims, and uses only the means that are strictly required by the situation. In other words, while it is difficult to exclude the possibility of violence as a last resort in situations where all else has failed (particularly in the more flagrant situations of colonization, genocide, or tyranny), clearly the legitimacy of self-determination is affirmed by one's willingness to engage in the democratic political game, not to bypass

33 In that respect, the most defensible case of secession is, of course, the "à l'amiable" sort in which both parties agree that they would be better off without each other (the Czech Republic and Slovakia come to mind).

it through violence. If Fanon's challenge was to theorize decolonization (i.e., a situation of radical oppression that may well have required the use of radical means, including violence), then most situations where self-determination is sought today are quite remote from that framework and would thus require means of a very different nature, including a willingness to submit to negotiations in good faith. The exclamation "it is them or us"[34] of the colonial predicament can surely not apply to aspirations to self-determination that are not dealing with such a radical denial of self. In the process of using minimal means, one also demonstrates one's fortitude and ability to earn through one's patience the eventual laurels of autonomy/independence.

Moreover, a legitimate movement for self-determination will always stop short of using some means, in the sense that no aspiration to self-determination could be worth resort to them. In particular, a project of self-determination that would require, for its material realization, the commission of genocide, crimes against humanity, ethnic cleansing, or grave human rights violations is one that should be ipso facto unworthy of recognition from a moral point of view (I realize, of course, that in practice international law has tended to gloss over such niceties). This also sets a limit to the sort of self-determination that can be sought based on the idea that some efforts at self-determination – for example, the search to create an ethnically pure state within an existing highly ethnically diverse territory – are simply off limits. In all cases, the argument is that a self-determination that needs to commit such crimes to come into effect negates that it has a valid basis.

To sum up, the emphasis on the process of self-determination (or self-determination *as* a process), including the means that are used to obtain it, is an interesting way of helping international law move beyond some misleadingly incontrovertible grounds (ethnocultural homogeneity upstream, or victory downstream). Instead, the international law of the recognition of self-determination can become a study of *how* the way in which one seeks self-determination validates one's argument that one has a right to its recognition. As such, it sets a particular tempo for the struggle for self-determination: a slow, responsive crescendo perhaps, but one that never degenerates into a shrill will to kill. Note, moreover, that the issue is not just one of means taken as such and in bland isolation from what is actually at stake: it is very much about evaluating whether the project is truly one of self-determination, and not something else in disguise. Acts speak louder than words, so to speak, and a precipitous resort to force when not merited by the circumstances, for

[34] Frantz Fanon, *The Wretched of the Earth* (New York: Grove Press, 1963), 84.

example, might betray that what is sought is something else than self-determination only: tyranny, a land grab, or a campaign of hatred.

4. CONCLUSION

The old idea of self-determination in international law was very wedded to an ontological concept of "a people" that has long been rendered outdated by our understanding of a people as always in a sense a form of political association, or at least a construction. A better understanding of what nation-states themselves really are (artificial political constructs) should have an incidence on our moral intuitions about who qualifies as a people whose self-determination is worthy of recognition. My suggestion is that in a context where peoplehood is no longer the decisive criterion and one moves from ethnographic classification to political arbitration, the case for self-determination becomes both more fluid and fragile (although also more interesting). The decline of a strong a priori entitlement to self-determination in some essentialized notion of "peoples" forces us to rethink the conditions under which any group might be able to claim to it. Such a quest should be characterized by a renewed attention to the legitimacy of self-determination as a process and how it further constitutes a people worthy of self-determination because they have deserved it. I believe that the resulting theory safeguards the centrality of the notion of "peoplehood" while not reifying it..

In short, the argument is that a claim to self-determination, whether for more autonomy or even secession, ought to at least be taken seriously normatively if it is made by a self-constituting people who make their case reasonably and politically, calibrating the means used to the goal sought while only making demands on the existing polity that are strictly necessary in a spirit of sensitivity to their politics' distributive outcomes, all the while refusing to utilize certain means that would nullify the validity of their claim. In fact, such a demand, as a demand for minority protection or autonomy, ought presumptively to be recognized in international law.[35] Whether secession is allowed is a more complex question but at the very least certain peoples might be seen as having, through their persistence and resilience, "earned" the right for their demand to be taken seriously and not dismissed out of hand based on some preference for the intangibility of arbitrary borders. In that case, merit is simply assessed more strictly given the potential for disruption. For example, unilateral secession is a priori shunned, to the benefit of a people earning secession through patient

[35] The question of what ought to be done to enforce it is a separate one, which I do not deal with here.

working within existing structures. However, the theory is also compatible with remedial theories of unilateral secession that see it as allowed when a people are being violently suppressed or systematically discriminated against.

The argument is not an entirely comprehensive one: it still calls for careful balancing and arbitrage between competing claims made by groups that may be roughly equally meritorious. Its strength, however, is that it does delineate the conditions in which the state or the international community cannot refuse to have a conversation on existing power or territorial arrangements. The specificity of the argument, moreover, is that it does not separate an a priori case for self-determination from the means used to obtain it in ways that open up the argument to the raw calculation of politics (e.g., justifying resort to illegitimate means to pursue a legitimate cause). Rather, in weaving the two together it offers an account that is both open at the level of primary principles and prudential in its application.[36] It avoids both unduly restrictive theories of when secession is permissible (e.g., only, as in the remedial theory, in response to threats to the integrity of a people) and unduly permissive ones (e.g., that maintain a right to self-determination even though that right has been exercised in ways that disqualify the idea that a people are worthy of it). The suggestion is that any search for a more expedited formula risks merely being an attempt to gloss over the finer moral details that will inevitably arise.

As will have become clear, the argument is also noteworthy for how it foregrounds certain political virtues – patience, stubbornness, resilience, the sheer will to make a case politically even in the face of great odds – as opposed to what the politics of nationalism have too often been synonymous with – shrillness, self-righteousness, and an opportunistic mix of the antipolitical (the unproblematized concept of peoples) and the narrowly legalistic (the right to self-determination seen as an entitlement to secession). Perhaps no idea has done more harm to international order and justice than the idea that self-determination is a right inherent in hypothetical peoples that dispenses them from political and democratic struggles and allows them to engage in a fight at any cost. It is arguably this danger that has led international law to gradually eviscerate the right to self-determination of much of its progressive content, in a way that may have made it potentially less bloody but only at the cost of fundamental impoverishment. The account I have provided, I hope, seeks to

[36] This is a little akin to the way in which just war theorists have long considered that the justness of a war at the jus ad bellum level depends not only on just cause but ultimately also on the means used at the jus in bello level to wage the war.

rescue some of the moral force and radicalism of the principle while building safeguards within it that are not merely prudential afterthoughts.

My critique of the international law of self-determination also draws from and feeds into critiques of rights as too often proceeding from misleadingly simple equations. However, it is also a quite special case of this critique, one that emphasizes the uniqueness of self-determination within the corpus of human rights. Because the "peoples" in the right to self-determination are a moving target, a brittle conceptual framework that constantly threatens to crumble under its own weight, I have argued that the existence of a people and the search for self-determination are coextensive, and that we simply have no easy way of knowing who is a people except through an attention to who is claiming self-determination. Similarly, I have argued that we have no easy way of knowing which people ought to have their right to self-determine recognized except through an attention to the nature of their struggles and how, under certain circumstances, these may in themselves bring about what they merely claim (traditionally) to derive from. Where the idea that rights are conditional on one having proved by one's actions that one is their legitimate subject would be eminently distasteful to the ordinary language of individual rights (this is a common critique of the focus on the old "dignity"),[37] it seems to be the only rational answer to the riddle of self-determining peoples, one that highlights the dignitas of being recognized as self-determining as the culmination of a process and the crowning achievement of efforts.

Finally, I should point out that while it is quite clear that I have been interested in an ideal theory-inspired critique of the law for the purposes of this chapter, I do not discount the possibility that the account I propose might under certain circumstances better reflect the reality of self-determination as a praxis, at least as it is understood by those who seek it. In this, I may have offered a moral vocabulary that better makes sense of the tension between the perception of self-determination by its actors, its spectators, and its potential arbitrators.

[37] Stéphanie Hennette-Vauchez, "A Human *Dignitas*? Remnants of the Ancient Legal Concept in Contemporary Dignity Jurisprudence," *International Journal of Constitutional Law* 9, no. 1 (2011): 32–57.

4

The Right to Exist and the Right to Resist

JENS DAVID OHLIN

Self-determination is rightly regarded as one of the highest collective rights protected by the UN Charter and international law. However, there is precious little positive law outlining the scope and content of this right because courts rarely pass judgment on claims regarding self-determination. Two notable exceptions, which prove the rule, are the Canadian Supreme Court decision on the Quebec Referendum and the International Court of Justice (ICJ) *Wall Opinion*, which recognized the Palestinian right of self-determination.[1] The question is why the concept of self-determination, given its universal recognition as central and indisputable, has yielded few other precedents. The problem stems from the legal concept to which self-determination attaches. On pain of circularity, the right belongs to nations or peoples, not states. Generally speaking, philosophers are more comfortable talking about peoples and nations, compared with lawyers raised with positivist tendencies who are allergic to adjudication of claims attaching to nations and peoples – legal entities that are notoriously difficult to define.[2] While the definition of states is codified and even has its own treaty – the Montevideo Convention – no similar instrument exists for nations or peoples.[3] The right of self-determination will only receive its due respect once international lawyers make peace with

[1] See *Reference re: Secession of Quebec*, [1998] 2 S.C.R. 217 (Can.); Legal Consequences of the Construction of a Wall in the Occupied Palestinian Territory, Advisory Opinion, 2004 I.C.J. 136, ¶ 88 (July 9).

[2] On different uses of the word "people" and "peoples," see Christopher W. Morris, "Peoples, Nations, and the Unity of Societies," in Carol C. Gould and Pasquale Paquino (eds.), *Cultural Identity and the Nation-State* (Lanham, MD: Rowman & Littlefield Publishers, 2001), 19.

[3] Convention on the Rights and Duties of States (Montevideo Convention), Dec. 26, 1933, 165 L.N.T.S. 19. For a critical discussion, see Thomas D. Grant, "Defining Statehood: The Montevideo Convention and its Discontents," *Columbia Journal of Transnational Law* 37 (1999): 403–57.

abstract collective entities and recognize that they form an essential backbone of the international legal system, and that they have rights and duties attached to them – a complicated and uncomfortable position for neopositivist international lawyers who are allergic to the concept of natural law.

This chapter therefore makes three elementary points regarding the core right of self-determination. First, although the right of self-determination has been inhibited by uncertainty surrounding its connection to the abstract concept of peoples or nations, these entities can be defined either through self-perceptions or other-perceptions, and either is sufficient to ground the right of self-determination. Second, the right of self-determination belongs to a cluster of legal rights, including the right to be free from aggression and genocide, which emerge from two natural rights: the right to exist and the right to resist autonomy-threatening attacks. Although one might think that a right of resistance is necessarily an outgrowth of the more primary right to exist (since resistance might be an instrumental method of securing existence), this chapter denies this common-sense intuition. This brings us to the third claim: the right of resistance is an independent, neo-Kantian right regarding the autonomy of collective groups, such as nations or peoples, that is not reducible to the right to exist.[4] The primary argument for its theoretical independence stems from a discussion of cases of futile self-defense, where it is certain that resistance will not achieve the continued existence of the defendant. But even in such cases where annihilation is inevitable and existence cannot be protected, the right of resistance persists.

Before continuing, an important word regarding methodology is in order. This is an exercise in political theory – a statement about the moral and political concepts underlying our current system of international law and international relations. However, many of the moral and political concepts are ones that are not explicitly recognized by our current legal system. It is therefore important to distinguish between two levels of conceptual analysis. First, there is the description of the current international legal system with reference to preexisting rights found in applicable treaties, judicial decisions from international or criminal tribunals, and rules of customary international law. Much of the analysis found in Section 1, on the right of self-determination

4 By using the phrase "neo-Kantian" I do not mean to suggest that Kant would have supported this argument. (Indeed, Kant was skeptical of the right to revolution.) I call my approach neo-Kantian to emphasize the role that autonomy plays in the overall structure of the argument. Also, as will become clear as the argument develops, my overall theory is largely nonconsequentialist and appeals to deontological considerations.

and its relationship to aggression and genocide, takes place at this level of positive analysis, although it ventures beyond the positive law when it considers a normative theory for explaining the concepts of nations and peoples. In contrast, the analysis in Sections 2 and 3 delves into the normative foundations of international law with reference to natural and moral rights that find no direct or explicit reference in the positive law.

1. THE PROBLEM OF DEFINITION

Lawyers are allergic – predictably so – to any talk of nations or peoples.[5] I am not talking here of law professors or legal scholars or political scientists who write about the law. I am talking about practitioners who advance claims in a court of law or make legal arguments in other legal domains, including in the court of world opinion. These lawyers are happy to talk about national rights, but in so doing they are referring to rights that attach to nation-states. But talk about rights that attach to nations *simpliciter* is noticeably absent from the dialogue of most international lawyers. Why is this so? Self-determination represents a significant outlier – a right that is universally recognized as central and indisputable in international law,[6] but unfortunately of very little practical significance.[7] Of course, the right has great rhetorical and political appeal when minority groups are pressing their claims for internal or external self-determination, but the right has little legal appeal when lawyers are making arguments.[8] Political leaders and diplomats may change their course when an appeal to self-determination is made, but lawyers rarely use the concept of self-determination as a hinge to make an argument.

Of course, there are notable exceptions. The Canadian Supreme Court concluded that the Quebec nation had the right of self-determination but also concluded that Quebecers' access to political participation in the Canadian

5 For criticisms regarding the vagueness inherent in the self-determination of peoples, see Edward A. Laing, "The Norm of Self-Determination, 1941–1991," *California Western International Law Journal* 22 (1992): 209, 221, citing Charles De Visscher, *Theory and Reality in Public International Law* (Princeton, NJ: Princeton University Press, 1968), 175.

6 See Lee Seshagiri, "Democratic Disobedience: Reconceiving Self-Determination and Secession at International Law," *Harvard International Law Journal* 51, no. 2 (2010): 553.

7 See Richard Falk, "The Rights of Peoples (In Particular Indigenous Peoples)," in James Crawford (ed.), *The Rights of Peoples* (Oxford: Clarendon Press, 1988), 17: "there persists a statist conception of rights"; cf. Antonio Cassese, *Self-Determination of Peoples: A Legal Reappraisal* (Cambridge, N.Y.: Cambridge University Press, 1998).

8 For a discussion, see Milena Sterio, *The Right to Self-Determination under International Law: "Selfistants," Secession, and the Rule of the Great Powers* (Milton Park: Routledge, 2013), 3.

government was sufficient to meet the standards of internal self-determination; no external right of secession was warranted.[9] Similarly, the ICJ concluded in the *Wall Opinion* that the Palestinians' right of self-determination was violated by the placement of the Wall and its associated denial of economic rights and free movement.[10] But these are exceptions that prove the rule. The more relevant example is to return to the Canadian case, and note that the Cree and other First Nations argued against the legality of a Quebec secession on the ground that they were a distinct nation and that their mandatory inclusion within the Quebec nation was itself a denial of *their* right of self-determination.[11] Neither the Canadian Supreme Court nor the relevant UN committees wanted to touch this argument, though it had some natural appeal.[12] The *reason* that no court wanted to address the substance of the argument is because resolving the argument required engagement in a pre-legal argument regarding the nature of the Quebec and Cree peoples, and whether they were logically distinct from each other. This was, in a sense, a sociopolitical question, not a legal one.

But is the indeterminacy inherent in the concept of nations or peoples any different from other concepts that lawyers deploy? Is there a rule of recognition for peoples? And how should a court answer such a question? Should it become a battle of the experts, with Ernest Gellner, Elie Kedourie, and Benedict Anderson appearing for the different parties to the case?[13] Arguably, one ought to have a coherent answer to the question, but inevitably this requires an inquiry into social scientific facts of the sort that make lawyers exceptionally nervous.[14] Lawyers rarely engage in these socioscientific inquiries, though there are exceptions.

Consider, for example, the early jurisprudence of the International Criminal Tribunal for Rwanda (ICTR), which was required to determine whether

9 See *Reference re: Secession of Quebec*, [1998] 2 S.C.R. 217 (Can.), ¶ 135. See also Michla Pomerance, *Self-determination in Law and Practice: The New Doctrine in the United Nations* (The Hague: Martinus Nijhoff, 1982), 37.

10 See Legal Consequences of the Construction of a Wall in the Occupied Palestinian Territory, Advisory Opinion, 2004 I.C.J. 136, ¶ 128 (July 9).

11 For a discussion of Cree claims to self-determination, see Robert A. Young, *Secession of Quebec and the Future of Canada* (Montreal: McGill-Queen's University Press, 1995), 108.

12 See Grand Council of the Crees (of Quebec), *Submission: Status and Rights of the James Bay Cree in the Context of Quebec's Secession from Canada* (Submission to the U.N. Commission on Human Rights, February 1992).

13 For examples, see Ernest Gellner, *Nationalism* (New York: New York University Press, 1997); Elie Kedouri, *Nationalism* (London: Hutchinson, 1960); Benedict Anderson, *Imagined Communities: Reflections on the Origin and Spread of Nationalism* (London: Verso, 1983).

14 Kosovo opinion punted this question purely because of the problem of definition.

the atrocities committed in Rwanda amounted to genocide.[15] In order to make this legal determination, the court was required to find that the attacks were committed with the special intent (dolus specialis) to destroy, in whole or in part, one of protected groups enumerated in the ICTR Statute (and genocide convention).[16] The list of protected groups is closed and not subject to judicial enlargement, and only includes national, ethnical, racial, and religious groups.[17] When confronted with this question, the ICTR was essentially relegated to a subsidiary academic inquiry into sociology and ethnography, without either the competence or the training to engage in these questions.[18] Moreover, the answer was certainly not self-evident. The attacks against the Tutsi were not motivated by national hatred, since both Hutus and Tutsi considered themselves to be members of the same Rwandan nation. Nor are Hutu and Tutsi racial classifications, and neither would consider themselves to be engaged in a racial struggle. Finally, religious identity cut across the Hutu and Tutsi divide, with many perpetrators and victims sharing the same religious identity. The most obvious solution would have been to declare the genocide as directed against a political group, that is, against enemies of the current regime, which included both Tutsis and moderate Hutus opposed to the "Hutu Power" movement.[19] Unfortunately, "political groups" are excluded from the closed list of protected groups, though proposals have been advanced to broaden the list to include vulnerable political groups.[20]

The ICTR finally settled on declaring the Tutsi to be an ethnical group subject to the protection of the Genocide Convention.[21] The Tutsi group is properly thought of as a tribal category, and calling it "ethnical" was

[15] For example, see Prosecutor v. Akayesu, Case No. ICTR-96-4-T, Judgment, ¶ 498 (Sept. 2, 1998), www.unictr.org/sites/unictr.org/files/case-documents/ictr-96-4/trial-judgements/en/980902.pdf.

[16] Ibid.

[17] See United Nations Security Council (SC), Resolution 955, "Statute of the International Tribunal for Rwanda," art. 2(2), Aug. 11, 1994, www.ohchr.org/EN/ProfessionalInterest/Pages/StatuteInternationalCriminalTribunalForRwanda.aspx.

[18] For a critical commentary, see the probing analysis found in Alexander Zahar and Göran Sluiter, *International Criminal Law: A Critical Introduction* (Oxford: Oxford University Press, 2008), 158.

[19] See David L. Nersessian, *Genocide and Political Groups* (Oxford: Oxford University Press, 2010), 2.

[20] Ibid., 205–07.

[21] Compare Prosecutor v. Akayesu, Case No. ICTR-96-4-T, Judgment, ¶ 511–13 (Sept. 2, 1998), concluding that Tutsi constituted a protected group by virtue of being a stable and permanent group though not an ethnic group per se, with Prosecutor v. Kayishema and Ruzindana, Case No. ICTR-91-1-A, Judgment, ¶ 34 (June 1, 2001), concluding that the Tutsi were indeed an ethnic group.

controversial.[22] First, contemporary readers will have no idea what was meant by the drafters of the Genocide Convention when they used the word "ethnical," because that word is no longer common parlance and has been replaced with the more current term "ethnic."[23] Most lay individuals would probably toss their hands in the air and give up if asked whether the Tutsi were an "ethnical" group. Scholars have reviewed the ICTR findings regarding the Tutsi as an ethnical group and have criticized it for its lack of scholarly sophistication from the perspective of rigorous ethnography.[24]

With regards to self-determination, the same pitfalls present themselves. In order to determine whether the right of self-determination applies in this or that case, it is logically necessary to determine whether the collective group in question is indeed a nation or a people capable of exercising the right of self-determination.[25] If there is no nation or people, the group has no right of self-determination, though they might have some group rights by virtue of their minority status within a particular state.

How should lawyers answer these questions? There is no universally recognized answer in the social science literature, though proposed definitions usually canvass a predictable landscape of overlapping commonalities.[26] Ernest Gellner, in *Nations and Nationalism*, famously offered the following two definitions of nationhood. The first definition stated, "Two men are of the same nation if and only if they share the same culture, where culture in turn means a system of ideas and signs and associations and ways of behaving and communicating."[27] Gellner's second definition is more extensive:

> Two men are of the same nation if and only if they recognize each other as belonging to the same nation. In other words, nations maketh man; nations are

22 See Zahar and Sluiter, *International Criminal Law*, 161–62 (see n. 18).

23 "An ethnical group was a sub-group of a national group; it was a smaller collectivity than the nation, but one whose existence could nevertheless be of benefit to humanity." U.N. GAOR, 3rd Sess., 74th mtg. at 98, U.N. Doc A/C.6/SR.74, reprinted in Hirad Abtahi and Philippa Webb, *The Genocide Convention: The Travaux Preparatoires* (Leiden: Martinus Nijhoff, 2008), 1400.

24 See Zahar and Sluiter, *International Criminal Law*, at 186 n. 171 (see n. 18), noting that "post-1994 historical works on Rwanda are tarnished by the misconceptions and mythologies surrounding the war of that year."

25 "No doubt there has been continuing doubt and difficulty over the definition of what is a 'people' for the purpose of applying the principle of self-determination. None the less, the principle appears to have a core of reasonable certainty." Ian Brownlie, "The Rights of Peoples in Modern International Law," in James Crawford (ed.), *The Rights of Peoples* (Oxford: Clarendon Press, 1988), 1, 5.

26 Sellers argues that nations are cultural units while peoples are territorial. See Mortimer N. S. Sellers, *Republican Principles in International Law: The Fundamental Requirements of a Just World Order* (Basingstoke: Palgrave Macmillan, 2006).

27 Ernest Gellner, *Nations and Nationalism* (Ithaca, NY: Cornell University Press, 1983), 6.

> the artefacts of men's convictions and loyalties and solidarities. A mere category of persons (say, occupants of a given territory, or speakers of a given language, for example) becomes a nation if and when the members of the category firmly recognize certain mutual rights and duties to each other in virtue of their shared membership of it. It is their recognition of each other as fellows of this kind which turns them into a nation, and not the other shared attributes, whatever they might be, which separate that category from non-members.[28]

The category of "nation" or "people" is usually established by virtue of their shared living space in a defined geographical area, a common ancestry, religious or linguistic affiliations, or social practices. However, any number of these commonalities can cut against each other.[29] Not every French speaker in the world is a member of the French nation, nor is every Catholic a member of the Holy See. On the other hand, there is a greater willingness to view every member of the Jewish diaspora, wherever they are located, as part of the Jewish People. Why the difference? One might argue that all Jews are potential citizens of the State of Israel by virtue of the right of return, and that this future citizenship ties the nation together. However, this has it exactly backwards. All Jews have the right of return to Israel because they are members of the Jewish People, not the other way around. If it were the other way around, there would be no rationale for the right of return.

All of this is just to say that defining the concept of nationhood or peoples is so fraught with definitional challenges that it is no surprise that lawyers are inclined to run from the concept with reckless abandon. Gellner's definition points the way toward a potential solution, one that might resolve the pathological uncertainty that burdens the concept. Gellner offers what amounts to a subjectivist theory whereby "members of the category firmly recognize certain mutual rights and duties to each other in virtue of their shared membership of it."[30] In other words, a group becomes a nation when its members *see* themselves as a nation, and recognize each other as standing in a unique relationship to each other that has moral, political, and potentially legal consequences, based on principles of partiality.[31] Benedict Anderson offered

[28] Ibid., 7. [29] Ibid. [30] Ibid.

[31] This subjective theory of identity was also advanced by the ICTR in Prosecutor v. Sylvestre Gacumbtsi, Case No. ICTR-2001–64-T, Judgment, ¶ 254–55 (June 17, 2004), www.unictr.org/sites/unictr.org/files/case-documents/ictr-01–64/trial-judgements/en/040617.pdf. For a subjective account of group identity, see Monika Ambrus, "Genocide and Discrimination: Lessons to be Learned from Discrimination Law," *Leiden Journal of International Law* 25, no. 4 (2012): 935–54. For a commentary on this view, see Frederic Mégret, "LJIL Symposium: A Comment on Ambrus by Frederic Mégret," *Opinio Juris*, December 20, 2012, http://opiniojuris.org/2012/12/20/ljil-symposium-a-comment-on-ambrus-by-frederic-megret/.

a more extreme version of this thesis by suggesting that these were imagined communities, a restatement of the view that is far more radical than the view adopted by Gellner, who shares a subjectivist inclination with Anderson but nonetheless is inclined to view these commitments and relationships as real.[32]

The subjectivist view has the benefit of clarity and potentially solves the definitional challenge, but at what cost? Groups become nations and become capable of exercising self-determination when they view themselves in that light, regardless of the underlying racial or ethnic or linguistic or religious connections – so what matters is the significance that individuals attach to them. The potential for boot-strapping oneself into the right of self-determination is quite severe here because a group of individuals would be owed the right of self-determination just for *thinking* that it is so and acting consistently with that belief. Is the right of self-determination really that susceptible to gamesmanship?

Although the view sounds radical, there are hints of its plausibility once one considers the crime of genocide and how individuals are considered a member of a protected group. One relevant question for making the determination in that context is whether the individuals involved view themselves as belonging to the same collective group, regardless of whether this group is based on objectively verified scientific facts on the ground.[33] It might, as it were, be based on mere mistakes. The standard story with regard to the Rwandan classifications was that their significance stemmed from the arrival of Belgian colonizers.[34] According to Philip Gourevitch, the Tutsi and Hutu classifications predated the arrival of the Belgians but the groupings were originally of little cultural or political significance.[35] When the Belgians arrived with their nineteenth-century pseudoscience, they started measuring foreheads and noses with rulers and "scientifically" explained the differences between the groups.[36] Hutus were physically stronger and more suitable for manual labor; Tutsis were more intellectual and suited for white-collar endeavors, thus paving their way for entry into the political class.[37] Hutus became second-class citizens, their resentment festering until it finally exploded during the Rwandan genocide of 1994.

[32] Anderson, *Imagined Communities*, 83–84 (see n. 13).

[33] Indeed, Zahar and Sluiter, *International Criminal Law*, 162 (see n. 18), view the subjective theory as incoherent for this reason.

[34] For example, see Philip Gourevitch, *We Wish to Inform You That Tomorrow We Will Be Killed With Our Families: Stories from Rwanda* (London: Macmillan, 1999), 56: "the Belgian colonials stuck with the Hamitic myth as their template and, ruling Rwanda more or less as a joint venture with the Roman Catholic Church, they set about radically reengineering Rwandan society along ethnic lines."

[35] Ibid., 57. [36] Ibid., 55–56. [37] Ibid.

The moral of this story – if it is indeed true – is that it did not really matter that the Belgian classification system was based on pseudoscience rather than objective fact. What matters is that the classification was deployed to structure the daily lives of Rwandans, to make decisions about who would do what and when they could do it. We are left then with two possible definitions, one involving self-perceptions and the other based on other-perceptions. Under the self-perception view, what matters is that the subjective self-ascriptions of the relevant individuals take their membership in the collective group as dispositive regarding their interrelations. In other words, the relevant individuals take their membership in the collective as both descriptively and normatively important, both in describing their current situation and in prescribing actions going forward. An example of the latter prescriptive function might include claims regarding the demands of partiality, and whether they owe a special loyalty to fellow members of the group, and how those claims of partiality ought to be weighed against the competing demands of cosmopolitan ethics.

In contrast, the other-perception view assumes that group membership can be negatively defined by other groups that view the relevant individuals as belonging to the relevant group.[38] The obvious basis for such prescriptions would be cases of genocide or persecution where the perpetrating group classifies the victimized individuals as belonging to a particular nation or people singled out for discrimination or annihilation. In such cases, what matters most is not the self-perception but rather the negatively defined other-perception, since it is the definitional criteria of the perpetrators that determines whether any particular individual will be subject to discriminatory or genocidal treatment.[39] If one reason why the law cares about the rights of nations and peoples is to protect them from genocidal attack and grant them a remedial right of self-determination, then it stands to reason that the law should be particularly sensitive to the criteria for group membership that gives rise to that unlawful treatment in the first instance.

The two views are not necessarily mutually exclusive.[40] An other-perception interpretation of group membership might trigger self-perception, or vice

[38] On this question, consider Rebecca Young, "How Do We Know Them When We See Them? The Subjective Evolution in.the Identification of Victim Groups for the Purpose of Genocide," *International Criminal Law Review* 10, no. 1 (2010): 1–22.

[39] Ibid. See also Prosecutor v. Sylvestre Gacumbtsi, Case No. ICTR-2001–64-T, Judgment, ¶ 255 (June 17, 2004) (see n. 31).

[40] It should be noted that both the self-perception and other-perception theories can be construed as *internal* to the remedial theory of secession – the well-known theory that justifies secession in order to remediate human rights abuses. In other words, some groups have rights of self-defense

versa, entangling the two in a dynamic relationship of mutual recognition. Consider first the obvious entailment. The victim group self-identifies in a particular way and the perpetrator group then adopts that definitional criterion as dispositive of group identity and uses it as a basis for discrimination. Most observers would view this as the most likely causal explanation. But consider a less obvious causal explanation: a perpetrator's perception of the victim group may eventually lead the victim group to self-identify in exactly the same way – but this time motivated by self-protection. Indeed, denying the existence or salience of one's group identity – in the face of a genocidal threat presupposing this identity – would appear to be wishful thinking in the extreme. The more likely response is to adopt the other-perception as self-perception and harness its logic for a remedial response, whether self-defense or self-determination. In either of those two scenarios, other-perception and self-perception are locked together in a dynamic relationship.

The question for both the other-perception and self-perception views is whether they are too subjectivist and are insufficiently tethered to the objective facts on the ground. Both rely on subjective perceptions without deeper reference to the objective facts of group identity, which surely are more grounded than our pure subjective mental states would suggest. There is a deeper objective reality out there.

The answer to this objection requires consideration of the more primary objection that group identity itself is overbroad as a definition of nations or peoples; plenty of groups, even those deserving protection from genocide, are not nations or peoples. The most obvious example would be members of a particular religion; they clearly deserve protection from genocide but no one would suggest that every religious group automatically satisfies the definitional criteria for nationhood or constitutes a people. Similarly, although individuals can be discriminated against for being female, women are neither a nation nor a people – this would be a category mistake. Consequently, subjective understanding of group membership, whether negatively or positively defined, would appear to be a necessary but not sufficient condition for constituting a nation or people. But what constitutes the rest of the definition?

In addition to a shared sense of culture or identity, as Waldron calls it,[41] a collective group must also have some interrelation as a functioning society in

and external self-determination (remedial secession) once independent statehood becomes the only way of protecting their legitimate interests to safety and security. However, the mere fact of remediation leaves open the question of *who* gets the remediation, i.e., what constitutes the relevant group and how it is defined.

41 "[T]he culture of a community is a way of doing things, particularly the things that are done *together*, throughout the whole course of human life: language, governance, religious rituals."

order to qualify as a nation or a people. In the context of a nation with a burgeoning claim of nationalism, that society might include a claim to full-blown statehood – the richest and most concrete type of society. However, there are other forms of society that do not entail statehood; indeed all that is required is a particular way of life. A society might be constituted by religious practices if they are sufficient to generate a particular way of life, as opposed to mere abstract theological beliefs, or they might be constituted by ethnic ties if, again, those ethnic ties result in a particular way of life. Other collective groups, such as women, do not form a distinct society with a unique form of living, if only because both genders usually combine together to form functioning societies.[42] In general, the connection to a particular territory, either real or imagined, past, present, and future, is often listed as a criteria for constituting a nation or people.[43] This might exclude a diaspora, although even a diaspora usually has a future or ideal connection with a particular territory – a would-be homeland, if you will.[44] But it seems as if territory and land is a mere proxy for a deeper notion, such as society or a way of life, that one usually associates with inhabiting a territory, though the connection is not, strictly speaking, logically necessary.[45] What is more essential is the social element, not the territory on which the social element is built.

See Jeremy Waldron, "Multiculturalism and Melange," in R.K. Fullinwider (ed.), *Public Education in a Multicultural Society* (New York: Cambridge University Press, 1996), 96.

42 That being said, there is nothing essential or necessary about this fact. As a matter of thought experiment, one could imagine a more futuristic example where women, or men, use advanced reproductive technologies to imagine a single-sex society. However, this is not the world we currently live in, due to the particular contingent state of biotechnological development.

43 For example, see M.N.S. Sellers, *Republican Legal Theory: The History, Constitution and Purposes of Law in a Free State* (Basingstoke: Palgrave Macmillan, 2003), 67, 138. The last definition of "peoples" might be a different sense from the one used in the present chapter because the right of self-determination applies to peoples who do not, as of yet, inhabit their own state.

44 On this point, see Avishai Margalit, "The Moral Psychology of Nationalism," in Robert McKim and Jeff McMahan (eds.), *The Morality of Nationalism* (New York: Oxford University Press, 1997), 74, 85.

45 However, it should be noted that if the national group wishes to claim some territory as the location for its state, it must explain why that specific territory is necessary or appropriate as the ground to instantiate its self-determination – a question that logically implicates the interests and claims that other national groups might have regarding that territory. For a general discussion of the relationship between territory and self-determination, see Cara Nine, *Global Justice and Territory* (Oxford: Oxford University Press, 2012), and Anna Stilz, "Nations, States, and Territory," *Ethics* 121, no. 3 (2011): 572–601.

2. THE RIGHT TO EXIST

Having identified the difficulties with the concepts of nations and peoples in Section 1, our task now shifts to understanding the particular rights that the international system attaches to these concepts. The previous section noted that although the right of self-determination is arguably the most important collective right enshrined in contemporary international law, its status is relatively underdeveloped, in particular because it stands in some tension with the statist right of sovereignty and noninterference that has been implicit in international relations since Westphalia. As such, the collective right of self-determination often clashes with the sovereign rights of existing states. Therein lies the dilemma.[46]

The standard assumption in international law is that while the right of self-determination might belong to abstract entities, such as non-self-governing colonial peoples, the other collective rights (such as self-defense) belong to state entities properly defined by international law. As such, the problem of definition, which threatens the full development of the right of self-determination, does not bleed into other areas of public international law, such as jus ad bellum, which can be pursued with more positive rigor.

For reasons explained in the following, this view is misguided. Simply put, even the positive rights associated with collectives, such as the right of self-defense, are positive expressions of underlying natural rights – natural rights that belong to collectives that long predate the formation of positive entities in the international system. Furthermore, the positive rights recognized under international law – the right to be free from genocide and aggression and to exercise self-defense despite the general prohibition on the use of force – are traceable to two core natural rights: the right to exist and the right to resist. The right of existence will be explained in this section and the second, the right to resist, will be cashed out in Section 3. Both are examples of the underlying political theory justifying our legal practices, not a description of the actual legal doctrine itself.

The rights to self-determination, freedom from genocide, and freedom from attack are all based on an underlying right of existence and flourishing. Unfortunately, the term "right to exist" has been hijacked by the Israeli-

[46] Of course there is also a more general tension between the collective and the individual and whether collective entities have independent moral significance – a moral conclusion rejected by some revisionist Just War Theorists and other moral individualists. A full defense of moral collectivism is beyond the scope of this chapter, which is limited to elucidating the moral foundation for core legal rights already attributed to groups under public international law.

Palestinian question – an important issue, to be sure, but one that is quite narrow when compared to the question presented here.[47] Our notion of the right to existence is much broader and of universal application. Consider the proposed Declaration of the Rights and Duties of Nations, which declared in 1916 that "Every Nation has the right to exist, and to protect and to conserve its existence."[48] The right is naturally limited to justified acts; no state may secure its existence through "unlawful acts."[49] Elihu Root, then president of the American Society of International Law, echoed the reporter in noting that the declaration's "every statement, far from being novel, is based upon the decisions of American courts and the authority of American publicists."[50] These rights are more than simply aspirational.

Consider first the right of self-defense. The right means that the collective group has the right to use defensive force to ward off an unjustified attack. In international law, the right is codified in Article 51 of the UN Charter, which states that "[n]othing in the present Charter shall impair the inherent right of individual or collective self-defence if an armed attack occurs against a Member of the United Nations, until the Security Council has taken measures necessary to maintain international peace and security."[51] Notice the reference to self-defense as an *inherent* right – or what in the French-language version of the Charter is referred to as "droit naturel."[52]

Although the case law and the jurisprudence on Article 51 is mostly restricted to positive sources, it is important to remember that the right stems from natural law, as the founders of international law such as Vattel,[53]

47 For example, see Lassa Oppenheim, *International Law: A Treatise*, 3rd ed. (London: Longman's, Green, and Co., 1920), 192.

48 See James Brown Scott, *The American Institute of International Law: Its Declaration of the Rights and Duties of Nations* (Washington, DC: American Institute of International Law, 1916), 87.

49 Ibid., 88.

50 See Elihu Root, "The Declaration of the Rights and Duties of Nations Adopted by the American Institute of International Law," *American Journal of International Law* 10, no. 2 (1916): 213.

51 UN Charter Art. 51.

52 "Aucune disposition de la présente Charte ne porte atteinte au droit naturel de légitime défense, individuelle ou collective, dans le cas où un Membre des Nations Unies est l'objet d'une agression armée, jusqu'à ce que le Conseil de sécurité ait pris les mesures nécessaires pour maintenir la paix et la sécurité internationales." UN Charter Art. 51 (French language version). For a full explanation of the significance of the French language version of Article 51, see generally George P. Fletcher and Jens David Ohlin, *Defending Humanity* (Oxford: Oxford University Press, 2008).

53 For example, see Emmerich de Vattel, *The Law of Nations, or, Principles of the Law of Nature, Applied to the Conduct and Affairs of Nations and Sovereigns* (London, 1797), 5 ("every nation is obliged to perform the duty of self-preservation"), 154 ("In vain does nature prescribe to

Grotius,[54] and other natural rights theorists recognized.[55] Some referred to it as self-preservation, others as self-defense, but the label did not matter. What is relevant is the similarity in the normative account: that is, that in the state of nature, even in the absence of law or civilization to enforce contractual rights, there existed an inalienable and natural right to respond with lethal force to protect oneself from existential annihilation. This was, in a sense, an outgrowth of a primitive right to *exist*.[56]

One can see the right to be free from genocide as a natural extension of this same right to exist. Although the right of self-defense is usually associated with states, as opposed to nations and peoples, the right to be free from genocide must, by definition, attach to more abstract entities such as nations. In particular, the Genocide Convention protects individuals belonging to the same national, ethnical, racial, or religious group.[57] Genocide as a *crime* is committed when a perpetrator commits a predicate act, with the intent to destroy, in whole or in part, one of the protected groups.[58] While much attention has been paid to the so-called dolus specialis for genocide – genocidal intent – far too little attention has been paid to the underlying predicate acts. According to the Rome Statute, for example, the predicate acts include: (a) killing members of the group, (b) causing serious bodily or mental harm to members of the group, (c) deliberately inflicting on the group conditions of life calculated to bring about its physical destruction in whole or in part, (d) imposing measures intended to prevent births within the group, and (e) forcibly transferring children of the group to another group.[59] What the list reveals is that the law prohibiting genocide protects the *group* interest. If

nations, as well as to individuals, the care of self-preservation, and of advancing their own perfection and happiness, is she does not give them a right to preserve themselves form every thing that might render this care ineffectual"), 217 ("We have seen what rights a nation derives, in a case of necessity, from the duty of self-preservation").

54 See Hugonis Grotius, *De Jure Belli et Pacis Libri Tres*, trans. William Whewell (Cambridge: J.W. Parker, 1853), 29, citing Cicero for the proposition that self-preservation is a "first principle" and that not even God can change it.

55 For more contemporary examples that echo aspects of natural law, see W. Michael Reisman, "The View from the New Haven School of International Law," *American Society of International Law Proceedings* 86 (1992): 118–25; Jean d'Aspremont, *Formalism and the Sources of International Law: A Theory of the Ascertainment of Legal Rules* (Oxford: Oxford University Press, 2011), 106.

56 See Ray T. Donahue and Michael H. Prosser, *Diplomatic Discourse: International Conflict at the United Nations* (Greenwich, CT: Ablex, 1997), 343.

57 Convention on the Prevention and Punishment of the Crime of Genocide art. 2, Dec. 9, 1948, 78 U.N.T.S. 277, 28 I.L.M. 754.

58 Ibid.

59 Rome Statute of the International Criminal Court art. 6, July 17, 1998, 2187 U.N.T.S. 90 (entered into force July 1, 2002).

genocide were a purely individual wrong, then it would be limited to cases where only individuals are killed or subject to serious bodily or mental harm. However, genocide includes situations where individuals are transferred from one group to another either by sterilization or by kidnapping. Hypothetically, these situations could effectuate the destruction of a protected group without killing a single person. Though no individual would be destroyed, the group itself would be destroyed, and that would be enough to constitute a moral wrong.

Why should such behavior not only be criminalized but also be declared one of the most imperative international crimes triggering the full machinery of international criminal justice? Some might complain that when compared with wartime atrocities where millions of civilians are killed, such group destruction does not – or ought not – rank high on our collective priority list. There are multiple answers. First, national and ethnic groups have an inherent moral worth not reducible to the individuals that compose them. The great multiplicity of national groups in our world community enriches the tapestry of human existence. If a national group perishes, humanity as such is harmed because the multicultural and cosmopolitan nature of humanity is an a priori good. Second, one might argue for a less collectivist answer. The group right to be free from genocide is derived from an individual right to human flourishing because an individual's membership in a cultural community is often a necessary condition for achieving human flourishing. This is a debatable assumption – one frequently asserted by communitarians but rejected by liberal cosmopolitans.[60] In any event, one need not resolve the familiar debate regarding group rights and whether they are irreducibly collective or whether they are derived from liberal individual rights.[61] Either way, there is a collective right to be free from genocide, either deducible from a prior individual right or simply an expression of a primary group right.

There are several reasons to support the group rights thesis. First, although human rights are individualistic, public international laws (and the associated rights regarding genocide, self-determination, and self-defense) are codified at the collective level. The *doctrine* of public international law deals with collectives. States are participants in the formation of public international law, through treaties and customary law, and states are the entities most clearly

[60] Compare Charles Taylor, *Hegel and Modern Society* (Cambridge: Cambridge University Press, 1979) and Michael Sandel, *Liberalism and the Limits of Justice* (New York: Cambridge University Press, 1982) with Will Kymlicka, *Liberalism, Community and Culture* (New York: Oxford University Press, 1989).

[61] For a good discussion, see Seyla Benhabib, *Democracy and Difference: Contesting Boundaries of the Political* (Princeton, NJ: Princeton University Press, 1996), 159.

bound by international obligations. (Although individuals might also be bound, this requires an extra, controversial step to explain.)[62] Furthermore, the relevant rights at issue are exercised at the collective level. Only the collective can exercise the right of self-defense under international law. To talk of an individual – or group of individuals – exercising that right is to make a category mistake; it is nonsense talk. Similarly, the right of self-determination, whether external or internal, is exercised at the collective level through the processes of secession and state formation.

Of course, this does not *conclusively* demonstrate that the prelegal foundation for these rights is not individualistic. It is certainly coherent to argue that the legal doctrine is collectivist, but the underlying conceptual theory is individualistic. Under this view, the group rights in international law would be justified only because, at the level of moral theory, the individuals are morally significant. To operationalize these rights, however, some of them are codified at the collective level. But the normative foundation might be individualistic through and through.

One way of getting at this dispute is to analyze whether the social contract is one-step or two-step. Under the one-step system, there is only one social contract that generates normative rules regarding municipal life and international relations.[63] Under the two-step system, though, the bargaining begins with individuals, either real of hypothetical, who agree on basic rules for a domestic society. Then, after a domestic society is formed, each society then bargains with other liberal societies to establish normative rules for international relations. Rawls's *Law of Peoples* is perhaps the most famous recent example of a two-tiered social contract theory.[64] A two-step social contract theory provides a greater place for collectives in its account than does a one-step theory because the two-step contract assumes that groups have interests that can and should be bargained for at the international level. Of course, the group interests might be parasitic on individual interests, or the group interests might have independent moral significance, but either way the international system is built on a codification of those group rights, the most primary of which is the right to exist.

Where necessary, when the right to exist is threatened by attack or genocide, the collective group has the right of self-determination. This is often

62 See Kate Parlett, *The Individual in the International Legal System: Continuity and Change in International Law* (Cambridge: Cambridge University Press, 2011).

63 For example, see Thomas Pogge, *Realizing Rawls* (Ithaca, NY: Cornell University Press, 1989); Charles R. Beitz, *Political Theory and International Relations* (Princeton, NJ: Princeton University Press, 1979).

64 See John Rawls, *The Law of Peoples* (Cambridge, MA: Harvard University Press, 1999), 32.

referred to as remedial self-determination – the easiest cases to justify.[65] In contrast, when the group is subject to neither mistreatment nor discrimination, it is unclear why the group's right to self-determination should trump the host state's sovereign right to noninterference and territorial integrity; indeed, this was the whole point of the Canadian Supreme Court's reference to internal and external self-determination. The latter (via secession) only becomes a legal right when the particular national group cannot achieve its rights within the federal system to which it belongs.[66] In the case of Quebec, the court argued, it had ample access to the political and legal resources to secure its autonomy, thus obviating the need for a remedial claim.[67] In the end of the analysis, all of these collective rights, including self-defense, freedom from genocide, and self-determination, are clustered together as expressions of a more fundamental right to exist that belongs to nations or peoples.

3. THE RIGHT TO RESIST

In the present section, I argue that the conceptual ground for these collective rights requires more than just positing the right to existence; I also argue that it requires positing a right of resistance that is normatively independent from the right to exist.[68] The argument for this conceptual independence is complex, but it can be summarized in the following way. Victims have a right to resist an unjust attack, whether couched in terms of self-defense or freedom from genocide, even in situations where the victim has no hope of surviving the attack. In such situations, the right to exist is normatively

[65] Compare Marc Weller, *Escaping the Self-determination Trap* (Boston: Martinus Nijhoff, 2008), 59, with Katherine Del Mar, "The Myth of Remedial Secession," in Duncan French (ed.), *Statehood and Self-Determination: Reconciling Tradition and Modernity in International Law* (New York: Cambridge University Press, 2013), 79, 85 (arguing that remedial self-determination "does not form part of the international law of self-determination").

[66] See *Reference re: Secession of Quebec*, [1998] 2 S.C.R. 217 (Can.), ¶ 126.

[67] There are other limitations to the right. The salt water thesis suggests that the right of self-determination is an antiimperial norm – a right that colonial peoples, geographically distant from their rulers, often separated by an ocean (hence salt water), can assert against empires. See G.A. Res. 1541 (XV), UN Doc. A/RES/1541 (Dec. 15, 1960) ("prima facie there is an obligation to transmit information in respect of a territory which is geographically separate and is distinct ethnically and/or culturally from the country administering it").

[68] See Frédéric Mégret, "Beyond 'Freedom Fighters' and 'Terrorists': When, if Ever, is Non-State Violence Legitimate in International Law?" (working paper on file with author) (discussing resistance to colonization, international crimes, aggression, and tyranny); Frédéric Mégret, "Beyond the 'Salvation' Paradigm: Responsibility to Protect (Others) vs the Power of Protecting Oneself," *Security Dialogue* 40, no. 6 (2009): 575–95.

insufficient to ground the victim's defensive force, since it is not necessary for securing its continued existence. Consequently, the only ground for the defensive force must be found in an independent right to resist. A full explanation follows.

Recent scholarship on the theory of self-defense has focused on the so-called success condition. For example, one prominent theorist, Daniel Statman, has concluded that the logic of defensive force includes a covert requirement that the defensive force is only justified if it is *successful* in stopping or averting the threat; otherwise the defensive force represents wasted blood.[69] I say "covert" here because Statman correctly notes that the success condition is rarely recognized in the law as a codified or explicit requirement for defensive force, yet it is lurking in the background.[70]

The success condition generates more than one anxiety with regard to defensive force. First, it suggests that defensive force, either in the criminal or in the international context, is impermissible if it will be ineffectual. So a defender confronted by a rapist would have no right to use defensive force that will be ineffectual; if that is the only defensive option, since successfully repelling the assault is impossible, the defender must forego all force entirely.[71] Simply injuring the attacker, if it will not stop the assault, is not permissible according to the success condition. Similarly, in the collective context, a state would not be permitted to exercise self-defense if the defensive force will not stop the invasion; the result of the defensive force would be needless killing that will fail to achieve any particular outcome. This suggests that the success condition occasionally counsels against the defensive use of force in both the individual and the collective contexts.

But there is a second concern suggesting that the success condition might counsel in favor of *greater* defensive force. Consider the following hypothetical example from the international context. An aggressor state invades and occupies a victim state, and a third-party vindicator decides to come to the rescue. The vindicator dislodges and pushes back the invading state from its ill-gotten gains, but ultimately decides against pursuing the retreating troops of the aggressor state all the way to its home capital.[72] Instead, the vindicator decides to respect the original territorial integrity of the aggressor state. Think

69 See Daniel Statman, "On the Success Condition for Legitimate Self-Defense," *Ethics* 118 (2008): 659–86.

70 Ibid.

71 "The shocking upshot of these historical comments is that, according to S, because the Jews of the Ghetto were not fighting for their lives, they were not morally justified in killing the Germans, at least not under the right of self-defense." Ibid., 665.

72 Statman has also discussed this issue in his written work.

here of Saddam Hussein after his invasion of Kuwait; expelling the Iraqi forces from Kuwait but respecting the territorial integrity of Iraq proper might prove to be an insufficient deterrent, either general or specific, and might result in a deadly counterattack against Kuwait and coalition forces. In this situation the success condition would provide a reason for a greater amount of defensive force, because the lesser amount of force would be ineffectual. Consequently, the proper way of understanding the success condition is that it pushes defensive force to either sides of the spectrum. Either the defendant should use enough overwhelming force to secure the legitimate aims of the defensive force, or the defendant should forego force entirely. Half-hearted measures that are ineffectual are morally impermissible because they result in needless killing without the positive benefits.

I disagree with the success condition because I think it produces absurd consequences, at both the individual and collective level, precisely because victims of aggression, whether individual or collective, have an inalienable right of resistance that is not predicated on the success of the defensive force. The reason for this conclusion is that defensive force vindicates the victim's autonomy regardless of whether it prevents the aggressor from consummating the attack. A full explanation follows.

The success condition rests largely on consequentialist grounds because it assumes that the failure to achieve a particular consequence – the successful prevention of the unjustified attack – is morally relevant. Failure to stop the attack means that the consequence of injuring the unjust attacker is a negative consequence that does not entail any positive consequences that could outweigh it. However, nonconsequentialists are less inclined to view the interaction in the same way. Let me put the point this way in thinking about individual defense: utilitarians and fellow travelers will be greatly worried if an agent uses deadly force but fails to succeed in saving his own life. In this situation, the defensive force is futile and the killing of the aggressor generates no *additional* utility – only the killing of an additional life or an injury to another person. It does not make the world a better place. So the original victim ought to abstain from defensive force. Similarly, the defensive force in international law would result in the killing of enemy combatants and civilians without any possible benefit to outweigh this killing.

To put the point sharply, it should come as no surprise that the success condition is important for utilitarians, because success is, after all, a *consequence*. But deontologists do not place "consequences" in such a privileged position in their moral system, so the fact that the defensive force might be futile does not animate a tension for them in the same way. This is not to suggest that consequences do not matter at *all* for deontologists, but rather that consequences matter far less for deontologists than they do for utilitarians, and therefore the success condition should matter much more for consequentialists than deontologists.

To understand the deontological intuitions here, consider the individual hypothetical again. A victim is being raped and her defensive force is futile and will fail to repel the attack, though it might injure the aggressor. Does the futility of the resistance require the victim to forego resistance altogether and submit meekly to the assault? There is something deeply distasteful about this conclusion and it ought to signal that something in the argument has taken a wrong turn, and the wrong turn cannot be corrected simply by asserting that the victim is defending her honor and that this is a nontrivial consequence.

For my intuitions, the outcome of this thought experiment is that success does not always matter, at the individual level, and this ought to give us pause for understanding the right to self-defense and the deeper principles from which it emerges. Utilitarians might be kept up at night by this example but only because their commitment to consequences is constitutive of their moral program and cannot be abandoned. For a nonconsequentialist, *resistance* itself to the moral wrong could in theory be elevated as an a priori good, which explains in part why futile resistance need not be abandoned in the face of a putative success condition. However, this route is unavailable to a pure consequentialist who must genuinely confront this counterexample and must either bite the bullet and hold that the futile defense is immoral or recast his or her moral theory.

To further the point, I think that the success condition is equally problematic at the collective level. The analysis necessarily assumes that merely deflecting an attack for a finite amount of time – say a month – qualifies as futile, thus triggering the concern about wasted blood. The problem with this view is that it assumes the basic *fungibility* of moments in time, something that there are good reasons to deny. Consider again the individual level. Say that an attacker has already deployed a poison that will kill his victim in a month and no antidote is available. The attacker comes back and decides to kill the victim a month earlier by shooting him with a gun. Is it wasteful to kill the attacker to stop the gun attack because the victim's death by poisoning is inevitable? This would only be the case if all moments in time are essentially fungible, if there is little difference in dying today and dying a month from now. Even if the difference is only a day, the day that the victim would spend with his daughter tomorrow has moral value. That is precisely why most criminal law jurisdictions do not recognize the inevitability argument. If an attacker shoots and kills you while you are falling to your death from a skyscraper, the shooter is still guilty of murder even if the attacker only robbed you of one second of your life.[73] The same is true in mercy killing cases.

Moving back to the collective level, the fungibility of time assumes that saving a state's existence, only if that brings a one-month reprieve from an inevitable defeat, would represent wasted blood. But the thirty days of survival is only fungible in this regard if it can and should be traded off with the time afforded to the attacking state – precisely the kind of balancing that a non-consequentialist might deny. In fact, such situations represent *partially* successful cases of self-defense because the attack is forestalled for a discrete unit of time, whether several days or several hours. And even a delay is a kind of success. Indeed, all cases of permanent success are just aggregations of individual cases of delay, all of which are morally significant.

However, there are other ways to reformulate the success condition problem in ways that would avoid the response just presented. Consider an unjust attack and assume that the defender's response will be not only ultimately ineffective, but immediately ineffective as well. In other words, the defensive force will not buy the defender any extra time at all. The death or injury associated with the unjust attack will occur at just the same moment in time whether the defender exercises force or not. Consequently, the defender does not gain even a second more of freedom by attempting to repel the assault. The only difference is that the defensive force will impose an extra harm on the unjustified aggressor.

Even in this scenario, the defender can and should exercise force against the unjustified attacker. However, the rationale for the defensive force has nothing to do with the success condition. Rather, the victim has the right to resist force, regardless of whether doing so secures his or her existence, because doing so is an expression of the defender's autonomy as both a moral agent and a legitimate object of moral concern. The right to meet force with force is a natural right that all agents are endowed with, and to succumb to force just because the defense will be ineffectual is to passively accept the unjustified aggression. Attempting to repel the assault, whether successful or not, represents a rejection of that assault and the unjustified intrusion that it represents. By fighting against an attacker, the victim asserts his or her right to bodily integrity, to the sovereignty of his or her own person. Indeed, there is something poignant about the victim who defies the attacker even when the defiance is ineffectual; in so doing, the victim stands with all victims of assault,

[73] These are often treated as cases of overdetermination. For recent analysis, see James G. Stewart, "Overdetermined Atrocities," *Journal of International Criminal Justice* 10, no. 5 (2012): 1189–218.

not just in solidarity, but also in compliance with a universal maxim that asserts that unjustified attacks violate the moral law and that defensive force against them is both meaningful and appropriate.

Consider Barbara Herman's well-known version of a Kantian right of individual self-defense.[74] Under her rendering, the right stems from the aggressor's impermissible use of the victim as a means to achieve a particular result – an act that violates the moral worth of the victim and violates the categorical imperative.[75] By acting passively – by failing to resist, as it were – the victim would be assenting to that aggression and its impermissible treatment of the victim as a mere means in violation of the universal moral law.[76] As such, the right of self-defense still applies even in cases where the defense will be ineffectual, because even passivity in the face of ineffectual self-defense would represent an assent to the impermissible actions of the aggressor.[77] Moreover, this argument applies just as much to collectives as it does to individuals.[78] When a nation or state acts passively in the face of an unlawful attack, it assents to the aggressor's impermissible use of the victim group as a mere means to achieve a particular aim. As such, the victim group ought to resist, even to the point of futility, in order to avoid assenting to the unlawful maxim deployed by the aggressor.

Might there be an important asymmetry between the collective and individual level here that suggests an objection to the present view? On the individual level, the harm imposed on the aggressor during an act of futile self-defense is a harm that is imposed on a truly culpable individual. For that reason, it seems strange for the analysis to allow the harm imposed on the culpable aggressor to outweigh the victim's reason to engage in the admittedly futile self-defense. But what about situations in which the harm is imposed on a third party? Would futile self-defense still be appropriate if the harm is imposed not on the culpable attacker but also on an *innocent* third party? Then the argument for the independent right of resistance becomes more difficult to muster.

One might think that this is precisely the situation posed by collective self-defense. On the international level, the harms imposed by futile acts of self-defense will be born by civilians and combatants on the side of the aggressor

74 See Barbara Herman, *The Practice of Moral Judgment* (Cambridge, MA: Harvard University Press, 1996), 129.

75 Ibid. 76 Ibid., 130.

77 Ibid. See also Whitley R. P. Kaufman, *Justified Killing: The Paradox of Self-Defense* (Lanham, MD: Lexington Books, 2009), 50–51.

78 Similarly, consider A.J. Coates, *The Ethics of War* (New York: Manchester University Press, 1997).

state. However, those civilians and combatants may or may not be the same individuals responsible for the original aggression. Once one pierces the veil of the state, the benefits and burdens of the original attack and the futile self-defense will not be distributed equally. Some individuals will receive the benefits while others will receive the burdens. At this point, the picture begins to look a lot more like imposing third-party burdens during the course of futile self-defense, which we just suggested was more difficult to justify.

The answer to this question is that we should not necessarily pierce the veil of the state in this situation. Although it is difficult to explain, the state or nation represents a collective group and there will always be distribution concerns within the group. However, like it or not, the international system is predicated on the idea that citizens and their nations will advance and retrograde together, as Francis Lieber once described it.[79] Although the benefits and burdens of warfare are not always distributed equally by sovereign governments, this does not entail that collectives do not act on the international stage. When an aggressor unjustly attacks a victim, the victim has a right of response whether or not the aggressor and victim are individuals or collective entities. Moreover, the actions of the collective are not fully explainable by simply reference to individuals.[80] So the reason why international law deals with collectives is not simply a matter of linguistic convenience, as mere shorthand, if you will. The *reasons* that a collective has for acting can only be explained if we take the nation or state as a bona fide collective.

4. CONCLUSION

In this chapter I have defended a unified conception of the core collective rights that are codified in international law: rights of self-defense, self-determination, and freedom from genocide. I have argued that these rights attach to abstract entities such as nations and peoples, rather than just nation-states in the positivistic sense of that expression. I have also shown that this cluster of rights can be traced to a deeper set of moral rights: the right to exist and the right to resist. Moreover, I have denied that the right of resistance can be derived from the right to exist, which would be more primary. Instead, I have

[79] See Instructions for the Government of Armies of the United States in the Field, General Order No. 100, April 24, 1863, art. 20. ("Public war is a state of armed hostility between sovereign nations or governments. It is a law and requisite of civilized existence that men live in political, continuous societies, forming organized units, called states or nations, whose constituents bear, enjoy, suffer, advance and retrograde together, in peace and in war.")

[80] See Christian List and Philip Pettit, *Group Agency: The Possibility, Design, and Status of Corporate Agents* (Oxford: Oxford University Press, 2011).

argued that the right to resist is an independent moral right because resistance is morally appropriate even in cases of futile self-defense. The warrant for this conclusion is that resistance represents a neo-Kantian expression of the defender's autonomy. By engaging in defense against the unjustified attack, the defender acts pursuant to a universal maxim that unjustified threats against another's sovereignty, whether individual or collective, ought to be negated by force.

5

Self-Determination in Three Movements

PATRICK MACKLEM*

When Arab, Asian, and Latin American delegations began to press the United Nations in the early 1950s to recognize a human right of self-determination, European officials expressed alarm, seeing their campaign as "a mere pretext for attacks on the colonial powers."[1] The upstart delegations had succeeded in blocking an effort to exempt colonies from the application of the draft covenant intended to transform the Universal Declaration on Human Rights into a legally binding treaty, and now they were setting their sights higher.[2] Especially outraged by these developments was a Belgian delegate, Fernand Dehousse, who stated that "[c]ertain delegations which had spoken in favour of the self-determination clause did not seem to be sufficiently interested in the solution of the question, but appeared to regard the clause in the negative sense, as a weapon for use against the colonial Powers."[3] His protests fell on deaf ears. In 1966, the right of self-determination was enshrined in the International Covenant on Civil and Political Rights and the International Covenant on Economic, Social and Cultural Rights.[4]

* William C. Graham Professor of Law. I am grateful for the comments by Fernando Tesón and an anonymous reviewer on an earlier draft of this essay. An earlier version of this chapter appears as Chapter 7 in Patrick Macklem, The Sovereignty of Human Rights (New York: Oxford University Press, 2015).

1 A.W. Brian Simpson, *Human Rights and the End of Empire: Britain and the Genesis of the European Convention* (Oxford: Oxford University Press), at 814.

2 For an illuminating account, see Roland Burke, *Decolonization and the Evolution of International Human Rights* (Philadelphia: University of Pennsylvania Press, 2010). See also Samuel Moyn, *The Last Utopia: Human Rights in History* (Cambridge, MA: Harvard University Press, 2010), at 84–119.

3 Summary Records of the Third Committee, 361st meeting, 7 Dec. 1951, A/C.3/SR. 361, paras. 11–12, as quoted by Burke, *Decolonization and the Evolution of International Human Rights*, at 158, n. 40.

4 International Covenant on Civil and Political Rights, art. 1, opened for signature 19 Dec. 1966, 999 U.N.T.S. 171 (entered into force 23 March 1976); International Covenant on Economic,

Opponents were right to see the campaign to recognize self-determination as a human right as an attack on colonialism. In fact, it is illustrative of a deeper role that the right of self-determination plays in the international legal order. The right of self-determination has become an instrument whose purpose is to promote a just distribution of sovereign power in the international legal order. It has come to assume this task because of three conceptual movements it underwent in the twentieth century that dramatically transformed its legal scope and content. The first had its origins in events surrounding the Paris Peace Conference in 1919, where self-determination's class of beneficiaries moved from the population of an existing state to potential populations within and across state boundaries. The second, a movement in legal status, from a principle to a right, coincided with international law's engagement with the dramatic decolonization projects that took root after the Second World War. The third movement is best understood in the context of self-determination's awkward relationship to central tenets of both public international law and international human rights law. It is a movement between legal orders, from its engagement with the international realm to an additional engagement with the domestic realm, from an entitlement that had the capacity to protect existing states or produce new states to one that also validates domestic constitutional reorganization of a political community. As a result of these three movements, the right of self-determination authorizes the formation of a new state by a colonized population and, more controversially, when an existing state fails to secure effective measures of political representation – what international law refers to as "internal self-determination" – for a people in its midst.

While these movements have been enlisted by others in support of distinctive claims about the contemporary legal salience of the right of self-determination,[5] less has been written, I believe, about their cumulative effect on the normative role that the right plays in the international legal order.[6] This essay proposes that these three movements yield a new role, or purpose, for self-determination in international law. Its new role is to mitigate adverse effects

Social and Cultural Rights, art. 1, opened for signature 19 Dec. 1966, 993 U.N.T.S. 3 (entered into force 3 Jan. 1976).

5 See, for example, Antonio Cassese, *Self-Determination of Peoples: A Legal Reappraisal* (Cambridge: Cambridge University Press, 1995); James Crawford, *The Creation of States in International Law*, 2nd ed. (Oxford: Oxford University Press, 2006), at 107–48. For an analysis of the problems posed by cultural and gender differences to the interpretation of self-determination, see Karen Knop, *Diversity and Self-Determination in International Law* (Cambridge: Cambridge University Press, 2002). For a literary portrait of self-determination, see Edward Morgan, "The Imagery and Meaning of Self-Determination," 20 *N.Y.U. J. Int'l Law & Pol.* 355 (1988).

6 A notable exception is the work of Allen Buchanan. See Allen Buchanan, *Justice, Legitimacy, and Self-Determination: Moral Foundations for International Law* (Oxford: Oxford University Press, 2004).

associated with how international law distributes sovereignty around the globe and how it authorizes its exercise by sovereign states. The right of self-determination is an instrument that stands to produce a more just distribution of sovereign power among collectivities that international law recognizes as states. The right of self-determination thus acts as an important conceptual bridge between the structure and operation of international law and global justice. Finally, this essay offers some reflections on some of the implications of this role, on what it means to speak of the distribution of sovereignty in international law, and on what it means to speak of self-determination as bridging international law and global justice.

1.

References to self-determination include the Charter of the United Nations, which lists the principle of self-determination as one of the purposes of the United Nations.[7] The Charter also calls for the promotion of a number of social and economic goals "with a view to the creation of conditions of stability and well-being which are necessary for peaceful and friendly relations among nations based on respect for the principle of equal rights and self-determination of peoples."[8] In addition, both the International Covenant on Civil and Political Rights (ICCPR) and the International Covenant on Social, Economic and Cultural Rights (ICESCR) provide that "all peoples have the right of self-determination [and to] freely determine their political status and freely pursue their economic, social and cultural development."[9]

Notwithstanding its present status as a human right, before World War I, the concept of self-determination – to the extent it received legal recognition – simply reinforced the then-existing distribution of sovereignty in the international legal order. In the words of Diane Orentlicher, "if international law enforced any conception of self-determination, it meant one thing: established states had a right to be left alone by other states."[10] The field traditionally understood self-determination as vesting in the entire population of an existing state, coextensive with sovereignty itself. Its object of

[7] United Nations, *Charter of the United Nations*, 24 Oct. 1945, 1 UNTS XVI, art. 1(2).

[8] UN Charter, art. 55.

[9] Art. 1, International Covenant on Civil and Political Rights (1966) 999 U.N.T.S. 171 in force 1976; art. 1, International Covenant on Economic, Social and Cultural Rights (1966) 993 U.N.T.S. 3 in force 1976.

[10] Diane Orentlicher, "Separation Anxiety: International Responses to Ethno-Separatist Claims," 23 *Yale L.J.* 1 (1998), at 22.

attention was the constituted power of a state and its autonomy and independence on the international stage.

International law's equation of self-determination with sovereignty existed at a time when international law extended legal validity to the colonizing projects of imperial powers. Although colonialism now undoubtedly constitutes a violation of a people's right of self-determination, for centuries international law authorized the colonization of peoples by sovereign states. It did so by comprehending the territory of a sovereign state as including the territory of any and all colonies under its imperial control.[11] A state's sovereignty thus extended to its colonial territories and colonized peoples. Any attempt by a colonial population to free itself of its colonial status was comprehended as a threat to the territorial integrity of its colonizing master and an international illegality. Sovereignty, and its latent synonym, self-determination, in other words, extended international legal validity to colonialism.

After the First World War, self-determination surfaced in international legal discourse as a principle relatively autonomous from the concept of sovereignty. It did so in discourse that justified the liberation of Eastern European nations under the yoke of foreign domination. The Paris Peace Conference and its aftermath saw the creation of Finland, Estonia, Latvia, Lithuania, Poland, Bulgaria, Yugoslavia, Czechoslovakia, and Turkey, and the splitting of Austria-Hungary into two separate countries. The ultimately futile geopolitical goal of creating buffer zones to restrain a resurgent Germany no doubt drove the politics of these acts of liberation. The most visible manifestation of this goal was the decision to establish joint occupation of the Rhineland for fifteen years in return for France abandoning its claim for a "free Rhine state."[12] Nonetheless, the principle that state boundaries should respect the self-determining identities of nations was what Woodrow Wilson unevenly relied on to justify, in normative terms, this radical political redistribution of

[11] *Case Concerning Right of Passage over Indian Territory (Portugal v. India)*, [1960] I.C.J. Rep. 6. With respect to mandated and trust territories, sovereignty was not viewed as vested in the administering power. Where it did vest, if it vested at all, was the subject of a debate whose "results, the luxuriance and variety of which are almost baffling." Quincy Wright, *Mandates under the League of Nations* (Chicago, IL: University of Chicago Press, 1930), at 90. See also Michael D. Callahan, *A Sacred Trust: The League of Nations and Africa, 1929–1946* (Brighton: Sussex Academic Press, 2004). For more discussion, see Crawford, *The Creation of States in International Law*, at 568–69.

[12] For discussion, see Patrick O. Cohrs, *The Unfinished Peace after World War I: America, Britain and the Stabilisation of Europe, 1919–1932* (Cambridge: Cambridge University Press, 2008), at 57.

sovereign power.[13] In fact, one of Wilson's advisors, Isaiah Bowman, envisioned the main function of the League of Nations to be the guarantor of "territorial integrity" of the nations of Europe, vested with the power to alter boundaries "if it could be shown that injustice had been done or that conditions had changed."[14]

During this period, self-determination served to legitimate the creation of states, and thus began to mean something more than a principle justifying the existing distribution of sovereignty. By regarding populations in addition to those of existing states as "self-determining," self-determination began its first movement, from a normative feature of the population of an existing state to one that can also characterize populations within and across state boundaries. Its object of attention now extended beyond constituted power to include constituent power – the power of a people to form a political community. In so doing, it began to assume the role of legitimating recalibrations of the distribution of sovereign power in international law.

Self-determination didn't perform this role in universal terms. Its relevance was primarily restricted to Europe and to peoples who international law deemed to be sufficiently developed to merit sovereign recognition. In 1919, the Covenant of the League of Nations declared that territories that had been annexed or colonized by Germany and the Ottoman Empire before World War I were inhabited by peoples "not yet able to stand by themselves under the strenuous conditions of the modern world."[15] These territories were administered by "mandatories" – sovereign states – whose administration in turn was supervised by the League Council and the Permanent Mandates Commission. Mandates were grouped into three categories depending on the degree of their "development," determining the extent to which they enjoyed political autonomy from their mandatory powers.[16] Mandatories were

[13] The normative and the geopolitical accounts may not be that far apart. See Zoran Oklopcic, "A Farewell to Rhetorical Arms: Unravelling the Self-Determination of Peoples," in Andrée Boisselle, Glen Coulthard, Avigail Eisenberg, and Jeremy Webber (eds.), *Recognition and Self-Determination* (Vancouver: University of British Columbia Press, forthcoming), 101–24, at 119 ("[s]elf-determination may be a battle cry for political emancipation, but it is, moreover, a rhetorical tool deployed by great powers through which they enlist select populations for the political projects that perpetuate their dominance").

[14] Memorandum by Isaiah Bowman (10 Dec. 1918), quoted in Cohrs, *The Unfinished Peace*, at 64.

[15] League of Nations, *Covenant of the League of Nations*, 28 April 1919, art. 22. See generally Wright, *Mandates under the League of Nations* (providing a contemporaneous account of the mandates system).

[16] Group A was comprised of territories in the Middle East, Group B was comprised of territories in Central Africa, and Group C was comprised of territories in South-West Africa and the Pacific. Wright, *Mandates under the League of Nations.*

responsible for the "tutelage" of peoples inhabiting mandates – in Woodrow Wilson's words, they were "tutors and advisors of these people"[17] – in accordance with "the principle that the well-being and development of such peoples form a sacred trust of civilization."[18]

This conception of self-determination in international law – one that legally validated the establishment of nation-states in Europe and the colonization of peoples elsewhere[19] – remained relatively constant until the aftermath of World War II. At the time of its enactment in 1948, the Charter of the United Nations simultaneously reaffirmed the "principle" of self-determination and the international legality of colonialism. Chapter XII of the Charter established the trusteeship system, a modified mandates system for the administration and supervision of remaining mandate territories now deemed trust territories. Trust territories were not the only colonies whose populations international law prevented from acquiring sovereign statehood in the name of self-determination. Chapter XI of the Charter governed "non-self-governing territories" over which member states at the time of its enactment asserted sovereignty outside of the trusteeship system. Chapter XI implicitly affirms the international legality of these colonial relations by setting forth a "Declaration" by members who exercise imperial power over colonies of this kind to act in the interests of the colonized populations in a variety of different ways. In the words of Samuel Moyn, "the United Nations, far from being the forum of a new and liberatory set of principles, appeared set at first on colluding in the attempted reimposition of colonial rule after the war."[20]

Soon after the UN Charter's enactment, however, international law performed a dramatic reversal on the international legality of colonialism. After a decade of efforts by the African, Arab, Asian, and Latin American delegations to attempt to persuade numerous UN bodies to recognize self-determination as a human right, the UN General Assembly enacted the

[17] Wilson Report to the Third Plenary Session of the Peace Conference, 14 February 1919, Foreign Office, Quai D'Orsay, PPW 55:176, as quoted by Anna Su, "Woodrow Wilson and the Origins of the International Law of Religious Freedom" (unpublished paper on file with author), at 25.

[18] Ibid. For more detail on the legal apparatus of the mandates system, see Crawford, *The Creation of States in International Law*, at 565–601.

[19] Compare Mark Mazower, *No Enchanted Palace: The End of Empire and the Ideological Origins of the United Nations* (Princeton, NJ: Princeton University Press, 2009), at 105 ("The 1919 settlement had barred the principle of national self-determination from Africa and southeast Asia but extended it across Central and Eastern Europe").

[20] Moyn, *The Last Utopia*, at 93. See also Mazower, *No Enchanted Palace* (arguing that the UN's creators envisioned it as an organization that would protect the interests of empire and that this vision was decisively reshaped by postcolonial states).

1960 Declaration on the Granting of Independence to Colonial Territories. Formally marking the beginning of self-determination's second movement, the 1960 Declaration, in the language of universalism, declared self-determination to be a "right" that entitles "all peoples" to "freely determine their political status and freely pursue their economic, social and cultural development."[21] The 1960 Declaration also continued self-determination's first movement by affirming that the right is vested in colonized peoples, populations that are not coextensive with the population of a state. It provided that the populations of trust territories and non-self-governing territories are peoples, and that these populations are entitled to "complete independence," or what has become known as "external" self-determination.[22]

The 1960 Declaration thus treats the right of self-determination as an instrument that addresses international law's complicity with colonialism. "With the official acceptance of the right to self-determination," according to Roland Burke, "the process of decolonization itself became a human right."[23] The elevation of self-determination to the status of a human right was a spectacular political achievement, one that underscored a dramatic transformation of the UN's stance toward colonialism. In Rupert Emerson's words, "[t]he earlier assumption that each colonial power should at its own discretion and in an unhurried way lead its dependent peoples to well-being and self-government gave way to the proposition that colonialism was an intolerable and illegitimate abuse to be done away with as speedily as possible by the international community."[24] The relationship between colonized and colonizer was no longer shielded from international scrutiny as a matter "essentially within the domestic jurisdiction" of a state.[25] The elevation of

[21] Art. 1, *Declaration on the Granting of Independence to Colonial Countries and Peoples*, GA Res. 1514, UN GAOR 15th Sess., Supp. No. 15, UN Doc. A/4654 (1960).

[22] Ibid., art. 5.

[23] Burke, *Decolonization and the Evolution of International Human Rights*, at 37. Burke provides a detailed historical account of the changing impact of decolonization on the UN human rights program. See also Jochen von Bernstorff, "The Changing Fortunes of the Universal Declaration of Human Rights: Genesis and Symbolic Dimensions of the Turn to Rights in International Law," 19 *Eur. J. Int'l L.* 903 (2008), at 912 ("The new Southern majority within the UN advanced the claims to liberation from racial discrimination and colonial rule in human rights terms; a political strategy that ultimately led to the inclusion of a common Article 1 on the right to self-determination in the two 1966 human rights covenants"). For a historical account from a British perspective of the anticolonial movement in the UN during this period, see Simpson, *Human Rights and the End of Empire*, at 300–22.

[24] Rupert Emerson, "Colonialism, Political Development, and the UN," 19 *International Organization* 484–503 (1965), at 486.

[25] UN Charter, art. 2(7).

self-determination to the status of a human right dramatically transformed colonialism into a matter of international concern.

Some have argued that self-determination's engagement with decolonization taints its normative status as an international human right.[26] Louis Henkin, for example, argued that self-determination was placed on the register of international human rights to be "used as a political weapon against colonialism or economic imperialism, not to enhance the rights of all persons against all governments."[27] Henkin cautioned that "its injection into the human rights covenants could only hamper progress on the covenants and reduce further the likelihood of adherence by important nations."[28] Crawford Young characterized the right of self-determination as an "instrumental norm for the anticolonial movement, a means to the transcendent end of immediate independence."[29] In Young's words, "the essential value" of democracy and self-determination "was their utility in the combat against colonial rule, rather than their intrinsic worth."[30]

These concerns confuse the legal value of the right of self-determination with the politics behind its legal production. What the history of the right of self-determination during this period illustrates is that the international legality of human rights is the product of deep political contestation over the international legal validity of the exercise of certain forms of power, not an inexorable step in the process of moral theory working itself pure on the international stage. The elevation of self-determination to the status of a human right was a spectacular political achievement by the Arab, Asian, and Latin American delegations at the United Nations. But the politics behind the legal production of the right of self-determination in international law – however spectacular – does not determine the role that it plays in the international legal order. The intent of those responsible for its entrenchment is but one factor in characterizing the purpose of the right. What this politics does suggest, however, is that the right of self-determination was meant by at least some of those responsible for its international legal existence to mitigate some of the adverse effects produced by how international law distributes sovereignty around the globe and authorizes its exercise by sovereign states.

[26] This discussion of the relationship between self-determination and decolonization is indebted to Burke, *Decolonization and the Evolution of International Human Rights*, at 35–58.

[27] Louis Henkin, "The United Nations and Human Rights," 19 *International Organization* 504, at 513 (1965).

[28] Ibid., at 513.

[29] Crawford Young, "African States and the Search for Freedom," in Robert H. Taylor (ed.), *The Idea of Freedom in Asia and Africa* (Stanford, CA: Stanford University Press, 2002), 9–39, at 32.

[30] Ibid.

The right of self-determination assumed this role in the context of decolonization, by the way it operated to redistribute sovereign power to redress international legal complicity in the colonizing projects of imperial powers.

Partly because of its radical potential, the 1960 Declaration gave rise to more questions than answers. For example, it stated that "[a]ny attempt aimed at the partial or total disruption of the national unity and the territorial integrity of a country is incompatible with the Purposes and Principles of the Charter of the United Nations."[31] So whereas the 1960 Declaration entitles colonized peoples to form their own states, it also reaffirms the territorial integrity of all states. Nor did the 1960 Declaration take explicit issue with international law's deep-rooted acceptance of the proposition that colonized territory is the territory of the colonizer. But if a state's territory includes the territories of its colonies, how can independence be achieved without disrupting the territorial integrity of colonizing powers?[32]

More importantly, if self-determination attaches to colonized peoples, then is it no longer coextensive with the entire population of an existing state? That is, does it have the potential to attach to some but not to all members of a state, to communities within states and across states? The 1960 Declaration states that all peoples possess the right of self-determination. It also declares that "alien subjugation, domination and exploitation" constitute violations of fundamental human rights. These forms of oppression presumably include colonization but reach beyond the colonial context. But the 1960 Declaration does not say that these forms of oppression violate the right of self-determination. And it restricts its discussion of the acquisition of independence to colonies. Does the right entitle a noncolonized people to sovereign statehood?

Some of these questions were clarified by the Declaration on Friendly Relations in 1970.[33] Partly the result of continued efforts by Arab, Asian, and American delegations to recast basic principles of international law, the 1970 Declaration provides extensive detail on principles commonly understood to be foundational to the international legal order, such as the prohibition on the use of force, the duty not to intervene in the domestic jurisdiction of any state, the principle of sovereign equality of states, and the principle of self-determination. In its elaboration of the meaning of self-determination, the

[31] 1960 Declaration, art. 6.

[32] To be precise, this question arose only with respect to non-self-governing territories. For more discussion, see Crawford, *The Creation of States in International Law*, at 568–69.

[33] *Declaration on Principles of International Law Concerning Friendly Relations and Cooperation among States in Accordance with the Charter of the United Nations*, GA Res. 2625, UN GAOR, 25th Sess., Supp. No. 28, UN Doc. A/8028 (1970).

1970 Declaration reaffirms the principle of territorial integrity but adds a crucial qualification. The 1970 Declaration made clear that the territory of a colony has "a status separate and distinct from the territory of the state administering it."[34] So while colonies possess separate territorial status, the territorial integrity of a colony and of a state is inviolable. The acquisition of sovereign independence by a colony via the right of self-determination, in other words, does not threaten the territorial integrity of a state.

Moreover, like the 1960 Declaration, the 1970 Declaration also states that all peoples, not simply colonized peoples, have the right of self-determination. It reiterates the language of "alien subjugation, domination, and exploitation" and says that these conditions constitute a denial of fundamental human rights.[35] But it also provides that these forms of oppression constitute a violation of the "principle" of self-determination. Theoretically this could cover a wide variety of circumstances. And the 1970 Declaration seems to qualify the commitment to territorial integrity even more than treating the territory of a colony as distinct from the territory of the colonizing state. It states that

> nothing in the foregoing paragraphs shall be construed as authorising or encouraging any action which would dismember or impair, totally or in part, the territorial integrity or political unity of sovereign and independent states conducting themselves in compliance with the principle of equal rights and self-determination ... and thus possessed of a government representing the whole people without distinction as to race, creed or colour.[36]

This suggests that the right can disrupt the territorial integrity of a state not "in compliance with the principle of equal rights and self-determination" and thus not "possessed of a government representing the whole people without distinction as to race, creed or colour."[37]

Taken together, the two declarations produced two specifications of the right. First, they treat the right of self-determination as an instrument of acquiring statehood in a colonial context where the parent state is geographically separate from the colony by deeming colonial territory to possess a legal status separate from that of the territory of the state administering it. Second, the declarations can plausibly be construed as treating the right of self-determination as an instrument of acquiring statehood, outside the colonial context, in cases of "alien subjugation, domination and exploitation," or where a surrounding state is not "in compliance with the principle of equal rights and self-determination" and thus not "possessed of a government representing the whole people without distinction as to race, creed or colour."[38]

[34] Ibid. [35] Ibid. [36] Ibid. [37] Ibid. [38] Ibid.

The first specification of the right of self-determination legitimated a very impressive record of decolonization. Between 1945 and 1970, seventy territories achieved independence.[39] Angola and Mozambique acquired independence in 1975, and Namibia, a territory once held by South Africa under a League of Nations mandate, acquired independence in 1990. The United Nations has consistently applied the right of self-determination to colonies seeking independence, typically organizing a referendum before the accession to independence. But given that there are very few formal colonies still remaining in the world,[40] what is the future of the right in terms of its second iteration, outside the colonial context?

While some applaud "the reluctant sunset of the concept of self-determination,"[41] others, in Orentlicher's words, are equally "reluctant to retire the right and have earnestly sought to find it new work."[42] One context where it does some work is in the context of foreign occupation of territory. In 1971, the International Court of Justice (ICJ) upheld a resolution by the UN General Assembly revoking South Africa's Mandate over Namibia after South Africa refused to hand over the territory to UN Trusteeship authority.[43] Part of the Court's reasons for upholding the resolution rested on the importance of the principle of self-determination. With the Mandate terminated, South Africa's continued presence in Namibia amounted to a foreign occupation in violation of international law.

Another context where self-determination has some salience, at least politically, is in relation to forced annexation of territory, as it did in the case of East Timor, which was annexed by Indonesia in 1975 and not liberated from foreign occupation until 1999. The UN Security Council was quick to enact a resolution calling "upon all states to respect the territorial integrity of East Timor as well as the inalienable right of its people to self-determination" and calling "upon the Government of Indonesia to withdraw all its forces from the territory without delay.[44] Although the ICJ followed suit with an enthusiastic endorsement of the

[39] Cassese, *Self-Determination: A Legal Reappraisal*, at 74–76.

[40] Cassese notes that the United States and British Virgin Islands, New Caledonia, Tokelau, Bermuda, and the Falklands/Malvinas, remain the "few unresolved problems," but also notes that the populations of at least some of these territories "do not want independence." Antonio Cassese, *International Law* (Oxford: Oxford University Press, 2001), at 286.

[41] Zoran Oklopcic, "A Farewell to Rhetorical Arms," at 102.

[42] Orentlicher, "Separation Anxiety," at 44.

[43] *Legal Consequences for States of the Continued Presence of South Africa in Namibia (South-West Africa) Notwithstanding Security Council Resolution 276* (1970) Advisory Opinion, [1971] I.C.J. Rep. 16.

[44] UN Security Council Resolution 384 (adopted on 22 Dec. 1975).

"irreproachable" right of self-determination of the people of East Timor, it dismissed the claim on technical grounds.[45]

Yet another area where self-determination has some relevance is in relation to Israel and Palestine. In an advisory opinion, the ICJ held that the Palestinian people constitute a people, that they possess the right of self-determination, and that the wall being constructed by Israel around the occupied territories violates their right of self-determination.[46] The Court said little about why the wall violates the right. The judgment alludes to territorial claims made by Israel to Jerusalem and certain settlements, with an unstated implication that the wall is including land that belongs to the Palestinians within Israeli territory.[47] The judgment is "significant as it demonstrated the judges' willingness to develop a legal rule for the first time (the existence of a noncolonial right of self-determination), and to apply it in a politically charged context."[48] But the Court does not address broader questions concerning self-determination and the Palestinians, leaving unclear the territory to which the right refers and what else it might vest in the Palestinian people. As a result, the judgment offers little insight on the relevance of self-determination to the vast majority of disputes we see arising these days, where a single state is comprised of two or more ethnic or religious or cultural groups. What role does self-determination play in these contexts? To answer this question, we want to first see the norm of self-determination in terms of its relationship to public international law and, second, in relation to international human rights law.

2.

Given its commitment to state sovereignty, public international law bears an awkward relation to the norm of self-determination. Despite – or perhaps

[45] *East Timor Case (Portugal v. Australia)*, [1995] I.C.J. 90, at para. 90. Specifically, the Court dismissed the claim of Portugal against Australia for entering into a an agreement with Indonesia that adversely affected the rights of East Timor, because Indonesia was not party to the case.

[46] *Legal Consequences of the Construction of a Wall in the Occupied Palestinian Territory*, [2004] I.C.J. Rep. 136. For commentary, see Frédéric Mégret, "A Sacred Trust of Civilization," 1 *J. Int'l L. & Int'l Rel.* 305 (2005).

[47] In this regard, the Court stated that the construction of the wall "gives expression in loco to the illegal measures taken by Israel with regard to Jerusalem and the settlements, as deplored by the Security Council. ... There is also a risk of further alterations to the demographic composition of the Occupied Palestinian Territory resulting from the construction of the wall inasmuch as it is contributing ... to the departure of Palestinian populations from certain areas." *Legal Consequences of the Construction*, at para. 122.

[48] Milena Sterio, *The Right to Self-Determination under International Law: "Selfistans," Secession, and the Rule of the Great Powers* (London: Routledge, 2013), at 94.

because of – its intimate relation to freedom, a paradox lies at the heart of self-determination: it both legitimates and challenges sovereign authority.[49] On one hand, sovereignty is the formal expression of the principle of self-determination in international law. Sovereignty provides a shield that protects the capacity of a people to determine freely the ways in which they wish to govern themselves, and authorizes state action to protect chosen arrangements from internal or external threat. On the other hand, self-determination, understood in light of the three movements identified here, threatens sovereignty to the extent that it acts as a justification for disrupting the existing distribution of sovereignty around the world by conferring the right to acquire sovereign independence – or external self-determination – on populations other than those of existing states.

That self-determination simultaneously promotes and threatens sovereignty is perhaps why international law is ambivalent about it. One can discern the ambivalence toward the norm in the way it appears in the UN Charter. The Charter does not specify what is meant by "self-determination." The Charter regards it only as a "goal" of the United Nations.[50] It does conceive of the norm as an instrument of state relations, as a means of "furthering the development of friendly relations among States,"[51] but it does not specify any state obligations it might engender beyond, as Cassese notes, the signaling of "the maturing of the political postulate of self-determination into a legal standard of behaviour."[52]

But self-determination also has an ambiguous relationship to international human rights law. On the one hand, and in some iterations, it is consistent with the emphasis in international human rights law on democratic governance.[53] And its second movement, from a principle to a right, was one to a *human* right, as expressed by the ICCPR and the ICESCR and the 1960 Declaration. On the other hand, although one can still characterize the right as a universal right, in that everyone participates in communal bonds of some sort,[54] it challenges international human rights law's emphasis on the

49 This insight is Martti Koskenniemi's. See Martti Koskenniemi, "National Self-Determination Today: Problems of Legal Theory and Practice," 43 *Int. & Comp. L.Q.* (1994), 241, 245 (identifying the "paradox" that national self-determination "both supports and challenges statehood").

50 UN Charter, art. 55. 51 Ibid. 52 Cassese, *Self-Determination of Peoples*, at 43.

53 See, for example, Thomas Franck, "The Emerging Right to Democratic Governance," 86 *Amer. J. Int'l L.* 46 (1992).

54 S. James Anaya, *Indigenous Peoples in International Law*, 2nd ed. (New York: Oxford University Press, 2004), at 5 ("self-determination derives from common conceptions about the essential nature of human beings, and it accordingly applies universally and equally to all members of humanity").

universality of human rights. To the extent that it vests governance rights in communities defined by nation and ethnicity, it possesses the potential to divide people into different communities, to create insiders and outsiders, and to distribute rights differentially among individuals. Insofar as self-determination discourse aligns itself with these kinds of movements, it carries the potential of running counter to universal principles that inhere in human rights ideals.

The hard cases are those where the logic of self-determination and human rights "lead in different directions."[55] International human rights law historically dealt with hard cases by avoiding them, limiting the ability of individuals and groups to assert a right of self-determination in a judicial or quasi-judicial forum. The decision of the Human Rights Committee to interpret the right as a collective right and thus not as subject to the Optional Protocol of the ICCPR[56] has eliminated the possibility that individuals could file a communication alleging a violation of the right. And, until recently, the 1960 and 1970 Declarations were typically understood as affirming what is known as the "salt water thesis," according to which sovereign independence could be attained, under the banner of the right, only by a geographically separate colonial population against its colonial master.[57] The ICJ's advisory opinion addressing the international legality of Kosovo's unilateral declaration of independence takes international law's avoidance of self-determination to a new level by failing to say anything meaningful about the nature of the norm.[58]

Perhaps partly in an effort to address this paradox, international law has for some time ceased to regard the right of self-determination in absolute terms, as

[55] Benedict Kingsbury, "Restructuring Self-Determination: A Relational Approach," in Pekka Aikio and Martin Scheinin (eds.), *Operationalizing the Right of Indigenous Peoples to Self-Determination* (Turku: Institute for Human Rights, Åbo Akademi University, 2000), 19–38, at 29.

[56] See *Lubicon Lake v. Canada*, CCPR/C/38/167/1984 (March 26, 1990), paras. 31.1, 32.2. Note that this is merely a procedural conclusion regarding the enforceability of the right under the Optional Protocol. There are other procedures under the Covenant that may implicate the right of self-determination. The right is subject to the scrutiny of the Committee under the mandatory reporting procedure and the optional procedure for interstate complaints. A reporting procedure is also available under the Covenant on Economic, Social and Cultural Rights, which, as noted, also contains a right of self-determination.

[57] See Cassese, *Self-Determination of Peoples*, at 59 for the view that that the drafting history supports this construction.

[58] *Advisory Opinion on the Accordance with International Law of Unilateral Declaration of Independence in Respect of Kosovo*, 2010 I.C.J. 141 (22 July 2010). For commentary, see Elena Circovic, "An Analysis of the ICJ Advisory Opinion on Kosovo's Unilateral Declaration of Independence," 11 *German L.J.* 895 (2010).

solely authorizing complete sovereign independence for a people subject to the sovereign authority of a state that is not their own. Instead, with this movement, the right is migrating from the international to the domestic realm, from an entitlement that only had the capacity to protect existing states or produce new states to one that also validates domestic constitutional reorganization of a political community. This movement reconceptualizes self-determination as possessing internal as well as external dimensions.[59] External self-determination refers to a right of a people to acquire sovereign independence. Internal self-determination refers to rights internal to the constitutional order which a people belongs, best understood as harboring a spectrum of constitutional and institutional possibilities that fall short of secession but which can nonetheless protect a community's identity, culture, territory, and self-governing capacity.[60]

The spectrum of institutional possibilities short of sovereign independence contemplated by internal self-determination ranges from guaranteed representation in the political institutions of the broader society to constitutional or legislative arrangements that secure a measure of autonomy for ethnic, cultural, and religious communities.[61] It also includes social, economic, or cultural rights

59 Although it has acquired prominence recently, the distinction between internal and external self-determination was present in the discourse of those advocating for its recognition as a human right as early as 1952. See Burke, *Decolonization and the Evolution of International Human Rights*, at 43, quoting Summary Records of the Third Committee, 454th meeting, 24 Nov. 1952, A/C.3/SR. 454, paras. 25 and 32 (noting that Dmitrios Lambros, a Greek delegate, "could not accept the subtle distinctions drawn by some representatives between individual and collective human rights and between 'internal' and 'external' self-determination").

60 For an account of the emergence of conceptions of international law as an international legal order legitimately capable of supervising the adequacy of systems of minority protection and more generally of intervening in "matters concerning groups formerly invisible behind the veil of sovereignty," see Nathaniel Berman, "'But the Alternative is Despair': European Nationalism and the Modernist Renewal of International Law," 106 *Harv. L. Rev.* 1792 (1993).

61 The African Commission on Human and Peoples' Rights, in *Katangese Peoples' Congress v. Zaire*, for example has ruled that article 20 of the African Charter on Human and Peoples Rights, which guarantees the right of self-determination, can be exercised through a number of different internal arrangements. The Commission listed independence, self-government, local government, federalism, confederalism, unitarianism, "or any other form of relations that accords with the wishes of the people but fully cognizant of other recognized principles such as sovereignty and territorial integrity." *Katangese Peoples' Congress v. Zaire*. For a summary of this case, see Annex VI of Eighth Annual Activity Report of the Commission on Human and Peoples' Rights, 1994–1995, Thirty-first Ordinary Session, 26–28 June 1995, Addis Ababa, Ethiopia, www.umn.edu/humanrts/africa/comision.html. For analysis, see Scheinin, Martin Scheinin, "The Right to Enjoy a Distinct Culture: Indigenous and Competing Uses of Land," in Theodore S. Orlin, Alan Rosas, and Martin Scheinin (eds.), *The Jurisprudence of Human Rights Law: A Comparative Interpretive Approach* (Turku: Institute for Human Rights, Åbo Akademi University, 2000), 159–222, at 182–183.

that recognize or provide a sphere of collective autonomy to a community critical to securing internal self-determination.[62] This spectrum offers different forms of legal pluralism to a community seeking a measure of autonomy from the state in which it is located. Establishing a plural legal order is no mean feat, and often communities enlist the discourse of rights in support of such an aspiration. Because it contemplates legal autonomy short of secession, a right of internal self-determination is a natural organizing principle for transformative political agendas aimed at introducing a plurality of legal orders.[63]

Internal self-determination's spectrum of institutional possibilities shares important conceptual affinities with the rights that minority communities possess in international law. Except perhaps with respect to indigenous peoples, minority rights typically are not understood as providing territorial or political autonomy to minority communities, but can be understood as occupying points on internal self-determination's spectrum of institutional possibilities that represent less of a threat to the sovereignty of a state. Both self-determination and minority rights have been received in international law in different ways over time. But they have not been received in international law in ways that affirm their conceptual affinities.[64] In the early twentieth century, when self-determination legitimated the redrawing of the map of Europe, minority rights were the province of the League of Nations. After World War II, when self-determination emerged as a right exercisable by those subject to colonial occupation or foreign domination, minority rights were contained by the paradigm of individual, and universal, rights. After the end of the Cold War, when self-determination revealed itself to possess internal dimensions, minority rights are understood not as a subset of a more general right of self-determination but as if they are distinct legal entitlements. Successfully asserting minority rights in international law is no easy task. Asserting the right of self-determination is an even more daunting challenge. The relative marginality of these two categories of human rights is inversely related to the threat that each poses to the territorial integrity and sovereign authority of states.

[62] Cassese, *Self-Determination of Peoples*, at 348 (arguing that bridging this gulf is needed and internal self-determination is a concept that helps in this respect). Gnanapala Welhenggama, *Minorities' Claims: From Autonomy to Secession* (Aldershot: Asgate, 2000), at 128 ("these two concepts, minority autonomy and internal self-determination, are increasingly being seen as two sides of the same coin"); see also F. Harhoff, "Institutions of Autonomy," 55 *Nordic J. Int'l L.* 31, 31–40 (1986) (exploring link between "autonomy" and "self-determination").

[63] This discussion draws from Patrick Macklem, "Militant Democracy, Legal Pluralism, and the Paradox of Self-Determination, 4 *Int'l J. Con. L.* 488 (2006), at 502–503.

[64] For this insight, see Ana Vrdoljak, "Self-Determination and Cultural Rights," in Franconi and M. Scheinin (eds.), *Cultural Human Rights* (Leiden: Martinus Nijhoff, 2008), 41–78.

Redesigning and disaggregating the right of self-determination to accommodate diverse forms of internal self-determination displaces but does not eliminate the paradox at its heart. In all of its manifestations, self-determination stands to legitimate and challenge sovereign authority. A form of internal self-determination can secure a measure of freedom for a people to determine its own future, yet its implementation often renders insecure the freedom of the broader population to protect chosen constitutional arrangements from transformation. There is no way of knowing in theory whether the recognition or establishment of a form of internal self-determination will produce stable or unstable forms of government. Will establishment or recognition promote intercultural harmony or will it harden collective identities, deepen divisions, and embolden a minority community to demand more and more concessions from the center? The right of internal self-determination, beyond vesting in a people a right to a form of autonomy short of secession, provides little guidance on which form is appropriate in any given context.[65]

Yet a wholly contextual determination of the appropriate form of constitutional arrangements that internal self-determination should assume in any given state threatens to undermine this goal. How can human rights law subject ethnic, religious, cultural, or national conflict to the rule of law if it cannot identify, in advance and with a certain degree of specificity, a legal framework in which contextual considerations can be brought to bear to assess whether a community is legally justified in seeking a measure of legal pluralism? Absent some kind of framework to assist in this task, the content of the right of internal self-determination remains unclear. Equally uncertain is the definition of "peoples" who are capable of asserting the right in either its external or more controversial internal form.[66] Nor is there anything approaching a consensus that international human rights laws that do receive unambiguous international legal recognition, such as civil and political and social and economic rights, possess collective dimensions that provide disaggregated protection to the various dimensions of the right to internal self-determination.[67] The indeterminacy

65 See Cassese, *Self-Determination of Peoples*, at 332 ("both customary and treaty law on internal self-determination ... do not furnish workable standards concerning some possible forms of realizing internal self-determination, such as devolution, autonomy, or "'regional' self-government").

66 See Knop, *Diversity and Self-Determination in International Law*, at 51–65, for a discussion of debates in the field concerning definitions of "peoples" (contrasting approaches that utilize categories from those that seek coherence).

67 See Allan Rosas, "Internal Self-Determination," in Christian Tomuschat (ed.), *Modern Law of Self-Determination* (Martinus Nijhoff: Dordrecht, 1993), 225–52, for discussion of debates in the field concerning the legal status of internal self-determination.

surrounding the right to self-determination has led James Crawford to identify another paradox at its heart: "that the international law of self-determination both exists and is obscure."[68]

Despite its indeterminacy, the emergence of a right of internal self-determination provided an opportunity to extend external self-determination's reach beyond the colonial context. While politically expedient, stopping self-determination's first movement by restricting the right to overseas colonies is difficult to justify on principled grounds. In part, this is because the extension to the colonial context changed the conceptual structure of the right by adding contingency as one of its properties. As a result of the declarations, whether a people other than the population of an existing state possessed the right of external self-determination became contingent on their status as a colonized people. As a contingent right, external self-determination attaches as a matter of circumstance, not as a matter of inherent right, rendering it more capable of migration among right-holders who are subject to roughly similar circumstances. It is also partly because of the wording of the 1970 Declaration, which deems "alien subjugation, domination and exploitation" to constitute a violation of self-determination and which makes respect for territorial integrity contingent on the presence of a "government representing the whole of a people."[69] But it is mostly because, normatively speaking, geographic location has little to do with why a colonized people possesses a right of external self-determination and therefore should have little to do with why other peoples might possess a similar right.

This has led some to attempt to specify the conditions under which a people outside of the context of colonialism might be entitled to exercise a right of external self-determination to acquire sovereign statehood. Christian Tomuschat, for example, offers a relatively narrow interpretation of the 1970 Declaration. Tomuschat argues that when a state engages in the genocide of a minority population, when it "turns itself into an apparatus of terror which persecutes specific groups of the population, those groups cannot be obligated to remain loyally under the jurisdiction of that State."[70] According to this line of thought, systematic and brutal persecution of a minority population disentitles the state from relying on its sovereign status and territorial integrity to

[68] James Crawford, "The Right of Self-Determination in International Law: Its Development and Future," in P. Alston (ed.), *Peoples' Rights* (Oxford: Oxford University Press, 2001), 10–67, at 10.

[69] 1970 Declaration.

[70] Christian Tomuschat, "Self-Determination in a Post-Colonial World," in C. Tomuschat (ed.), *The Modern Law of Self-Determination* (Martinus Nijhoff: Dordrecht, 1993) 1, at 9.

prevent secession by that population.[71] Hurst Hannum interprets the 1970 Declaration more broadly, as stating that a state will not be considered representative "if it formally excludes a particular group from participation in the political process."[72] According to Hannum, however, a state that has a democratic, nondiscriminatory voting system but whose whole political life is dominated by an ethnic majority would not be unrepresentative within the meaning of the Declaration.

> Whether one takes a narrow or broad view is less important than the structural relationship between internal and external determination ushered in by self-determination's third movement. This relationship, which sees an external right triggered on the violation of the internal right, builds on the contingent nature of the right first introduced by the text of the two Declarations. Internal self-determination is an inherent right, a universal minimum core of entitlements that flow from the fact of communal bonds and communal identity, which entitles "a people to choose its political allegiance, to influence the political order in which it lives and to preserve its cultural, ethnic, historical or territorial identity."[73]

A right of external self-determination is a contingent right – contingent on the failure of the state in which a people lives to accommodate its aspirations for internal self-determination. In this light, Frederic Kirgis Jr. speaks of "degrees of self-determination, with the legitimacy of each tied to the degree of representative government in the state."[74] In his words,

> The relationship is inverse between the degree of representative government, on the one hand, and the extent of destabilization that the international community will tolerate in a self-determination claim, on the other. If a government is at the high end of democracy, the only self-determination claims that will be given international credence are those with minimal destabilizing effect. If a government is extremely unrepresentative, much more destabilizing self-determination claims may well be recognized.[75]

[71] For a theoretical defence of this position, see Allen Buchanan, *Justice, Legitimacy, and Self-Determination: Moral Foundations for International Law* (Oxford: Oxford University Press, 2004), at 331–400.

[72] Hurst Hannum, "Rethinking Self-Determination," 34 *Va. J. Int'l L.* 1 (1993), at 17. Later in this article, Hannum makes it clear that he is not of the view that the presence of such conditions would be a sufficient trigger for the right of external self-determination.

[73] Morton H. Halperin and David Scheffer, *Self-Determination in the New World Order* (Washington, DC: Carnegie Endowment for International Peace, 1992).

[74] Frederic Kirgis, Jr., "The Degrees of Self-Determination in the United Nations Era," 88 *Am. J. Int. L.* 304 (1994), at 306.

[75] Ibid.

An alternative way of characterizing this relationship is to regard internal self-determination as demanding an ongoing relationship with the state from which the group seeks a measure of distance, and therefore internal self-determination identifies rights and duties that articulate the terms and conditions of this relationship. In contrast, external self-determination entails the dismantling of existing relationships that exist between a people and the state in which it finds itself.[76]

The relationship between internal and external self-determination was publicized by the Supreme Court of Canada's judgment in the Secession Reference.[77] At issue in the case was whether there was a legal basis for the province of Quebec to unilaterally secede from Canada. In the course of its reasons, the Court characterized the right of self-determination in international law as not including a right of secession except in "in only the most extreme of cases and, even then, under carefully defined circumstances."[78] Echoing the text of the 1970 Declaration, it stated further that "a state whose government represents the whole of the people or peoples resident within its territory, on a basis of equality and without discrimination, and respects the principles of self-determination in its own internal arrangements, is entitled to the protection under international law of its territorial integrity."[79]

The Court drew a distinction between external and internal self-determination, specifying that external self-determination is available where a colony wishes to break free of its colonial status, and "where a people is subject to alien subjugation, domination or exploitation outside a colonial context."[80] It also suggested that external self-determination may also be available, as a last resort, where a people is blocked from the meaningful exercise of its right to internal self-determination, although it did note that "it remains unclear whether this third proposition actually reflects an established international law standard."[81]

76 This is Benedict Kingsbury's idea, although he speaks of a distinction between relational and end-state approaches to self-determination, and does not explicitly equate this distinction with the distinction between internal and external self-determination: see Kingsbury, "Restructuring Self-Determination: A Relational Approach," in Aikio and Scheinin (eds.), *Operationalizing the Right of Indigenous Peoples to Self-Determination*, 119–37.

77 *Reference re: Secession of Quebec*, [1998] 2 S.C.R. 217.

78 Ibid., at para. 129. See also Committee on the Elimination of Racial Discrimination. General Recommendation XXI(48), UN doc. A/51/18, pp. 125–126, para. 6 ("In the view of the Committee, international law has not recognized a general right of peoples unilaterally to declare secession from a State").

79 Ibid., at para. 130. 80 Ibid., at para. 133.

81 Ibid., at paras. 134, 135. Rainer Bauböck argues that the Court reached this (tentative) conclusion by misreading the 1993 Vienna Declaration on Human Rights, which contains

For present purposes, what is important is not whether international law now accepts that self-determination includes internal rights that, when violated, give rise to a right of external self-determination. It is instead that it is moving from an entitlement that only had the capacity to protect existing states or produce new states to one that also validates domestic constitutional reorganization of a political community. This movement, together with the right's previous movements from a principle that refers to the population of an existing state to one that potentially refers to populations within and across state boundaries, and from a principle to a right, has changed the normative role that self-determination plays in the international legal order. As the following seeks to explain, self-determination now mitigates adverse effects produced by how international law distributes sovereignty around the globe and authorizes its exercise by sovereign states. Self-determination, in other words, is an important bridge between the structure and operation of international law and global justice.

3.

As anyone from a state with an active secessionist movement will attest, not all claims of sovereignty possess international legal validity.[82] International law sorts claims of economic and political power made throughout the world by

language similar to that in the 1970 Declaration referring to "the whole people without distinction of any kind." Rainer Bauböck, "Paradoxes of Self-Determination and the Right to Self-Government," in András Sajó (ed.), *Global Justice and the Bulwarks of Localism* (The Netherlands: Koninklijke Brill NV, 2005), 100–27. Although he defends a conclusion similar to that reached by the Court on normative grounds, Bauböck argues that "a right to internal self-determination for a particular group within a larger state obviously presupposes some distinction for a particular group from 'the whole people belonging to the territory,'" and "if internal self-identification is interpreted as a right to political autonomy, then a positive identification of the group and of the territory within which the group enjoys self-government is needed." Ibid., at 111. Thus, for Bauböck, the term "people" in international law, with the exception of colonial populations and foreign occupation, still only refers to the entire population of a state.

An alternative reading of this phase, however, is that the phrase is referring to the entire population of a state but that "people" in international law can additionally refer to populations not coextensive with a state's population, as in the case of a people whose internal self-determination is being denied by the state in which it is located. Compare James Crawford, "The Right of Self-Determination in International Law: Its Development and Future," in Philip Alston (ed.), *People's Rights* (Oxford: Oxford University Press, 2001), 7, at 59–60 (construing the Court's position as consistent with "both the view that self-determination applies to peoples in the ordinary sense of the term and is not confined to the whole population of existing states, and the view that several peoples may coexist in relation to a particular territory").

82 This section draws from Patrick Macklem, "Human Rights in International Law: Three Generations or One?" 3 *London Review of International Law* (forthcoming).

validating some claims of economic and political power as sovereign authority and rejecting others as international illegalities. By legally validating some claims of sovereign power and refusing to validate others, international law organizes international political reality into a legal order in which certain collectivities possess legal authority to rule people and territory. Sovereignty, in international law, is a legal entitlement to rule people and territory that the field confers on the multitude of legal actors that it recognizes as states. International legal rules determine which collectivities are entitled to exercise sovereign authority and over which territory and people such authority operates. International law thus effectively performs an ongoing distribution of sovereignty among certain collectivities throughout the world.

International law performs its distribution of sovereign power by a set of rules and principles that relate to the acquisition and maintenance of state sovereignty. Claims of sovereign power possess legal validity in international law only under certain conditions and in certain circumstances. As we have seen, international law provides that a state whose government represents the whole of its population within its territory, consistent with principles of equality, nondiscrimination, and self-determination, is entitled to maintain its territorial integrity under international law and to have its territorial integrity respected by other states.[83] But international legal rules also determine which collectivities are entitled to exercise sovereign authority and over which territory and people such authority operates. As we have also seen, the field entitles a collectivity to form a state and wield sovereign power if it constitutes a "people" and has experienced severe and ongoing injustices such as colonial rule or alien subjugation, domination, or exploitation.[84] Finally, international law also confers legal validity on a claim to sovereignty by a collectivity if it manifests certain properties that international law stipulates as conditions of acquiring statehood.[85]

[83] See, for example, UN General Assembly, Declaration on the Occasion of the Fiftieth Anniversary of the United Nations (1995), GA Res. 50/6 (the right of self-determination "shall not be construed as authorizing or encouraging any action that would dismember or impair, totally or in part, the territorial integrity or political unity of sovereign and independent States conducting themselves in compliance with the principle of equal rights and self-determination of peoples and thus possessed of a Government representing the whole people belonging to the territory without distinction of any kind").

[84] According to some formulations, international law also entitles a people to form a state and assume sovereign power if it is denied any meaningful exercise of its right to self-determination within the state of which it forms a part. See, e.g., *Reference re: Secession of Quebec*, [1998] 2 S.C.R. 217.

[85] Article 1 of the Montevideo Convention on Rights and Duties of States (1933) 165 L.N.T.S. 19, for example, lists the following criteria of statehood: a permanent population, a defined territory, a system of government, and a capacity to enter into relations with other states.

These avenues of obtaining and maintaining sovereign statehood are the means by which the international legal order distinguishes between legal and illegal claims to sovereign power. International law brings legal order to international political reality by sorting the countless claims of sovereign power that have defined global politics for centuries according to a binary opposition between legal and illegal claims. By legally validating some claims of sovereign power and refusing to validate others, in other words, international law organizes international political reality into a legal order in which certain collectivities possess legal authority to rule people and territory. In doing so, international law effectively performs an ongoing distribution of sovereignty among certain collectivities throughout the world.

International law thus brings legal order to international political reality by processing the countless claims of sovereign power that have punctuated global politics for centuries by sorting them by a binary opposition between legal and illegal claims of sovereignty. This has the effect of legally including certain political communities, and legally excluding others, in a dynamic and systemic international distribution of sovereign authority. Its dynamic nature arises from the presence of rules and principles that authorize reallocations of sovereignty occasioned by the demise of existing states and the creation of new states by right or recognition. These rules and principles render the distribution of sovereignty capable of recalibration and realignment in light of new political developments deemed to possess international legal significance. Its systemic nature is a function of the fact that its distributional reach envelops all states in its structure and operation, treating all as formal equals in terms of the legal nature and scope of their sovereign power.

What does it mean to speak of self-determination as mitigating some of the adverse effects of international law's distribution of sovereignty? The distributional consequences of the ways in which international law organizes global politics into an international legal order are manifold. Our international legal order confers sovereignty on some collectivities and denies it to others. It has validated the sovereign power of some collectivities for centuries; it has recognized the sovereignty of other collectivities only recently. It episodically recalibrates the distribution of sovereign power that it performs, transferring peoples and territories from some sovereign legal actors to others. Not only does it legalize an international distribution of sovereign power, but it also validates countless ways in which sovereignty can be and is exercised. It confers on states broad powers to exercise sovereign power in ways that can benefit and harm their populations. By geographically dividing the globe into a finite set of sovereign states, and legally recognizing sovereignty as including exclusive rights to a state's territory and resources, international law also determines what belongs to whom, and thus validates a global distribution of wealth and resources. And by empowering sovereign states to establish international instruments and institutions that legalize certain economic and social relations at the expense of others, it provides international legal validity to myriad processes of economic and social globalization that dramatically affect the nature and levels of poverty and inequality throughout the world.

As a result of the three movements it experienced, the right of self-determination engages with but a few of these features of the structure and operation of the international legal order. In its external manifestation, it operates as a mechanism that has the potential to rearrange the distribution of sovereignty that international law performs by specifying the legal conditions under which a particular collectivity – as of right – is entitled to claim sovereign independence. Granted, its specifications remain unclear outside the context of colonization. There does not appear to be a consensus that a right of external self-determination arises in the context of violations of internal self-determination. Nor does international law offer much specificity as to the content of self-determination or the nature of violations that would trigger external self-determination. Nonetheless, the right of self-determination, as a legal mechanism, has the capacity to alter the distribution of sovereignty in the world. Self-determination also engages with another basic feature of the structure of international law, namely, that it authorizes the exercise of sovereign power by legal actors it recognizes as states. In its internal manifestation, the right provides a frame of reference for comprehending certain limits on the exercise of sovereign power by requiring domestic constitutional arrangements to internally respect the self-determination of peoples within their midst.

What does it mean to speak of self-determination as a bridge between the structure and operation of international law and global justice? Implicit in the performance of self-determination's functions are normative claims that relate to the justice of the international legal order. The movement from a principle that refers to the population of an existing state to one that potentially refers to populations within and across state boundaries reflects a critique of the distribution of sovereignty relating to the class of beneficiaries in whom it vests. The movement from principle to right represents the field's acknowledgement that there are questions of justice surrounding how sovereignty is acquired and how it is justified and exercised, and these questions should be asked through the juridical prism of a right. And the movement from an external conception to one that also possesses internal dimensions identifies normative concerns with the freedom that international law otherwise vests in sovereign powers to organize their domestic constitutional arrangements free from external interference.

The content of the right provides insight into the nature and thrust of these normative claims. By specifying that colonized peoples have a right to external self-determination and sovereign independence, self-determination rights the wrong, so to speak, of the fact that colonialism possessed international legal validity. It deems this particular feature of international law to be unjust and seeks to mitigate its adverse effects. More controversially, and perhaps part of the reason for the controversy, it tentatively specifies that a people whose internal self-determination is being systematically violated possesses a right to acquire sovereign independence. What's controversial is not that the systematic violation of internal self-determination is unjust. It is what the right holds out as remedy: sovereign independence. In both iterations, the right of external self-determination operates an instrument whose purpose is to promote a more just distribution of sovereignty in the international legal order.

In contrast, the right of internal self-determination operates as an instrument that promotes the just exercise of sovereign power by states, by requiring them to respect the rights of peoples within their midst. The dynamism that new political developments, deemed to possess international legal significance, impart to the distribution of sovereignty is the backdrop to the role that the right of internal self-determination plays in international law. This is partly a function of the fact that international treaties episodically modify the distribution of sovereign power by transferring sovereignty over territory and people from one sovereign actor to another. In so doing, they create majorities and minorities. Minorities exist in relation to majorities, and majorities exist because international law distributes sovereign power over territory and people to certain collectivities and not others.[86] Comprehending the right of internal self-determination in terms of the role it can play in monitoring the justice of the distribution of sovereign power reveals that its normative status lies in the fact that it serves as an instrument to mitigate injustices associated with the

[86] Compare Hans Kelsen: "the concept of a majority assumes by definition the existence of a *minority*, and thus *the right of the majority* presupposes the *right* of the minority to exist. From this arises perhaps not the necessity, but certainly the possibility, of *protecting* the minority from the majority. This *protection of minorities* is the essential function of the so-called *basic rights* and *rights of freedom*, or *human and civil rights* guaranteed by all modern constitutions of parliamentary democracies." Hans Kelsen, "On the Essence and Value of Democracy," in Arthur J. Jacobson and Bernard Schlink (eds), *Weimar: A Jurisprudence of Crisis* (Berkeley: University of California Press, 2000) 84–109, at 100 (emphasis in original). See also Patrick Macklem, "Minority Rights in International Law," 6 *Int'l J. Const'l L.* 531 (2008).

kinds of recalibrations of sovereign power that international law treats as possessing international legal force.

The dynamic nature of the distribution of sovereign power is also partly a function of the fact that international law includes certain collectivities and excludes others from its distribution. International law excluded indigenous peoples, for example, from the outset from its distribution of sovereign power and included them within the sovereign power of states established on the territories they inhabited since time immemorial. This process of exclusion and inclusion is an ongoing one. International law continues to exclude and include indigenous peoples in its distribution of sovereign authority by refusing to recognize that they possess a right of self-determination entitling them to acquire sovereign statehood. Instead, indigenous peoples have rights of internal self-determination, which entitle them to extensive protection associated with their identities, cultures, territories, and forms of governance.[87] The right of self-determination possessed by indigenous peoples in international law thus speaks to some of the adverse consequences of international law's exclusion of indigenous peoples from the distribution of sovereign power.[88]

Comprehending the right of self-determination in international law in these terms challenges traditional accounts of the role of human rights in international law, namely, that they protect universal features of what it means to be human.[89] On the account offered here, the right of self-determination is not so much a formal expression of what justice requires as a matter of abstract morality as it is an international legal instrument that seeks to do justice in the world in which we live. The current status of the right of self-determination law underscores the fact that human rights in international law have less to with essential features of our common humanity and more to do with how international law organizes global politics into an international legal order.

87 See United Nations Declaration on the Rights of Indigenous Peoples, A/Res/61/295 Ann. 1 of 13 Sept. 2007.

88 For more discussion, see Patrick Macklem, "Indigenous Recognition in International Law: Theoretical Observations," 30 *Mich. J. Int'l L.* 177 (2008).

89 A. John Simmonds, *Justification and Legitimacy: Essays on Rights and Obligation* (Cambridge: Cambridge University Press, 2001), at 185 ("human rights are rights possessed by all human beings (at all times and in all places), simply in virtue of their humanity") (emphasis deleted). Jack Donnelly, *Universal Human Rights in Theory and Practice*, 2nd ed., (Ithaca, NY: Cornell University Press, 2003), at 18 ("[h]uman rights are, literally, the rights that one has simply because one is a human being"); see also Alan Gewirth, *Human Rights* (Chicago, IL: University of Chicago Press, 1982).

6

Self-Determination for National Minorities

ALAN PATTEN

1. CONCEPTIONS OF SELF-DETERMINATION

My discussion will be structured around a distinction between three different ideas of self-determination, which I refer to as the *statist*, the *democratic*, and the *nationalist* conceptions. Each of these conceptions is invoked in international affairs, often as part of a principle that states and other actors are said to have a weighty reason to obey.

The statist conception equates self-determination with the familiar idea of state autonomy. Understood in these terms, self-determination is an enduring notion in international thought. The principle of self-determination imposes a negative duty on states to refrain from interference in one another's affairs.

A variety of justifications for such a principle are often repeated. One standard argument claims that a general norm of noninterference makes a significant contribution to international peace and security. Understood as state autonomy, self-determination excludes various pretexts that states have historically offered for going to war, and thus diminishes the likelihood of war and the need for anticipatory militarization.

A second kind of argument connects the state with its people. It is argued that the citizens of a state have interests in determining the development of their own society. When outsiders intervene, they deny citizens the opportunity to realize this interest and convey the message that citizens will never get their act together to reform their own society. A distinct but related idea is that, given differences of culture and tradition, outsiders are at significant risk of misjudging the needs of a society targeted for intervention. One size does not fit all, and thus states have no business imposing what works in their own societies onto other peoples and societies. Michael Walzer's influential attempt to ground the "moral standing of states" in a notion of "communal integrity" draws on both of these ideas.[1] A presumption against foreign interventions leaves space for the political community's own politics to determine outcomes, and it reflects the privileged epistemic vantage point of citizens of that community relative to outsiders.

The democratic conception of self-determination takes as its point of departure this shift in moral accent from state to people. Suppose we accept for the moment that self-determination matters because of the value for a people of being able to shape and determine its own affairs. We must immediately confront the possibility that a state's structures might themselves be substantial impediments to a state population's interests in this area. The internal character of the political system in authoritarian states may be such that nobody could think there is any determination by the people of their own affairs that could be worthy of protection or respect.

The democratic conception takes seriously this possibility and insists that self-determination involves both a negative and a positive condition. Negatively, it requires nonintervention. But, positively, it requires the presence of institutional structures through which the people can engage in a meaningful way in the shaping and determining of their own affairs.

Paradigmatically, those institutional structures are democratic ones, but the approach need not rule out the possibility that a broader range of inclusive structures, such as Rawls's "decent consultation hierarchy," might satisfy the positive condition.[2] There is also scope, under the heading of the positive condition, to interpret the requirement of democracy or inclusion in a more or less procedural manner. The requirement might focus narrowly on how collective decisions for the society get made, or it might take a broader look at the degree to which the individuals who make up the people are treated as full or equal members.[3]

Since the negative and positive conditions may pull in different directions, there is no reason, on the democratic conception, to think that a concern for

[1] Michael Walzer, "The Moral Standing of States: A Reply to Four Critics," *Philosophy & Public Affairs* 9:3 (1980), pp. 209–29.

[2] For discussion of institutional arrangements in this broader range, see John Rawls, *The Law of Peoples* (Cambridge, MA: Harvard University Press, 1999); Joshua Cohen, "Is There a Human Right to Democracy?," in *The Egalitarian Conscience: Essays in Honour of G.A. Cohen*, ed. Christine Sypnowich (Oxford: Oxford University Press, 2006), pp. 226–48, and "Minimalism about Human Rights: The Most We Can Hope For?," *Journal of Political Philosophy* 12:2 (2004), pp. 190–213; and Charles Beitz, "The Moral Standing of States Revisited," *Ethics and International Affairs* 23:4 (2009), pp. 325–47, and *The Idea of Human Rights* (Oxford: Oxford University Press, 2009).

[3] Ronald Dworkin argues that rule by the people implies not just democratic procedures but the protection of various substantial rights. *Freedom's Law: The Moral Reading of the American Constitution* (Cambridge, MA: Harvard University Press, 1997).

self-determination always implies noninterference. In some cases, there may be reasons internal to the idea of self-determination for thinking that some form of interference or intervention is justified.[4] The international community might support human rights campaigners or a democratization movement in some state and believe reasonably that they are promoting self-determination along one of its two required dimensions.

The nationalist conception of self-determination focuses on a condition that is highlighted by neither the statist nor the democratic views. On the nationalist view, the world is home to a number of different sociocultural groups that can be thought of as nations or peoples. States may be pivotal in creating and maintaining nations and peoples, but, as a conceptual matter, such groups are not equivalent to the populations of states. A particular state may be home to more than one national group, and a particular national group may be spread across more than one state.

On the nationalist conception, it is peoples understood in this sociocultural sense that ought to be self-determining. Self-determination, in other words, has a *boundary* condition. A people is self-determining only if it is able to determine its own affairs through its own political structures. For this condition to be satisfied, there needs to be congruence between the boundaries of the political unit and the boundaries of the sociocultural one.[5]

I shall have much more to say about the nationalist conception throughout this paper. For now, let me draw attention to a point that has already been implicit in the language used to describe the three conceptions. Associated with each conception is a specific claim about who the subject or "self" is of self-determination. If the statist conception focuses on the self-determination of the state, and the democratic conception highlights the self-determination of the people defined as the citizens of the state, then the nationalist

[4] Beitz, "The Moral Standing of States Revisited," makes a related argument. In Beitz's view there are several reasons to value what he terms "internal self-determination," and reflection on these reasons should guide claims about the nature and normative implications of self-determination. One such reason is the instrumental connection between self-determination and the protection of rights and interests. A second is "developmental": self-determination may help a community to develop certain capacities required for effective governance. And a third is "constitutive": individuals may identify with their political community and value its political agency. Against Walzer, Beitz argues that considerations of self-determination do not exclude the legitimacy of humanitarian interventions against rights-violating authoritarian regimes. It is not that self-determination is outweighed by other values, but that the reasons for caring about self-determination in the first place are conflicted in this sort of case.

[5] Ernest Gellner defines nationalism as "primarily a political principle, which holds that the political and national unit should be congruent." *Nations and Nationalism* (Ithaca, NY: Cornell University Press, 1983), p. 1.

conception's concern is with the self-determination of peoples, where peoples are understood as sociocultural groups having their own sense of national identity.

My aim in this paper is to reflect on which of these conceptions of self-determination is most suitable for adoption into a principle of international law or practice. To keep the discussion focused, I shall assume, for the most part, that the democratic conception is more acceptable than the statist one. Most political theorists gravitate toward a version of the democratic view, and even self-identifying statists, such as Walzer, seem to incorporate weak versions of the democratic conception's positive condition into their idea of self-determination.[6] The main question to be considered is whether the democratic conception is all that is needed, or whether a further step to the nationalist conception is also worth taking. For reasons that will be explored in the following, many commentators are dubious about the nationalist view. The democratic conception, they suggest, is based on important values of democracy, inclusion, and equal membership that are plausibly regarded as matters of fundamental justice. By contrast, the basic concepts and normative commitments associated with the nationalist conception are harder to pin down, and the values involved – to the extent that they can be identified – do not seem like matters of grave moral significance.

Although there is much to be said for this skeptical position, I shall take the opposing view. I think that failure of self-determination in the nationalist sense should sometimes be regarded as a matter of legitimate international concern. A failure to make space for national self-determination does involve a kind of injustice – even if not a "fundamental" injustice – and it is reasonable for the international community to take proportionate measures aimed at preventing and remedying that situation.

2. A MODERATE VERSION OF THE NATIONALIST CONCEPTION

The nationalist conception is often characterized in ways that make it seem extreme and unpalatable. One instance of this tendency occurs when it is assumed that, on the nationalist conception, the boundary condition can be *substituted* for the positive condition. This version of the nationalist conception holds that it does not matter for self-determination whether democratic

6 For instance, Walzer responds to the objection that the perpetuation of a state regime may be a matter of bare military force by insisting that the successful use of military force to maintain a regime is typically predicated on some reasonable level of social support. Walzer, "The Moral Standing of States," pp. 219–22.

structures are in place so long as the authoritarian, or nondemocratic, structures that are in place are in some sense controlled by members of the relevant national group, so that the boundary condition is met.

A second tendency in the interpretation of the nationalist conception is to assume that the congruence between political and national that it calls for must take the form of the nation-state. According to this version of the nationalist conception, states should not contain more than one nation, and nations should not be spread over more than one state. Once this understanding of the nationalist conception is locked into place, it is but a few short steps to the worry – famously articulated by Wilson's Secretary of State, Robert Lansing – that self-determination is a "phrase loaded with dynamite." Given that state boundaries do not align very well with existing national groups, a principle of national self-determination will immediately raise the specter of endless instability and violent conflict.

The version of the nationalist conception that I shall defend avoids both of these tendencies, and in this sense is more moderate than the view that critics often have in mind. On a moderate nationalist view, it is necessary that the negative condition, the positive condition, and a boundary condition *each* be satisfied. It is not enough for self-determination that the state be free from external interference and that it constitute itself in a democratic or broadly inclusive manner. Its democratic or inclusive structures must themselves be organized within particular boundaries so as to empower national groups. Equally, however, it is not sufficient that the boundary condition be satisfied, if the positive or negative conditions are not. The moderate nationalist conception rejects the idea that, so long as national groups are given space to determine their affairs in a way that fits with their own beliefs and traditions, they are self-determining even if they determine those affairs in an authoritarian manner.[7] On the moderate nationalist view, in other words, the relationship between the boundary and positive conditions is one of addition rather than substitution. Thus the view offers little cover to actual or aspiring nationalist authoritarian regimes that insist on being left alone by the international community.

A second distinctive feature of the moderate nationalist conception is that it does not claim that national minorities ought, in general, to possess their own state. To satisfy the boundary condition, it is sufficient that some meaningful form of internal autonomy be given to national minorities. This may involve federalism, devolution, or some other form of regional autonomy, which seeks

[7] This suggestion is defended by Walzer in "The Moral Standing of States," and is criticized by Beitz, "The Moral Standing of States Revisited."

to empower a national minority by making them the local majority within a territorial unit of the state. Or it might conceivably involve some form of nonterritorial autonomy in which the structures of representation are designed in such a way that a national minority has control over some of its own affairs.[8]

The moderate nationalist conception, as I understand it, thus focuses on internal rather than external state boundaries, and in this sense on internal rather than external self-determination.[9] It does not rule out the possibility that external self-determination (e.g., secession) might be an appropriate remedy for a persistent, unjustifiable failure on the part of a state to offer internal self-determination to national minorities. But the moderate nationalist conception does not imply any general or "primary" right on the part of national minorities to choose their own political status.[10]

So the version of the nationalist conception that I want to defend is moderate in two key respects. First, the conception accepts that democratic or inclusive structures are an essential condition of self-determination and thus avoids the objection that it ends up legitimating authoritarian nationalist regimes. And, second, it regards internal substate political arrangements as an adequate vehicle for the self-determination of national minorities: there is no requirement that every national group have its own state. Of course, it is one thing to announce this moderate position as the view to be defended; it is another to defend it with an argument that really does justify the moderate conception without entailing the extreme and unpalatable positions with

[8] For discussion of the nonterritorial alternative, see Rainer Bauböck, "Multinational Federalism: Territorial or Cultural Autonomy," Working Paper, accessed at http://dspace.mah.se/bitstream/handle/2043/690/Workingpaper201.pdf?sequence=1.

[9] On internal versus external self-determination, see Antonio Cassese, *Self-Determination of Peoples: A Legal Reappraisal* (Cambridge: Cambridge University Press, 1995). In general, internal self-determination is a matter of what internal arrangements of self-government there are, while external self-determination is a matter of external borders. Typically, a concern for internal self-determination is identified with the presence or absence of democratic institutions. On my view, internal self-determination is also a matter of whether and how internal boundaries are drawn (e.g., federal subunits). In the closing pages of his book (pp. 348–65), Cassese considers internal autonomy arrangements and also uses the term "internal self-determination" to characterize them. Internal boundaries are a major topic in the political theory literature. See, e.g., Will Kymlicka, *Multicultural Citizenship* (Oxford: Oxford University Press, 1995), *Finding Our Way* (Oxford: Oxford University Press, 1998), and *Politics in the Vernacular* (Oxford: Oxford University Press, 2001); Margaret Moore, *The Ethics of Nationalism* (Oxford: Oxford University Press, 2001), pp. 139–41; Allen Buchanan, *Justice, Legitimacy, and Self-Determination: Moral Foundations for International Law* (Oxford: Oxford University Press, 2004).

[10] Allen Buchanan, "Theories of Secession," *Philosophy & Public Affairs* 26 (1997): 31–61, distinguishes between "primary" and "remedial" rights to secession, and argues for the latter over the former.

which the nationalist conception is often associated. Without such an argument, the restriction to the moderate nationalist position will seem ad hoc, and the arguments themselves will seem untenable.

I think the arguments I lay out in the following do favor the moderate nationalist conception over other variants of the nationalist view. They point to reasons for thinking of the boundary condition as a supplement to, rather than a substitute for, the positive condition. And they point to reasons for thinking that self-determination appropriately takes an internal rather than an external form in the usual circumstances of modern pluralistic societies.

3. SUBJECT POPULATIONS AND INDIGENOUS PEOPLES

One approach to evaluating the competing conceptions of self-determination is by asking which is most consistent with widely endorsed developments in international law and practice. A virtue of the nationalist conception is that it can help to make sense of some important cases. The subject populations of overseas colonies and indigenous peoples are two categories of cases in which many commentators would agree that there are strong claims to self-determination. It is widely thought that the populations of overseas empires ought to have had the right freely to determine their own political status: it was appropriately up to them whether they wished to become an integral part of the colonial state or whether they wished to become an independent state of their own. This right, and the associated "salt water test," which limited the right to the populations of overseas colonies, was recognized by the international community in the postwar years.[11]

Likewise, many commentators would accept that indigenous peoples have a right to self-determination.[12] It might not be feasible, in many instances, for such peoples to form their own independent states, but they should at least be able to enjoy autonomy or self-government within the larger state in which they find themselves. In recent years, this right has been formally recognized

[11] The "salt water test" is the phrase used to describe the doctrine laid out in UN General Assembly Resolution 1541 (1960), Annex, Principles IV and V. For the phrase, see, e.g., Hurst Hannum (ed.), *Documents on Autonomy and Minority Rights* (Dordecht: Martinus Nijhoff, 1993), p. 23.

[12] S. James Anaya, *Indigenous Peoples in International Law* (New York: Oxford University Press, 1996); Will Kymlicka, *Politics in the Vernacular; Multicultural Odysees* (Oxford: Oxford University Press, 2007); and "Minority Rights in Political Philosophy and International Law," in *The Philosophy of International Law*, ed. Samantha Besson and John Tasioulas, (Oxford: Oxford University Press, 2010), pp. 377–96; Buchanan, *Justice, Legitimacy, and Self-Determination.*

by the international community. The UN Declaration on the Rights of Indigenous Peoples (UNDRIP) (2007) affirms that indigenous peoples have a right to "self-determination" (Art. 3), the exercise of which may involve a "right to autonomy or self-government in matters relating to their internal and local affairs" (Art. 4).

These cases are significant for our discussion because they involve attributing a right of self-determination to groups that can be understood as social and cultural in character. In neither kind of case is the subject of self-determination considered to be the whole population of an existing or even previously existing state. In the colonial case, the group wielding the right to self-determination was in practice often defined by administrative boundaries established by the colonial power. But these boundaries were clearly not the whole story, since, according to the salt water test, a group defined by the same kind of administrative boundaries but located on the historic territory of the imperial power would not have the same right. A plausible interpretation of this set of facts is that the subject population of an overseas colony possesses a right to self-determination at least, in part, because of its social and cultural distinctiveness vis-à-vis the population of the colonial power.[13]

The connection with the nationalist conception is even clearer in the case of self-determination by indigenous peoples. These groups are clearly not defined as the population of an existing state or as the population of an administrative unit of an existing state. Nor did they typically possess states in the recent past, although they often do claim to have had their own institutions of self-government. What is generally true of indigenous peoples is that they are culturally and socially distinct from the majority population of the state.

Based on these considerations, one might think that aspects of the nationalist conception of self-determination are already present in international law and practice. A full embrace of the nationalist conception would be a matter of making these anticipations of that conception more explicit and applying them more consistently across other kinds of cases. It would mean, for instance, extending the self-government rights enjoyed by indigenous peoples to all national minorities.

It should be said that advocates of the democratic conception resist this whole line of argument. They deny that subject populations of overseas colonies or indigenous peoples enjoy self-determination rights *qua* cultural

[13] This is supported by the text of UN General Assembly Resolution 1541, which refers to a "territory which is geographically separate and is distinct ethnically and/or culturally" (Annex, Principles IV and V).

or social groups. Instead, the fundamental feature of these groups is that they have been, and in many cases continue to be, particularly vulnerable to the rights abuses and forms of exclusion that are salient under the democratic conception.[14] The democratic conception can allow for the possibility that territorially concentrated populations that are denied equal membership may have remedial rights to self-government of some form. From the perspective of the democratic conception, then, the developments relating to decolonization and indigenous peoples do not imply any commitment to the nationalist conception. Instead, these cases showcase the remedial rights that can be defended by the democratic conception, rights that may extend beyond the colonial and indigenous cases but do not extend to all national minorities.

There is more that could be said about this particular argument. One might wonder what the democratic conception would say about the theoretically possible (even if historically rare) case of an overseas colony governed on the basis of democratic principles. For instance, I suspect that many observers would judge that the present-day inhabitants of Nouvelle-Caledonie have a basic right to freely determine their own political status.[15] And one might also wonder what the democratic view would say about indigenous peoples whose members are genuinely treated as equal citizens by the state in which they live. The democratic conception implies that the rights to internal self-determination announced in the UNDRIP should be reconsidered in the future if indigenous peoples find themselves consistently governed in a democratic or inclusive manner. This is not the position generally taken by indigenous peoples themselves, however, nor is it anticipated in the UNDRIP.

I will not explore these issues further here. I think there is a suggestive case for the nationalist conception based on consistency with the treatment of decolonization and indigenous peoples. But it seems clear that the case is hardly a decisive one. Proponents of the democratic conception have their own interpretation of the precedents in question, and they might also question whether the nationalist interpretation is in danger of proving too much. To the extent that international practice regarding decolonization has shown deference to tyrannical post-colonial regimes (e.g., Idi Amin's Uganda), precedent seems to prefer authoritarian over moderate nationalism. To defend the

[14] For arguments in this vein, see Charles Beitz, *Political Theory and International Relations* (Princeton, NJ: Princeton University Press, 1979), pp. 92-105; and Buchanan, *Justice, Legitimacy, and Self-Determination*, ch. 9. Will Kymlicka attributes a similar "remedial" view of indigenous self-determination to James Anaya. Kymlicka, *Politics in the Vernacular*, ch. 6.

[15] By agreement with French authorities, they are entitled to hold a referendum on secession in between 2014 and 2018. I am suggesting, however, that there is a more basic claim here that does not depend on the fact of an agreement.

moderate nationalist conception, a deeper argument is called for. It is necessary to explain why something that is normatively important would be lost or ignored by stopping at the democratic conception and not taking the further step to the moderate nationalist one.

4. CONCEPTUALIZING NATIONAL MINORITIES

Given doubts about an argument based on existing law, it is best to look for a deeper justification of the nationalist conception. The conception faces a number of serious challenges. First, and most basically, there is a challenge to its ontology. Is the concept of a national minority a coherent one? Second, even if a coherent notion of national minority can be specified, is there a good reason to think that self-government for such a minority has any special value? Third, even if the first two challenges can be met, it is questionable whether providing self-government to national minorities is a matter of justice. Finally, even if all of these challenges can be answered, it may be that institutionalizing a right to self-government in international law or practice would have objectionable consequences.

We might call these the problems of *ontology*, *value*, *justice*, and *institutions* respectively. In this section, and the three that follow, I shall say something in response to each challenge. I consider them one by one, but it is worth noting that the most difficult form of challenge attacks along several fronts at once. Such attacks allow that a given objection might be answered in a particular way, but insist that answering it this way makes it even harder to handle one of the other objections.

The result of the discussion, I hope, is more than a catalogue of responses to criticisms of the nationalist view. The theoretical and normative basis of such a view should come into focus, and the reasons for endorsing it over an account of self-determination that stops with the democratic conception should become apparent.

At first glance, the problem of ontology may seem strange to some readers. There are standard lists of national minorities familiar from news reports and discussed in political science and law. These lists include, to mention just a few examples, the Quebecois, the Scots, the Catalans, and the Russian minorities in various states that once were part of the Soviet Union. The lists do not seem especially controversial and are not typically accompanied by any caveat about relying on a problematic category.

However, when state officials first seriously struggled with the problem of identifying distinct nationalities, in the years after the First World War, they did find the task to be much more difficult than was expected. The various standard criteria for identifying national groups – language, ethnicity, self-identification – all led to different conclusions.

In recent years, the problem of defining and identifying national groups has become intertwined with concerns about essentialism. Can national groups be identified in a manner that does justice to their invariably heterogeneous, dynamic, contested, and interrelated character? And can a nonessentialist account of national groups avoid reducing them to mere patterns of discourse (like seventeenth-century witch-talk) having little positive normative resonance?

I believe that there is a way of identifying distinct national groups that neither essentializes them nor reduces them to mere patterns of discourse.[16] An ontology of groups can avoid essentialism by focusing, at the fundamental level, not on the traits (beliefs, values, etc.) that all members of the group supposedly share in common, but on the social lineage of the (heterogeneous, contested, fluid) traits that members do have. On a social lineage account, individuals belong to the same group when they are, to an appropriate degree, the products of a common social environment. They share in exposure to a common set of social institutions and practices, and (in part for this reason) they interact more intensively with one another than they do with individuals outside the group. Or at least this was true of them earlier in their lives. Individuals belong to a *distinct* group – for instance, a minority group, rather than the majority – when the common social environment that they share or shared is to, some degree, isolated from the environment that forms others. The institutions and practices that create a common social experience for the minority group are not and were not present (to the same extent) in the lives of the majority, who instead are or were subject to a different set of institutions and practices.

This characterization of groups is too broad in the sense that it is likely to include groups that are not specifically *national* in character. For a group to be national, three further conditions are needed. The first is that the distinctive social environment that gives rise to the group is *multidimensional* in character. That is, there are a number of different institutions and practices that each exert a common influence on members of the group and that do not exert such an influence on nonmembers. In a paradigm case, a national minority is concentrated in its own territory, separated geographically from the majority population. It possesses its own distinct language, and its own institutions of government, administration, and education. The religion professed by most of its population is different than the dominant religion among the majority. In part because of these various differences, the minority are

16 I draw at this point on Alan Patten, "Rethinking Culture: The Social Lineage Account," *American Political Science Review* 105:4 (2011), pp. 735–49.

treated by the media, and by businesses, as forming their own market. In these ways, and perhaps others, a whole series of structures, which influence the socialization of individuals, coincide in impacting all and only the members of the group. In virtue of these several different dimensions of distinctness, the social experience and formation of members of the group is quite different from that of nonmembers.

In practice, actual national minorities fall short of this paradigm in various ways. Like the Scots, they may speak the same language as the national majority. Or like the Catalans, they may practice the same religion as the majority. In addition, even where there is "isolation" along some or all of the dimensions, it may be quite modest in degree. The members of the minority may live interspersed amongst members of the majority, and interact with them in many contexts. Institutions of administration or government that are peculiar to the minority may be a thing of a past, living on only in the narratives and identity of members of the group. There will certainly be forms of commerce, technology, and economic organization that encompass minority and majority alike and, indeed, some that are global in their reach. The important point is that distinct national groups pass a threshold level of social and historical isolation from the majority population that is discernible along a number of different dimensions.

Second, for the group to be considered "national," the distinctive social environment that makes it a group must generate a distinctive pattern of beliefs, values, concerns, and allegiances – what might be called a distinct *culture*. It need not be that everyone in the group shares the same beliefs, values, concerns, and allegiances. This would be to fall back into essentialism. But the frequency with which different beliefs, values, and the like are held among the minority should diverge from the pattern among the majority if the group is to count as a national minority for the purposes of my account. This second, *cultural* condition is not logically entailed by the multidimensional social isolation condition. But it should be clear that the two conditions are contingently quite highly correlated. It would be surprising if a group formed under conditions of multidimensional social isolation did not exhibit a distinctive pattern of beliefs, values, and concerns, relative to others whose formative influences are quite different.

A third requirement of a national group is that there be a widespread sense of identification with and valuing of the group formed by the distinctive social environment. It need not be true of everyone, but many people should think of themselves as members of the group, value their membership, and – importantly, if the group is to be considered a *national* one – want the group to be self-governing with respect to at least some matters. Again this *identity* condition is not necessitated by the first condition, but there is likely to be a contingent association of the two. Where an identity is present, this may reinforce the tendency to social isolation, as members of the group prefer, in certain contexts, to interact with other members. And where there is social isolation, based on a distinctive set of common institutions and practices, this may engender an attachment to those institutions and practices, and to one's fellows who have also been formed by them. It may engender, that is, an identity.

In summary, then, a national group is a group of people who are formed by a distinctive, multidimensional social environment, who exhibit a distinct culture as a consequence, and many of whom have a national identity focused on the group in question. I believe that this account picks out all or most of the groups that are commonly mentioned as national minorities, and does so without falling into the essentialist trap or reducing such minorities to a normatively dubious social construction. Some of the characteristic features of nations that I am drawing attention to here, such as the presence of distinctive beliefs and concerns, and the widespread desire for self-government, are familiar from standard accounts in the literature.[17] The twist I am proposing is to think of members of a national group as sharing a common social lineage. The social lineage account can embrace the idea that nations are settings in which certain beliefs, preferences, and identities are especially prevalent while at the same time accommodating the fact that typically not everyone in the group shares these beliefs and attitudes.

5. THE VALUE OF SELF-GOVERNMENT

As we saw before, a second challenge to the nationalist conception of self-determination is to explain why it would matter to members of a national minority that they enjoy self-determination. The general shape of my answer to this challenge is quite conventional. Like several other theorists who have discussed the issue, I shall describe two main benefits of self-determination.[18] The first highlights the instrumental value of self-determination; the second its intrinsic value.

[17] See, e.g., Joseph Raz and Avishai Margalit, "National Self-Determination," in Joseph Raz, *Ethics in the Public Domain: Essays in the Morality of Law and Politics* (Oxford: Oxford University Press, 1994), pp. 125–45; Yael Tamir, *Liberal Nationalism* (Princeton, NJ: Princeton University Press, 1993); David Miller, *On Nationality* (Oxford: Oxford University Press, 1995); Moore, *The Ethics of Nationalism*; and Wayne Norman, *Negotiating Nationalism: Nation-Building, Federalism, and Secession in the Multinational State* (Oxford: Oxford University Press, 2006).

[18] Raz and Margalit, "National Self-Determination"; Miller, *On Nationality*.

The instrumental benefit relies on the idea that a national minority is defined, in part, by a common culture. As we saw, this does not mean that everyone in the group shares the same values, beliefs, concerns, and the like, but it does mean that certain values, beliefs, and concerns are more prevalent (and others are less prevalent) than they are among the national majority. Self-determination makes it easier for members of a group to express their distinctive values and preferences in political decisions and outcomes. When a group is in the majority in a constituency, it has greater power to bring about decisions and outcomes that reflect commonly held beliefs, values, and concerns than would be the case if its members are thrown into a collective decision-making process dominated by a culturally distinct majority.

It is easy enough to see how this argument might go for the cases of overseas colonial subjects or indigenous peoples. Relative to the ones that prevail in the metropolitan or national majority, the dominant beliefs, values, and concerns within the colonized or indigenous group are likely to be quite distinct. Whereas carving out jurisdictional spaces in which such a group can be self-governing helps to ensure that laws and public decisions more fully reflect its distinctive beliefs and approaches, this sensitivity to the group's particular concerns would be much less likely were its members to constitute only a small minority in a much larger jurisdiction. The argument seems particularly strong in the case of indigenous peoples, but there is no categorical reason not to apply it to other national minorities. An argument of this kind was often made by Scots in favor of devolution, and is echoed again today by Scots who favor full independence. The pro-devolution Scots maintained that Scottish political values were systematically thwarted during the Thatcher years (when the vast majority of Scottish MPs were in opposition) and that devolution would make it harder for this to happen again.

So self-determination is valuable for members of national groups, then, in the straightforward sense that it allows them to more easily express and realize their distinctive (non-self-determination-related) values and preferences. One way to put this point is by saying that, *all else being equal*, it is good when individuals can be governed by political decisions and outcomes that "fit" with their own values and traditions. When there is a fit of this kind, individuals are "at home" in their public life and institutions. Public life is understandable and meaningful to them – familiar and comfortable. As we noted earlier, this notion of "fit," or what Walzer also terms "communal integrity," is sometimes offered as a reason for *dropping* the positive condition (democratic institutions) in favor of the boundary condition. My claim is that "fit" is indeed relevant, but its relevance plays out as part of the case for autonomy for national minorities *within* democratic or inclusive institutions. It is implausible to regard the values related to "fit" as canceling or outweighing the values realized by democracy, since the instrumental benefits of democracy may themselves be very substantial. But acknowledging this point is consistent with insisting that "fit" is relevant to how democratic institutions are organized.

A familiar objection to this instrumental argument is that it tacitly relies on a form of essentialism. Although the concept of culture appealed to by the argument is avowedly nonessentialist, the real work might seem to be done by a different concept according to which everyone who shares a culture holds some distinctive set of values and preferences. If essentialism is truly being foresworn, then presumably it is more accurate to say that self-determination will help some members of the group and hinder others. Scots with Thatcherite values might have done better in realizing their values in a unitary Britain than under devolution. The decisions and outcomes made in a Britain-wide forum were likely to be a better "fit" with their values.[19]

This objection raises an important point. It suggests that we should regard the claim that self-determination has instrumental value for members of the group as shorthand for the weaker claim that it has instrumental value for *some* members of the group. But, for our purposes, the weaker claim should suffice. Suppose it is granted that both the majority and the minority in a national group have some claim to a jurisdiction in which their values and preferences are able to flourish. And suppose that the majority preferences do better in a substate jurisdiction (e.g., in decisions made by the Scottish Parliament) and the minority's preferences do better in the state-wide setting (e.g., in decisions made in Westminster). An argument for self-determination (i.e., empowering the Scottish national identity by assigning some powers to the Scottish Parliament) could still be made in one or other of two ways. One could argue that, if forced to choose one or the other, it is more important to achieve a fit with the preferences of the majority in the group. Or one could argue that, under a system of devolution or federalism, jurisdictions are assigned in such a way as to fit with the majority in some areas and with the minority in other areas, thereby achieving a kind of equality or evenhandedness. The second of these possibilities anticipates the proposal to be offered in the next section for handling situations in which there is more than one national group present on the territory on which some particular group is seeking self-determination.

The intrinsic benefits of self-determination can be described more succinctly. Two variants of the argument can be distinguished, one of which

[19] For an objection of this form, see Beitz's Afterward to *Political Theory and International Relations*, pp. 191–98. See also Waldron, "Two Conceptions of Self-Determination," in Besson and Tasioulas, *Philosophy*, pp. 397–413.

relies on a particular view of cultural preservation, while the other makes do without it. The cultural variant starts from the premise that people often value their culture and desire its preservation. It adds to this a nonessentialist conception of what it means to preserve a culture. Preserving a culture is not a matter of preserving any particular value or tradition, since no particular value or tradition is definitive of the culture. Instead, a culture is preserved over time when its members – rather than the members of the majority society – retain control over the mechanisms of cultural transmission from one generation to the next, even if the substantive values and preferences of the new generation diverge quite markedly from those of their elders. On this view, self-determination is valuable because it is one of the mechanisms by which members of the national minority control the socialization of members of the next generation.

The second variant of the intrinsic argument maintains that the value of self-determination derives simply from the fact that the aspiration to collective self-determination is one of the constituting features of a shared national identity. To have a national identity is to have a set of attitudes and dispositions, one of the most important of which is the desire for some degree of collective self-determination. The self-determination of some particular national identity group is a good for individuals in that group in the simple sense that it accommodates, or gives expression to, the desire for self-determination shared by (most) people with that identity. The accommodation of this desire may in turn be one of the sources of self-respect for some individuals. Their respect for themselves may, in part, be a function of the respect that is publicly accorded their identity group through the creation of institutional jurisdictional spaces in which the group can be self-determining.[20] Where respect is at stake in this way, the claims about justice considered in the following should be given added weight.

6. JUSTICE AND SELF-DETERMINATION

Self-determination is valuable for national minorities in several different ways. It allows many in the group to more effectively realize their values and preferences and to enjoy the Walzerian good of communal integrity. And it

[20] On the connection between self-respect and self-government, see Charles Taylor, *Reconciling the Solitudes* (Montreal: McGill-Queens Press, 1993); Margalit and Raz, "National Self-Determination"; David Copp, "Democracy and Communal Self-Determination," in *The Morality of Nationalism*, ed. Robert McKim and Jeff McMahan (Oxford: Oxford University Press, 1997), pp. 284–85; and Moore, *Ethics of Nationalism*, pp. 59–61.

offers an important tool with which to preserve the minority's culture and to provide the more direct satisfaction of the desire for self-determination itself.

The question we must now explore is how the values associated with self-determination should figure into an account of what is owed to persons as a matter of justice. For the most part, the arguments for the value of self-determination appeal to ways in which various values and preferences of individuals would be satisfied by such an arrangement. But, since there is no general right to have one's values and preferences satisfied, an additional step in the argument needs to be completed. One could accept that self-determination is valuable in the ways that I have outlined and still not think that that any issue of justice is at stake. And, even if one thought that some form of justice were involved, one might question whether the injustice involved in denying a national minority self-determination should be of any concern to those who frame international law and conduct international affairs.

A first step in completing the argument is to observe that the self-determination of national groups is a good that can be distributed more or less equally depending on political arrangements.[21] At one extreme, for instance, political arrangements might not provide any space for self-determination at all to some national group. At the same time, those with a different national identity may, in this situation, readily be able to identify with the political community in which collective decisions are made. It may be both the case, for instance, that they think of the entire state, and all fellow citizens, as forming their community of belonging and that it is at this statewide level that political decisions are made.

On the other hand, self-government need not be so unequally distributed. Constitutional arrangements can be put in place, for example, that empower people with a substate national identity – through federalism or devolution – while at the same time providing a degree of self-determination to statewide national identity holders as well – through the retention of certain democratically

[21] This paragraph and the next few borrow from Alan Patten, "Democratic Secession from a Multinational State," *Ethics* **31**:4 (2002), pp. 558–86. See also Alan Patten, "Conception Libérale de la Citoyenneté et Identité Nationale," in *Nationalité, Citoyenneté et Solidarité*, ed. Michel Seymour (Montréal: Éditions Libre, 1999), pp. 232–56; "Equality of Recognition and the Liberal Theory of Citizenship," in *The Demands of Citizenship*, eds. Catriona McKinnon and Ian Hampsher-Monk (London: Continuum), pp. 193–211; and *Equal Recognition: The Moral Foundations of Minority Cultural Rights* (Princeton, NJ: Princeton University Press, 2014). The general suggestion that minority rights are rooted in a notion of fairness or fair treatment is quite familiar in the literature. See, e.g., Kymlicka, *Multicultural Citizenship* and *Politics in the Vernacular*; Joseph Carens, *Culture, Citizenship, and Community* (Oxford: Oxford University Press, 2000); and Moore, *The Ethics of Nationalism*.

controlled powers by the central state. Provided that significant functions and responsibilities are assigned to each level, a kind of rough equality in self-determination is worked out.

Consider again the case of Scottish devolution. This arrangement enhances equality in two different respects. First, and most obviously, devolution brings about greater equality between citizens in Scotland with a Scottish national identity and citizens in England who have a British national identity. The Scots enjoy some degree of self-determination in the association that they value, and can expect to enjoy some of the instrumental and intrinsic benefits outlined earlier that derive from this arrangement. Because of the powers retained in Westminster, Britain-identifiers in England enjoy self-determination alongside all British citizens, although they do not get to participate in determining for the Scots those questions that are assigned to the Scottish parliament.

Second, devolution enhances equality *within* Scotland between those whose identity is primarily Scottish and those whose identity is primarily British. Whereas the creation of uniquely Scottish institutions, including a Scottish parliament, gives public expression to the Scottish identity, retaining certain powers and responsibilities in London gives a public, political life to the British identity. This second relationship of equality helps to explain why the goods associated with self-determination do not count in favor of secession or a massive delegation of powers to the substate authority. A devolution, or a secession, that assigned too many powers to the substate authority would end up denying equal opportunity for self-determination to citizens of the substate unit who maintain a statewide identity. Had the Scots voted to secede in the September 2014 referendum, a valuable form of equality would have been undermined. Herein lies my reason for thinking that the argument I have been developing for the nationalist conception of self-determination favors the moderate version rather than a stronger version of that conception, which justifies, or even demands, a state for each nation.

Once it is noticed that the opportunity for self-determination can be distributed more or less equally to members of different intrastate national groups, it becomes plausible to think of self-determination as a matter of justice. For the various reasons reviewed in the previous section, it can matter a great deal to people whether the group they identify with enjoys self-determination or not. Nobody has a claim of justice that all the things that matter to them will be guaranteed in full. But people do plausibly have a claim of justice to equal treatment in the distribution by public institutions of resources and structures that provide opportunity to attain the goods that matter to them.

In previous work, I have argued that the notion of equal treatment that is being invoked here can be rooted in a fairly fundamental principle of liberal thought – the principle of liberal neutrality.[22] All else being equal, a liberal state ought not to be taking sides among the different preferences and attachments of its citizens. Of course, it should take sides when liberal values themselves are at stake, but there is a large range of preferences and attachments that are permissible from the standpoint of liberal values. Toward these permissible preferences and attachments, the state should extend neutral treatment: relative to an appropriate baseline, it should confer equivalent benefits to, and impose equivalent burdens on, the pursuit and enjoyment of the different preferences and attachments that people have. A scheme of public institutions that gives some space for self-government to national minorities and some to those who identify with the national majority does a better job of realizing neutrality in this sense than either a unitary state or a state that has been dismembered by secession.

The principle of liberal neutrality is itself grounded in an even more basic idea in liberal thought: the idea that the state should leave its citizens with a fair opportunity to pursue and enjoy the preferences and attachments that they in fact have. The fundamental principle of the account, then, is an individual one: fair opportunity for individuals to pursue and realize their conceptions of the good. But the argument is that group recognition and self-determination can be consequential for the pursuit of individual conceptions of the good. Fair treatment of individuals thus requires attention to be paid to (among many things) the fair treatment of groups. Because fair opportunity for individuals is the fundamental concern, the account being offered here does not justify – and indeed counsels against – the political accommodation of groups and group structures that treat individuals (be they members or nonmembers) in a harmful, oppressive, or otherwise unfair manner. There is continuity at the deepest level of the theory between individual human rights and the moderate nationalist conception of self-determination: both have a common source in fundamental individualist principles of liberal thought.

As I mentioned earlier, it is possible to accept this argument and still think that self-determination is not a matter of justice as far as the international community is concerned. On this kind of view, devolution-seeking Scots would have a claim of justice against fellow Britons, but there would be no issue of justice as far as the rest of the world is concerned.

22 Alan Patten, "Liberal Neutrality: A Reinterpretation and Defense," *Journal of Political Philosophy* 20 (2012), pp. 249–72. I argue for the connection between neutrality and minority rights in *Equal Recognition*, chapters 4–5.

But this position seems confused to me. If one accepts the democratic conception of self-determination, then one should be open to the idea that justice claims that, in the first instance, are internal to some state can end up a matter for international concern if they are not satisfactorily resolved within that state. Consider the case of a state that denies basic freedoms of speech or association to an ethnic minority in its population. The members of that minority have a justice claim, which in the first instance is directed at the state and at fellow citizens. But if this justice claim is consistently overlooked or rejected, then, on the democratic conception at least, there are grounds for the international community to take remedial actions of some sort. In addition, given the risk of rights violations occurring, there may be grounds for international monitoring and advocacy efforts, even directed at states where no actual rights violations in need of remedy are occurring. The key point is that nothing about where the claim of justice is directed in the first instance is relevant to whether a persistent injustice (or danger of such injustice) might be a matter of international concern.

A possible response might be to argue that the denial of self-determination is not a *fundamental* injustice and that only fundamental injustices ought to be of international concern. This sort of argument would differentiate the denial of self-determination case from the freedoms of speech and association ones that were just mentioned.

I would accept that denial of self-determination does not rise to the level of a fundamental justice. And I would accept that conflicts between fundamental and nonfundamental justice ought to be resolved in favor of the former. But I see no reason to believe that, as a general matter, international concern should be *limited* to matters of fundamental justice.

It is true, of course, that certain expressions of international concern would be out of proportion to a nonfundamental injustice. Military intervention would not be justified, nor would other severe responses (e.g., blockades, far-reaching economic sanctions, expulsion from important international organizations) that are appropriately reserved for extreme cases involving grave moral urgency. Nor, for that matter, would it be proper for the international community to use recognition as a tool for promoting nonfundamental justice, except perhaps in cases where the injustice is strongly resistant to domestic correction and where the risks to the continued realization of fundamental justice are minimal. As a general matter, it is wrong to undermine or disrupt existing states that are doing a tolerably good job of providing fundamental justice to their citizens.

But none of this rules out *proportionate* measures taken by the international community to encourage and incentivize the realization of nonfundamental justice within particular domestic contexts. The mere fact that a particular right or principle is announced in an international covenant or declaration can enable domestic actors to advocate more effectively for the realization of that right or principle. More substantively, the international community can monitor and report on the condition of national minorities, and it can offer various forms of training and organizational and material support to minorities that are denied self-government. In addition, international organizations (e.g., the European Union) might make respect for self-determination in the nationalist sense a condition for accession or for the receipt of particular benefits. All of these mechanisms, which fall short of recognition as well as more coercive measures, are instruments that international actors might wield to encourage and incentivize compliance with the nationalist conception consistent with a norm of proportionality.

7. INSTITUTIONALIZING NATIONAL SELF-DETERMINATION

A final challenge to the nationalist conception concerns its acceptance into international law and practice. Would the development of a general norm of guaranteeing self-determination for national minorities lead to adverse consequences of various kinds? As we saw near the start of the paper, one argument in favor of the statist conception is that it eliminates any of the possible adverse consequences associated with empowering states (or other international actors) to intervene in one another's affairs. This may seem excessively conservative in that it ignores possible benefits flowing from a practice of international concern. But it is possible that the balance of considerations is different when one examines (as we have done in much of the paper) the choice between the democratic and nationalist conceptions. It might be argued that the democratic conception gets the balance about right between the benefits of international concern, on the one hand, and the risks of adverse consequences, on the other.

To explore this possibility, let us consider two kinds of adverse consequences that are sometimes associated with national self-determination.[23] The first is connected with the fact that, in contrast with indigenous peoples, many national minorities are irredentist in character. They speak the same language as, and share a cultural heritage with, the majority population of

[23] Both are discussed by Will Kymlicka: "Western Political Theory and Ethnic Relations in Eastern Europe," in *Can Liberal Pluralism Be Exported?: Western Political Theory and Ethnic Relations in Eastern Europe*, eds. Kymlicka and Magda Opalski (Oxford: Oxford University Press), pp. 13–105, and *Multicultural Odysseys*.

some neighboring or nearby state. The national identity of these minorities often expresses itself as a desire for greater cultural and political connection with the "homeland" state and its majority population. When nationalist minorities have this irredentist character, intrastate struggles for internal self-determination can lead to interstate tensions and conflict. Since the nationalist conception legitimates such struggles for internal self-determination, and encourages outsiders to take an interest in their success, the worry is that it will end up destabilizing the interstate relationships that are also implicated. The drive for internal self-determination may diminish the possibilities for peaceful cooperation between neighboring states and raise the likelihood of distrust, enmity, and violent conflict.

A second adverse consequence arises from the fact that members of national minorities may not think that internal self-determination is sufficient. They may instead think that the benefits of self-government will be realized most fully through independent statehood. This sentiment may be especially strong amongst political elites, (would-be) government workers, and others who would gain tangibly from independent statehood. Although the nationalist conception is meant to legitimate internal self-determination only, and indeed the justice argument of the previous section condemns secession in some instances, the worry is that internal self-determination may serve as a stepping stone to external self-determination. The very institutions of intrastate autonomy may be used by secessionist elites as a platform to mobilize for further separation from the state. This possibility would seem to allow for a state that is home to national minorities to be open to internal autonomy "in theory," but to reject it "in practice" on the grounds that it jeopardizes its own territorial integrity and national security. The anxiety about national security is especially plausible when the concerns about irredentism and secessionism are both present. In such a situation, a state may fear that extending territorial autonomy to a national minority may produce a chain of events that leads to the loss of territory to a historic, neighborhood rival.[24]

This is an important set of challenges to the nationalist conception, and I do not think that it is possible to exclude the possibility that institutionalizing such a conception would have the adverse consequences that are predicted. However, there are ways of minimizing the risks of such consequences, and there are also risks on the other side. No configuration of international law and

[24] See Kymlicka, *Multicultural Odysseys*, for a detailed account of the tendency for national majorities to "securitize" ethnocultural relations by claiming that accommodations for minorities would pose an existential security threat to the state. Kymlicka finds the tendency to be especially pronounced in post-Communist Europe.

practice is without some risks. The best that can be done is to try to make the risks as tolerable as possible.

One reason for downplaying the risks of adverse consequences was introduced in the previous section's discussion of proportionality. The injustice involved in denying internal self-determination to a national minority is, on its own, a nonfundamental one. International action to remedy such an injustice should be proportionate to this nonfundamental character. Most importantly, such action should not undermine the capacity of states to continue delivering fundamental justice to their citizens. This constraint places significant limits on what "homeland" states can do to promote the claims of their kinsfolk who are a national minority in a neighboring state. They cannot escalate their pressure beyond a certain point, for example by issuing ultimatums, threatening economic reprisals, arming guerrillas, and so on, without running foul of the proportionality constraint.

Of course it is true that the risk does not disappear simply by noting the constraint's theoretical importance: homeland states might simply ignore the constraint. But this is a very general possibility and is not peculiar to institutionalizations of the nationalist conception. If the democratic conception were to be the established norm of international law and practice, homeland states might still come to the assistance of their ethnic kin in other states in defiance of any proportionality constraint. There is nothing magical about any of the conceptions of self-determination we have been considering. Moreover, there is at least some reason to hope that the nationalist conception would do better than the democratic one at limiting extralegal intrusions by states in one another's affairs. Compliance with international norms is more likely, all else being equal, if those norms are regarded as legitimate. If no space is made for a practice of international concern for national minorities denied internal self-determination, then homeland states may simply conclude that international norms should be ignored in this area and that they ought to take extralegal measures in a unilateral way. By contrast, the possibilities opened up by the nationalist conception reduce the "strains of commitment" to international norms, and make it a bit more likely (again, all else being equal) that states will comply with such norms.

In addition, if one is seriously concerned about the excessive zeal of homeland states for the self-determination rights of ethnic kin in neighboring states, then this may be a reason for taking the practice of international concern out of the hands of particular states and placing it instead in the hands of international bodies and organizations.[25] Defending such a proposal

[25] For a suggestion along these lines, see Cassese, *Self-Determination of Peoples*, pp. 344–46.

is beyond the scope of the present paper. The point is simply that endorsing the nationalist conception does not automatically entail new permissions for particular states to protect "their" kinfolk in other states.

Let us turn now to the worry that internal self-determination would serve as a launching pad for efforts to mobilize external self-determination. The key to addressing this concern is for international law and practice to offer a firm guarantee of the territorial integrity of states that do an adequate job of following the nationalist conception. To a degree, this guarantee is already established. There is no right to unilateral secession in international law, and there is certainly no such right in cases where there is no pattern of serious injustices calling to be remedied. However, to say that there is no right to secede is not equivalent to saying that (basically just) states have a right to territorial integrity. It may be that additional norms need to be developed that make it clearer to states that they can extend internal autonomy to national minorities, generally govern in an adequately just fashion, and feel secure that the international community will not support or recognize a unilateral attempt to secede.

As an illustration of such a mechanism, one might imagine the European Union adopting a two-part policy toward states seeking membership in the union. It might insist (1) that candidates for admission adopt or credibly commit to adopting a meaningful scheme of internal autonomy for national minorities. At the same time, the EU could itself commit to (2) refusing membership to any group that sought to use such a scheme as a stepping stone to full independence. Faced with loss of membership in the EU, it is unlikely that groups benefited by internal autonomy would try to propel themselves onward to independent statehood.

Admittedly, none of these considerations fully rule out the possibility that a state might harbor legitimate fears about its territorial integrity should it establish autonomy arrangements. In part for this reason, claims to self-determination made by national minorities should not be considered to have preemptory force. They can be outweighed by other considerations, such as a reasonable fear that self-determination would lead to one or more of the adverse consequences described in this chapter. To say that the value of self-determination is "outweighed" in these contexts is not, however, to say that it disappears from the scene altogether. Even though states are not obliged to establish self-determination in these contexts, a residue of the underlying values still remains. States ought to work, over time, to build up the conditions that are propitious for self-determination, such as friendly relations with neighbor states, observance of human rights, and participation in international organizations that protect the territorial integrity of just states. In this sense, national majorities should not lock a rejection of autonomy for national minorities into their long-term constitutional structures, but ought to lay the groundwork for an eventual adoption of such arrangements when the conditions are ripe.

8. CONCLUSION

The view of self-determination elaborated in this paper has been defended before. In the early 1990s, as European institutions struggled to deal with nationalist conflicts that erupted with the collapse of communism, the idea that national minorities should enjoy a right to internal autonomy arrangements came briefly into fashion. Several European bodies proposed a norm along these lines, arguing that it was a reasonable compromise between secession, on the one hand, and the unitary structures of the nationalizing state, on the other. Reflecting this context, perhaps, Cassese concluded his influential 1995 book, *The Self-Determination of Peoples*, with a call for the extension of a right to internal self-determination to encompass autonomy for national minorities.[26]

Despite this brief burst of enthusiasm for what I have called a nationalist conception of self-determination, international law and practice have shown little sign of moving in the direction that Cassese and other reformers were advocating. The main obstacles to reform are political. As a general rule, state officials tend to be skeptical of any proposal that would open their states up to additional monitoring and interference by the international community. As we saw in the previous section, in some contexts states may have legitimate fears that internal autonomy schemes would lead to the loss of territory through secession and/or to intra- or interstate violent conflict.

In addition to the political obstacles, however, there have also been intellectual ones. There is widespread skepticism among liberal-minded actors that national self-determination is an attractive and weighty idea. My aim in the present paper has been to address these intellectual obstacles. I have sketched a moderate version of the idea and argued that it is coherent and appealing. Although it would be unwise for the international community to insist that every state abide by norms of internal self-determination in the near future, the promotion of such norms is a worthy long-run goal of international politics.

[26] See also Hurst Hannum, *Autonomy, Sovereignty, and Self-Determination*, rev. ed. (Philadelphia: University of Pennsylvania Press, 1996 [1990]), Conclusion.

7

Self-Determination, Dissent, and the Problem of Population Transfers

MATTHEW LISTER*

1. INTRODUCTION

Many of the major self-determination movements of the twentieth century did not go smoothly, but resulted in forced or semiforced transfers of groups of people from one country to another. Famous examples include the compulsory "population exchange" between Greece and Turkey in 1923,[1] the population transfers that accompanied the independence of India and its split with Pakistan in 1947,[2] and the expulsion of most of the Palestinian population from the area that became Israel after 1948. Somewhat lesser-known examples include the expulsion of ethnic Georgians from Abkhazia[3] and (more recently) South Ossetia,[4] with the help of Russia, and the exchange of populations between Armenia and Azerbaijan in relation to the ongoing Nagorno-Karabakh dispute,[5] as well as the continuing slow-motion transfer of Serbs from Kosovo to

* Visiting Assistant Professor of Legal Studies and Business Ethics, Wharton School of Business, University of Pennsylvania.

1 See, for example, the papers in Renee Hirschon (ed.), *Crossing the Aegean: An Appraisal of the 1923 Compulsory Population Exchange between Greece and Turkey (Studies in Forced Migration, Vol. 12)* (New York, Berghahn Books, 2003).

2 See, for example, Yasmin Khan, *The Great Partition: The Making of India and Pakistan* (New Haven, CT: Yale University Press, 2007).

3 See Human Rights Watch, "Georgia/Abkhazia: Violations of the Laws of War and Russia's Role in the Conflict," www.hrw.org/reports/1995/Georgia2.htm, and, for more recent events, Elesya Vartanyan and Michael Schwirtz, "Georgians Forced Out of Abkhazia, EU Monitors Report," *New York Times*, Dec. 7, 2009.

4 See Brian Whitmore, "One Year After 'Independence', Abkhazia and South Ossetia in Legal Gray Zone", *Radio Free Europe/Radio Liberty*, Aug. 26, 2009, www.rferl.org/content/Year_After_Independence_Abkhazia_South_Ossetia_In_Legal_Gray_Zone/1808101.html.

5 See "Nagorno-Karabakh," www.globalsecurity.org/military/world/war/nagorno-karabakh.htm.

Serbia.[6] This last example, in particular, helps highlight the connection, in many historical instances, between population transfers and so-called "ethnic cleansing."

Forced population transfers are not, of course, supported by major theorists of self-determination and secession.[7] The problems that make population transfers extremely common in actual cases of self-determination and secession, however, are not squarely faced by many theories of self-determination. And, I shall argue, certain leading theories of self-determination and secession would make population transfers almost inevitable in practice, even if not called for or sanctioned in theory. This is a major stumbling block for any attempt to move from an abstract account of self-determination towards a working theory.[8] If our goal is to provide a "coherent set of principles to distinguish legitimate form illegitimate secession,"[9] and to set "just terms for secession,"[10] we need to be able to provide an account that is able to deal with the inevitable problem of population transfers.[11]

In this paper I will take a first step towards addressing this problem. I shall show how any approach to dealing with secession, including "primary rights" accounts, "remedial rights only" accounts, and even "consensual" accounts,[12]

[6] For a timeline of developments, including fairly recent ones, see www.bbc.co.uk/news/world-europe-18331273.

[7] Secession is, of course, only one form of self-determination. I will largely focus on cases of secession, in part because they provide clear cases for my purposes and in part because secession has been the focus of the most sustained discussion in the relevant literature. However, much of what I say will also apply to cases of decolonization and to at least some internal autonomy agreements, though I will have little directly to say about the last item. My thanks to Tim Sellers for insisting, at the conference where these papers were first presented, on the need to make these distinctions.

[8] I am enthusiastic in following Allen Buchanan's lead in thinking that theorists of global justice and international law should work hard to see how their views could be instantiated, and the likely results of adopting a theory, and agree with him that doing so requires us to consider real cases whenever possible. For relevant attempts by Buchanan to do this, see "The Quebec Secession Issue: Democracy, Minority Rights, and the Rule of Law," in Stephen Macedo and Allen Buchanan (eds.), *Secession and Self-Determination: Nomos XLV* (New York: New York University Press, 2003), 238–71; "Self-Determination, Secession, and the Rule of Law," in Robert McKim and Jeff McMahan (eds.), *The Morality of Nationalism* (New York, Oxford University Press, 1997), 301–23; and, more generally, "Introduction," in Allen Buchanan, *Human Rights, Legitimacy, and the Use of Force* (New York, Oxford University Press, 2010). For some doubts about Buchanan's actual implementation of this plan, see Lister, "Are Empiricism and Institutions Enough?", 2 *Transnational Legal Theory* **127** (2011).

[9] Buchanan, "Self-Determination, Secession, and the Rule of Law," 303.

[10] Buchanan, "Self-Determination, Secession, and the Rule of Law," 308.

[11] This problem is essentially ignored on the "just terms" suggested by Buchanan, for example. "Self-Determination, Secession, and the Rule of Law," 308.

[12] The details of these different approaches to secession and self-determination will be given in the following.

must be able to deal with the inevitable problem of population transfers, if it is to be a complete and plausible theory. I shall also show how population transfers, to the extent that we can always expect them to take place, can be made as just as possible, in light of any approach to the problem of secession. I will not here attempt to adjudicate between different approaches to secession and self-determination. My goal in this paper is not to give an account of secession rights, but to highlight an essentially unexplored problem that arises internally within most of the leading approaches. To that extent, my argument may be seen as a friendly addition to all of the approaches listed here, showing how they may try to meet an objection which they have not yet faced. It may be that the need to deal with the problem of population transfers will make some theories of secession seem "too expensive" and so not plausible, but if so, this is a problem that proponents of such theories will need to squarely face.

2. WHAT ARE "POPULATION TRANSFERS," AND WHY SHOULD THEORISTS OF SELF-DETERMINATION AND SECESSION ADDRESS THEM?

What is a "population transfer," as used in this paper? If we look at historical cases, such as those noted earlier, we see that they often involve the forced movement of people in a clear and unequivocal way. But sometimes these movements of people have been "negotiated" and semivoluntary. That is to say, the exchange of populations has been voluntary from the perspective of the states involved in the negotiation, but is not necessarily experienced as voluntary from the perspective of the people who are made, or encouraged, to move. In all of these cases, both the forced and the negotiated ones, there has been significant suffering[13] for those who were required to move. But, I shall argue, this is not a strictly necessary part of the problem. The issue I am most interested in here is not just that people are made to suffer from population transfers, though this is important and very often the case. Even if significant suffering can be avoided, I will argue, the problem must still be dealt with.

Put most abstractly and generally, a "population transfer," as I will use the term, is when the process of self-determination, by a part of an existing state or territory, causes a significant group within that territory to leave, either from

[13] By "suffering" I mean to include material deprivation, physical injury or harm, and subjective states of dissatisfaction. So, one may have suffered from being included in a population transfer even if one has not been subjected to physical or material harm, if one was made to move against one's will, this leads to subjective dissatisfaction. Of course, in many cases all three forms of harm will go together. My thanks to Jerry Vildostegui for encouraging me to be clear on this point.

the "new" state to the old, "parent" state, or from the parent state to the new one, or to some third state, so as to avoid being in the state from which the people have moved.[14] My general claim is that most normative theorists of self-determination, where this includes at least discussions of secession and decolonization, and perhaps some internal autonomy agreements, have ignored this phenomena. But population transfers are ubiquitous in nearly all actual and likely cases, and give rise to significant moral considerations that cannot be legitimately ignored, even, I will argue, in "ideal theory" discussions of secession.[15]

Given that population transfers are an obvious and salient problem in actual cases of secession, but have been ignored, to a large degree, in theoretical discussions, I am in the somewhat paradoxical position of arguing that they are important not only in practice, but also in theory. However, I will show that any theory of self-determination, including a theory of secession, must provide an account of this phenomena and how it is to be dealt with if it is to be complete. (This is not to argue that only a complete theory may be worthwhile. Even a partial theory is often an important step, and I do not claim to provide a

[14] I do not intent this category to cover all possible types of movement between the parent and the new state, but only that which is directly or primarily motivated by the desire to not be in the new (or old) state as such. So, for example, movement from the new state to the old, or vice versa, motivated merely by better economic opportunities in the other state would, at least in many cases, not count as a population transfer on my account. Of course, in real life, motivations are rarely "pure," and so it may be difficult to know if particular instances of movement between parent and new states falls under my account or not. My only comfort here is that this sort of problem seems to me to be very common in normative theory, and that there is nothing to do but to face it and do as well as we can in applying our theories to concrete cases. My thanks to Jerry Vildostegui for pushing me on this point.

[15] Of course, this problem has not been completely ignored by normative theorists – it is often briefly noted by those working on the subject, and international lawyers have been somewhat better on this than have philosophers, but even those who have noted the problem have not, I shall argue, given it the sort of significant attention that it deserves. And it is often confused with the distinct problem of guaranteeing minority rights within the new state. As I shall show, while this is of course important, it cannot suffice to fully solve the problem addressed in this paper. The issue has been considered much more regularly by those working in forced migration studies, an importantly interdisciplinary field. But this material has been largely ignored by philosophers and other normative theorists working on self-determination and secession, and the discussion within forced migration studies has also largely, though not completely, taken place without the input of philosophers. For a helpful over-view of this field, see Francois Crepeau, et al., *Forced Migration and Global Processes: A View from Forced Migration Studies* (Lanham, MD: Lexington Books, 2006). This mutual process of ignoring relevant literature is unfortunate, and I hope this paper contributes to breaking down some of these barriers. I should note a particularly good article from the forced migration studies field that is likely to be of use to many normative theorists working in the area, and that I shall refer to in the following Michael Barutcisk, "Population Exchanges in International Law and Policy," in Hirschon, *Crossing the Aegean*, 23–37.

complete theory, even of this phenomenon. Rather, my point is simply that without an account of this phenomenon, a theory cannot be complete.) More importantly, without an account of how to deal with population transfers, we cannot know if a particular theory of self-determination is plausible or not, as this is a completely expectable phenomenon, one with significant moral implications, but one that has been widely ignored in the literature.

This raises the question of why, if this problem is as important as I have claimed, it has been so widely ignored or downplayed. There are, I believe, at least two reasons for this. First, most historical cases, such as those noted earlier, involve grave injustices of a sort that theorists of self-determination or secession essentially all find unacceptable. So, the idea seems to be that, if the theorist or international lawyer focuses on "just" cases of secession, on whatever account of secession she or he is working with, and rules out obviously unjust acts as generally impermissible, then she or he need not consider this problem. Those taking this line of thought assume that all population transfers must be forced transfers. This is a mistake. As I shall show, the theories of secession I will discuss here entail significant moral obligations to those who will, almost inevitably, leave their homes during the process of self-determination, even if this move is completely voluntary.

A second, related, idea is that this problem is essentially just a sub-aspect of the problem of refugees, and so it is best dealt with via a theory of refugees and what is owed to them, rather than directly as part of a theory of self-determination. I will show, however, that both of these reasons for not dealing with the problem of population transfers directly within a theory of self-determination are mistaken.

First, in what follows I will show that the core injustice involved in many population transfers, even beyond the suffering that usually accompanies them, is not distinct from the injustice that legitimates secessionist movements and other attempts at self-determination. If I am correct in this claim, then a theory of secession that is based on a particular set of causes must deal with the problem of population transfers, as these same causes explain the core of the injustice of population transfers. This is made clearer when we note that the problem of population transfers is often caused, or at least precipitated, by the group seeking to secede, even when this group is justified in doing so on a particular theory.[16] If the injustice that accompanies population transfers is intimately tied in to the normative justification for secession and other forms

[16] That this is so in many historical cases is well shown by Michael Barutcisk. See Barutcisk, "Population Exchanges in International Law and Policy," 24–27. Barutcisk, in this paper, addresses primarily cases that involve significant wrongdoing by one or both sides to the

of self-determination, as I shall argue, then a theorist cannot ignore the issue by focusing on (usually imagined) "just" cases of secession.

Second, I contend that this problem cannot just be assimilated to the problem of refugees. The problem of population transfers, though not completely distinct from the problem of refugees, is in some ways broader and in others narrower. (That is, while some people subject to a population transfer are refugees, and some refugees have been subject to an involuntary population transfer, each group contains significant subsections that do not fall in the other.[17]) Dealing with the problem of population transfers, for example, will involve duties on the part of states that do not fit into the refugee paradigm. In particular, the movement of people in question may be caused by acts that do not involve or amount to persecution, and yet, I shall argue, the "causing" state may still have obligations to those who leave, on any plausible theory of secession. If I am correct, then the most plausible grounds for ignoring the problem of population transfers are not valid, and anyone wishing to craft a theory of secession must be able to deal with this problem.

3. APPROACHES TO SECESSION

Theories of secession are typically divided into two main approaches: "primary rights" accounts and "remedial rights only" accounts. In addition to these two approaches, I shall also discuss so-called "consensual" cases of secession.[18] While I will look at these approaches in turn, and will discuss the particular problems that arise on each, I will here claim that each approach must provide a mechanism for dealing with population transfers, as these movements of people are inevitable on all accounts, given their own terms. This is so since, on each of the accounts, doing what justice requires with regard to secession or self-determination rights will be just the sort of thing that gives rise to the movement of people we are here interested in. Furthermore, this movement of people could only be prevented with further injustice, by forcing people to

dispute, but as this is both common and expected in cases of secession, his lessons are well worth attending to.

[17] For an account of who does or should fall under a definition of refugees, see my paper, "Who Are Refugees?", 32 *Law and Philosophy* 645 (2013).

[18] Allen Buchanan has done more than most to show how "consensual" secession differs from "contested" cases, where the latter group includes both primary rights and remedial rights approaches. See Buchanan, "Self-Determination, Secession, and the Rule of Law," 304, and "The Quebec Secession Issue," 240–01. As I will try to show, even in the case of "consensual" secession, the problem of population transfers inevitably arises. This issue is not addressed by Buchanan in these accounts.

remain in a state they do not wish to remain in.[19] If this is right, then any approach to secession is likely to create significant injustices. We might take this to show that secession is never or only very rarely allowed. But if these injustices that arise with population transfers can be dealt with in other ways, and the injustice removed or at least significantly ameliorated, then the theory might be saved. I shall now show how the problem arises on each account of secession, and how it might be dealt with, starting with the primary rights account.

4. PRIMARY RIGHTS ACCOUNTS OF SECESSION

The core idea of a primary rights account of secession is that secession can be justified without needing to be based on any injustice on the part of the "parent" state or society.[20] The "primary right" in question may have a number of different bases. I will focus on two main versions. One, presented by Christopher Wellman in his important book *A Theory of Secession*, bases this right on the idea of freedom of association. The other, developed by David Copp, grounds a primary right to secession in democratic principles.[21] Importantly, neither of these accounts depends on the controversial claim that a primary right to secession follows from the right of a "nation" to have its own state. Wellman's account is at least compatible with some nationalist arguments (Copp explicitly rejects the idea that nationalism is relevant for self-determination[22]), but is broader than the typical nationalist argument, and could appeal to those who reject nationalist grounds.[23] I will focus primarily

[19] I do not, of course, mean this as a necessary truth. But nearly all of our experience, and, I will argue, the logic of the theories themselves show this to be extremely likely – likely enough that any theory that hopes to be workable must be able to deal with the problem. States that largely prohibited emigration, such as the former Soviet Union and East Germany, were rightly seen as deeply unjust for having done so.

[20] Of course, injustice, real or perceived, by the parent state might motivate secessionist groups, but on the primary rights account this would merely be a matter of psychology, and not the primary moral justification for secession.

[21] See, David Copp, "Democracy and Communal Self-Determination", in McKim and McMahan, *The Morality of Nationalism*, 277–300. The democratic process is also important for Wellman, in that it is a majority vote in a territory that determines which rights of association are relevant. Christopher Heath Wellman, *A Theory of Secession* (New York: Cambridge University Press, 2005), 62. But Copp's account seems to me to place democratic virtues at the center of the argument in a way that Wellman does not. This difference will be only minimally important for what follows, so I will not dwell on it at any length.

[22] Copp, "Democracy and Communal Self-Determination," 283–90.

[23] Wellman, *A Theory of Secession*, 97–127.

on Wellman, as his view is more fully developed, but will consider Copp's alternative account when useful.

Wellman puts his view into brief form by claiming that "Any group has a moral right to secede as long as its political divorce will leave it and the remainder state in a position to perform the requisite political functions."[24] (Copp provides a similarly strong brief formulation: "Societies with a territory and a stable desire for self-government have the right to constitute themselves as states,"[25] though he develops the necessary conditions for a society constituting itself as a state somewhat differently than does Wellman.) Importantly, though Wellman's view is "statist" in that it accepts that living in a state is a necessary condition, given the world we find ourselves in, for living a good life,[26] his account is also individualistic, in that the basis of the right mentioned earlier is that, "people should be left free to be the authors of their own lives."[27]

On Wellman's account, it is wrong to prevent a group that wants to, and would be able to, form a viable state from doing so if it is able to do so without wronging others.[28] Here, however, we reach a problem that Wellman, and many others in the primary rights camp, do not squarely face. Agreement to form a new state will essentially never be unanimous. Some of the population in the secessionist area will want the status quo.[29] Why is this a particular problem here? After all, any political decision will have losers – those whose desires are not satisfied by the choice and whose interests may be set back by the decision taken. If this were just another political decision, like any other, then those who lose out would not need any special compensation, and could not claim to be wronged.[30] But, I shall claim, proponents of a primary rights view cannot see this as just another political decision. If they did, then a *statewide* choice in favor of keeping the state together, as opposed to a regional

24 Wellman, *A Theory of Secession*, 1.

25 Copp, "Democracy and Communal Self-Determination," 278.

26 Wellman, *A Theory of Secession*, 16–17.

27 Wellman, *A Theory of Secession*, 2.

28 Wellman, *A Theory of Secession*, 57.

29 Indeed, as Donald Horowitz has argued, the presence of local minority members within the secessionist region is often one of the contributing factors in motivating the secessionist desires. See Horowitz, "A Right to Secede?", in Macedo and Buchanan, *Secession and Self-Determination*, 53–54. This point is also noted by Barutciski, "Population Exchanges in International Law and Policy," 26. Horowitz here focuses on ethnic minorities, but while these have been important and salient historical cases, there is no reason to limit the consideration to such groups.

30 Importantly, I am not advancing the claim, made by some libertarians, that any setback to interest caused by changes in government policies is a wrong requiring compensation. For a view like this, see Richard Epstein, *Takings: Private Property and the Power of Eminent Domain* (Cambridge, MA: Harvard University Press, 1985).

one to break away from the parent, would not be unjust. But with this, the supposed right to self-determination would disappear.[31]

Here we note that any attempt to fix the "optimal group" for a vote on secession will be artificial. There are no "natural" groupings that tell us where the boundaries of a vote should be placed. This is a larger problem than Wellman and other primary rights proponents realize, I shall show, and sets up the case for demonstrating how, on the primary rights account's own terms, an injustice is done to the "losers" in a vote for secession. In any case we can consider, we could redraw the boundaries so that the actual losers would win. But if the boundaries are arbitrary – that is, nonnatural and not self-determining – then there is no pretheoretical case for drawing them one way or another.

Recall now that the validity of the choice by the secessionist group to break away, on a primary rights account, depends on the idea that it is an important good to be able to live in a viable state of the sort that one wants. As Wellman puts the point, "A group's members are disrespected when the group's right to self-determination is violated."[32] If this good is denied someone without very weighty reasons, then, on the primary rights account, the rights of the person in question are violated. And, importantly, on Wellman's account, it not a group as such whose rights are violated when it is prevented from forming a state of the sort it wants, but rather the individuals who make up the group.

This raises the question of which group is the proper one for the analysis. Wellman takes his lead form Charles Bietz and holds that "The people should decide who the people are."[33] David Copp takes a similar path when he holds that "Societies with a territory and a stable desire for self-government have the right to constitute a state",[34] and that a group that is not currently a state has the liberty to hold a plebiscite within the relevant territory to decide this question.[35] But neither of these approaches can work on its own; as it will essentially always be possible to find groups of "people," or "societies with a territory and a desire for self-government", that choose the unionist, rather than the secessionist, outcome, negating the secessionist claim. So, we must push further if the primary rights account is to be coherent.

31 The idea of a statewide choice to divide an existing state arises in so-called "consensual" cases of secession, but as I shall show shortly, the problem of population transfers arises again in these cases, too.

32 Wellman, *A Theory of Secession*, 57.

33 Wellman, *A Theory of Secession*, 60, citing Charles Beitz, *Political Theory and International Relations* (Princeton, NJ: Princeton University Press, 1999), 106.

34 Copp, "Democracy and Communal Self-Determination," 280.

35 Copp, "Democracy and Communal Self-Determination," 279–801.

Copp's account, I will claim, offers us no help here. Copp holds that "all and only societies that are relevantly 'territorial' and 'political' have the right to self-determination,"[36] and that "societies are groups of an appropriate kind to form states."[37] But this, especially on a primary rights account, where we are assuming that the secessionist group is not facing injustice, does not give us any reason to treat the would-be secessionist group as the relevant "society" rather than the larger, pro-unionist group. This is perhaps especially true on an account such as Copp's, which rejections nationalism and cultural ground as legitimate ways for determining the boundaries of societies.[38]

Wellman, on the other hand, does offer us a reason for picking smaller, pro-secession groups as the relevant unit, as opposed to the larger, pro-union group. But, as we shall see, this very reasoning takes us to the heart of the problem of dissent and population transfers. Wellman says that "Our goal must be to construct politically viable states that include as many separatists and as few unionists as possible."[39] Why should this be? I think it must be because, on Wellman's account, we wrong those who do not want to join the new state when we include them. The logic of the primary rights account pushes us, it seems, relentlessly towards this conclusion.

Importantly, the wrong that is done to the dissenters who are included in the new state, as there inevitably will be, is not just or primarily that their preferences are not met, or even that their interests are set back.[40] This is, I would contest, a completely typical and nonproblematic feature of any political process, at least when not motivated by unacceptable grounds.

36 Copp, "Democracy and Communal Self-Determination," 290.

37 Copp, "Democracy and Communal Self-Determination," 292.

38 Copp notes that in the case of "societies" without a territory of "their own," providing a state to the society would necessarily involve "moving populations around in order to create space for the society," and recognizes that this is, at least, problematic. Copp, "Democracy and Communal Self-Determination," 295. He seems not to notice that no "society" has exclusive control of a territory, and so this "moving populations around" is in fact the typical and expected outcome of self-determination of the sort he supports. See again Barutciski, "Population Exchanges in International Law and Policy," 28, for useful discussion on this point.

39 Wellman, *A Theory of Secession*, 59.

40 Interestingly, Buchanan suggests that it might be part of a requirement of just secession that people who suffer loss in value of private property because of secession be compensated for this. While this might sometimes be reasonable, I do not think it is plausible as a general requirement. Loss in value of private property because of changes in government policy and regulation is a perfectly normal and, I think, unproblematic occurrence, and only a few extreme libertarians, such as Epstein, think compensation is owed for this. Loss in value of private property due to secession, then, seems to me to be a mere political loss, unlike the loses I shall discuss here. See Buchanan, "Self-Determination, Secession, and the Rule of Law," 308.

Rather, here it is the very right, one taken to be particularly weighty by the primary rights theorists, that gives legitimacy to secessionist cases that is violated by incorporating dissenters into the new state against their wishes. Recall Wellman's claim that "a group's *members* [that is, the individuals, not the group itself] are disrespected [and so wronged, on this account] when the group's self-determination is violated."[41] But this is just what happens to the dissenters who are trapped in the new state. As Buchanan aptly points out, the right of a local majority to secede is the right to deprive the local minority of its citizenship, or to determine its citizenship unilaterally.[42] But this unilateral determination of the citizenship of a minority by a majority is just the wrong that the primary rights account was meant to remedy.

We should note that the new state, arguably, does not violate the right to self-determination of those who populate what remains of the parent state. But those dissenters trapped in the new state – and there always will be such – have, on the primary rights account's own terms, their right to self-determination violated. To see this, recall Wellman's claim that "a group of citizens who are able and willing to perform their requisite political functions have a right to group self-determination."[43] This, however, applies to the undivided parent state as well. Furthermore, Wellman says, it is the "political capacities of the group" which "explain why it is entitled to political self-determination."[44] But before a case of secession, the future dissenters were part of a group with this capacity – the undivided state – and afterwards they are not. It is just the secession movement that destroys the capacity in the dissenters. On Wellman's own account, this is to wrong them.

It is important to note that this sort of wronging need not involve political persecution or other similar rights violations, such as rendering the dissenters stateless.[45] This is one reason why the problem of dissent and population transfers cannot be assimilated to the problem of refugees. But the wronging that does take place is still the same sort of wronging that makes, on the

[41] Wellman, *A Theory of Secession*, 57. Emphasis is mine. Copp makes a similar statement: "It is an unjust lack of regard for a person to fail to give him or her authority over decisions that affect only his or her own life; it is similarly an unjust lack of regard to fail to give this person equal authority with other members of his or her society over political decisions regarding that society." Copp, "Democracy and Communal Self-Determination," 292. Of course, a decision by a group to secede from a state never affects just that group – it necessarily also affect the inevitable dissenters as well.

[42] Buchanan, "Self-Determination, Secession, and the Rule of Law," 315.

[43] Wellman, *A Theory of Secession*, 57. [44] Wellman, *A Theory of Secession*, 58.

[45] In actual cases of secession this is an all-to-common and predictable result, a feature that generally seems to be ignored by theorists of secession. Surely the plausible results of following a theory deserve as much consideration as do the hoped-for ones.

primary rights account, suppression of secessionist movements itself a wrong. Furthermore, we can see now that the typical solution offered to the "losers" in a secessionist movement, such as having made sure that they had "meaningful input" in the decision to secede or not, as suggested by Diane Orentlicher, cannot suffice.[46] This would be a sufficient answer only if the harm suffered by the dissenters were a typical political loss. But as we have seen, the primary rights view must deny this. Similarly, while protecting the rights of the minority dissenters in the new state is certainly required, it again cannot be sufficient on the primary rights account, as this will not remedy the wrong suffered, and, on the primary rights account, protecting minority rights would not have sufficed to make succession unacceptable in the first place, either. So, by the very logic of the primary rights account, the secessionist group will have both harmed and wronged the inevitable dissenters. It will have deprived them of an important good, and a good they had a right to.[47]

What follows from this? There is a temptation, one I am liable to, to say that this argument shows that a primary rights account of secession is inconsistent and so must be rejected. This, I think, is probably too strong. If we can show that the secessionist group can nullify the wrong to the dissenters in some way, can provide compensation to them, then this problem can be met.[48] It is here that the problem of population transfers reemerges.

Now, in most real-world situations like this, the dissenting group is either directly forced out or subjected to conditions that make members' lives difficult, if not strictly intolerable. We see this even in supposedly benign

[46] Diane F. Orentlicher, "International Responses to Separatist Claims," in Macedo and Buchanan, *Secession and Self-Determination*, 30.

[47] We can also expect further harms to follow, of course. Most secessionist movements are followed by a period of "nation building", and as Anna Stilz has nicely noted, nation building will almost always be seen as oppressive, and sometimes extremely coercive, by those who are outside the dominant group. See Stilz, *Liberal Loyalty: Freedom, Obligation, and the State* (Princeton, NJ: Princeton University Press, 2009), 143. This should not be ignored, as it often is, by theorists of secession, but it is not our main focus here.

[48] Some other discussions of secession have talked about compensation as an element of just terms of secession, but none, to my knowledge, have been addressed to the issues raised here. As noted, Buchanan has suggested that compensation to individuals for loss of property value may be required, though I have suggested reasons to doubt this. More typical are calls for compensation to the "parent" state, to repay investments in infrastructure and the like. (See, for example, Copp, "Democracy and Communal Self-Determination," 280.) But none of these accounts addresses the wrong that is done to dissenting individuals, on the primary rights account's own terms, when they are trapped in the new state. Some historical negotiated population transfers have included calls for compensation, though the exact justification for and nature of the claims was often unclear, and any compensation actually paid could not plausibly be called sufficient. See Barutciski, "Population Exchanges in International Law and Policy," 30–33.

examples of secession, such as that of the Baltic states from the Soviet Union.[49] That this is both very common and completely predictable is largely ignored by those pressing the primary rights account.[50] This is essentially completely ignored by both Wellman and Copp. The completely foreseeable result is, most often, either the involuntary, or at best semivoluntary, transfer of populations (the slow-motion ethnic cleansing of Serbs by Kosovars in Kosovo provides a typical example[51]) or else in a continuing unstable state (Moldova, with the unresolved status of Trans-Dniester, might provide an example[52]). As I will show, however, the problem is not limited to cases of forced or semiforced transfers, as predictable and typical as those are.

If the primary rights account is to be plausible as anything more than a mere classroom example, it needs to be able to deal with this sort of completely predictable problem. And it will not suffice for proponents of the primary rights account to say that they do not sanction the sort of bad acts noted here. This is so for two reasons. First, because the sort of response noted is completely predictable on a primary rights account, and a theory, if it is to be plausible, must be able to account for its predictable results.[53] Second, and

49 See, for example, David Greene, "Russian Minority Struggles in Post-Soviet Estonia," *NPR*, Aug. 23, 2010, www.npr.org/templates/story/story.php?storyId=129333023. Similar situations exist for ethnic Russians in the other Baltic States. The utterly cavalier attitude of the Estonian president is particularly worth noting.

50 This fact is noted by Donald Horowitz, but he takes it to be a strong reason against recognizing a right to secession, a conclusion I do not here want to draw. See Horowitz, "A Right to Secede?", 55–56.

51 See International Crisis Group, "Setting Kosovo Free: Remaining Challenges," Sept. 10, 2012, www.crisisgroup.org/en/regions/europe/balkans/kosovo/218-setting-kosovo-free-remaining-challenges.aspx. Of course, the Kosovo situation involved other significant injustices as well, though the crisis started with the declaration of a unilateral right to secede by the Kosovars.

52 See Will Englund, "Transnistria, the Breakaway Region of Moldova, Could Be Russia's Next Target," *Washington Post*, March 24, 2014, at www.washingtonpost.com/world/europe/transnistria-the-breakaway-region-of-moldova-could-be-russias-next-target/2014/03/24/c68c50a4-be46-4042-a192-6813e93380bc_story.html

53 In recent years a view has developed, inspired by the work of Gerald Cohen and his followers, that political philosophy need not be action-guiding, but needs only to provide an ideal. This ideal need not have any practical connection with real life. For this idea, see Cohen, *Rescuing Justice and Equality* (Cambridge, MA: Harvard University Press, 2008), 229–73. This strikes me as quite wrong in general, but as particularly implausible if we are hoping to set rules for regulating behavior. For helpful discussion on the general philosophical point, see Gerald Gaus, *The Order of Public Reason* (New York: Cambridge University Press, 2010), 176. That theories of secession, among others, should have to account for their predictable results, and not just the desired ones, is an assumption of this paper. While I do not defend this assumption here, it seems to me to be a reasonable one for anyone who wants political philosophy to be taken seriously, for if the predictable results are not considered, why should anyone care about the theory at all?

more deeply, even if these predictable bad acts are avoided, the dissenters, who are trapped in the new state, will be, as noted, wronged on the internal logic of the primary rights account. The most plausible solution, it seems, is to compensate the dissenters by providing them means to engage in a truly voluntary population transfer, if they so wish.

It may seem odd or even paradoxical that a "population transfer" may be, in one case, part of the problem, and, in another, a potential solution to the problem. But the difference here is due to the voluntary nature of the transfer in the latter case. It will usually be, at best, problematic to force someone from a territory in which she or he lawfully resides without her or his consent.[54] But providing the same person with the option of assistance in moving from one country (say, from the new country to the parent state) may be not morally problematic, but, rather, morally required, at least on the internal logic of the primary rights account. Of course, this must not be seen as an alternative to having full rights in the new state, but as an additional option made available to the dissenters, to compensate them for the wrong done to them on the primary rights account's own lights. In this way the new state may "buy out," so to speak, those who did not wish to be incorporated into the new state, and who had their rights to association and self-determination violated against their will.

What would such compensation come to? It would not necessarily be required that those who dissented from the secessionist movement get payments or compensation that would make them just as happy as they were before the political split, or that would make them indifferent to the outcome. For one thing, this might turn on idiosyncratic valuations that could not be part of the sort of right that the primary rights account was meant to protect. More importantly, at least some of the setback to interest faced by the dissenters will be of the sort that losers in any political dispute will face, and losers in a political dispute are not generally entitled to compensation merely because their interests did not prevail. What is required, by the internal logic of the primary rights account, is that the new state take steps to help any dissenters who wish to do so to relocate to the remaining part of the parent state in a way that puts them in as close to a situation as they were in before, from the perspective of the rights claimed by the primary rights account, as is possible

[54] Such actions will nearly always, perhaps always, be problematic, but sometimes might be the least bad option. As Barutciski notes, "Insisting on certain principles in times when urgent action is needed can be unprincipled if the result is inaction." Baructciski, "Population Exchanges in International Law and Policy," 26. Though it is unpleasant to consider, it is possible that significantly less life might have been lost, for example, in the break-up of the former Yugoslavia if negotiated, though perhaps not completely voluntary, population transfers had been accepted early on.

and feasible. It is beyond the scope of this paper, and my expertise, to suggest every step that might be required, but as an example, we might think that the new state would have the obligation to ensure that the departing dissenter could sell her or his residence or business at the prevailing pre-split market rate, perhaps by being a buyer of last resort. Other steps may be required as well, but these are likely to be context-dependent and beyond the power of philosophical discussion to discern.

This requirement will put some burden on what remains of the parent state as well, mostly notably an obligation to accept the dissenters back into it as full members. This seems normatively unproblematic, as the dissenters should still be seen as citizens of the old state. But it is the new state that has the primary burden to put the dissenters into something like the situation they were in before.[55] This may be very expensive, and this expense might make secession, on the primary rights account, less attractive, but it is a cost that the new state must be willing to pay, if, by the logic of the primary rights view, it wants to be justified in breaking a formerly viable state to create a new one.[56]

5. REMEDIAL RIGHTS ONLY ACCOUNTS OF SECESSION

I will now turn to "remedial rights only" accounts of secession, and show how they, too, must be able to deal with the problem of population transfers if they are to be complete and plausible. Here I shall take Allen Buchanan as my primary representative of the remedial rights view. As Buchanan presents the case, a remedial rights approach sees secession as "a remedy of last resort against sever and persistent injustice," where the injustices "must be of such

[55] Let me reiterate that this does not mean that the dissenters must be indifferent between their situation pre- and post-split, only that they are compensated for the rights violation that the primary rights account suggests they have undergone. As noted, this compensation will often, perhaps typically, take the form of facilitating a voluntary population transfer.

[56] This requirement would also go a significant way towards making other parts of Wellman's view more coherent. Recall that Wellman claimed that we should try, in any vote on secession, to craft a territory so as to include as many secessionists, and as few unionists, as possible, and also held that a bare majority in a given territory is enough to justify secession. While not strictly incompatible, these two clauses together will tend to lead to significant numbers of dissenters being included, as this will often be the way to include as many secessionists, numerically, as possible, compatible with a bare majority of secessionists. The second clause will also lead, predictably, to including desirable territories in the plebiscitary region, even if these territories have a majority of dissenters, so long as this will not lead to a majority of dissenters overall. But the need to pay compensation to dissenters would discourage would-be secessionists from casting their nets as wide as possible, even when this meant including a large number of dissenters, and also from engaging in "land-grabs" by including desirable territories, even though they would not have a local majority of dissenters.

consequence as to void international support for a state's claim to the territory in question."[57] These injustices, Buchanan contends, include at least genocide and massive violations of basic individual human rights, unjust annexation of territory, and possibly, though more controversially, the persistent violation of internal autonomy agreements.[58]

In a case of secession supported by a remedial rights account, a part of a state breaks away, not primarily to exercise a right to association or self-

[57] Allen Buchanan, *Justice, Legitimacy, and Self-Determination: Moral Foundations for International Law* (New York: Oxford University Press, 2007), 337–8.

[58] Buchanan, *Justice, Legitimacy, and Self-Determination*, 351–52. In earlier work Buchanan had suggested that "discriminatory redistribution" within a state – the transfer of wealth from one region (or perhaps social or ethnic group) to another within the state – might be a ground for remedial secession, though even then he held that there were practical worries with this. See Buchanan, "Self-Determination, Secession, and the Rule of Law," 310–13. My purpose here is not to evaluate supposed grounds for justifying a remedial right to secession, though I will note, briefly, that it does not seem likely to me that any but the most extreme examples of "discriminatory redistribution" would plausibly "void international support for a state's claim to the territory in question." Mississippi, after all, is a persistent net importer of wealth and benefits from the rest of the states in the United States, a problem largely guaranteed by the U.S. constitution's system for representation, but this would not, I would think, justify the rest of the United States "seceding" from Mississippi. Violations of internal autonomy agreements, at least without other significant violations of civil or human rights, also seem at least a problematic ground. This is so because the justification for such agreements may deteriorate over time, leading to cases where the maintaining of such agreements leads to more injustice than their removal. Similarly, such agreements are often no more than one way of coming to a political settlement within a state, and as such might not be required by justice in themselves. To suggest that such agreements must be maintained, even in the face of changed circumstances, seems to me unjustified, and for "outsiders" to attempt to adjudicate these disputes, at least so long as there are not major human rights violations, would itself be a major violation of the right to self-determination. Outside adjudication, absent consent to a court to do so, would also be an illegitimate use of force. On this point, see my paper, "The Legitimating Role of Consent in International Law," 11 *Chicago Journal of International Law* 663 (2011). Finally, even the "unjust annexation" ground seems to me more problematic than Buchanan suggests. Buchanan's primary example is the annexation of the Baltic States by the Soviet Union. While not completely implausible, I will contend that this is also not as clear an instance as is suggested. The Soviet Union "annexed" the Baltic states in 1939, but they had been independent only for twenty-two years, and that only due to a peace treaty forced on the Soviet Union by an occupying (German) army intent on reducing Russian territory. This independence resulted in the expulsion of a large number of Russians who had been living in the Baltics before World War I. These Russians were living in the future Baltic states because it was at the time part of the Russian empire. Estonia had been part of the Russian Empire since the sixteenth century, and Latvia and Lithuania since the seventeenth. The inclusion of the Baltics in the Russian empire was the result of many wars over centuries, in some of which the Baltic States, particularly Lithuania, and their allies were the aggressors. How to adjudicate these matters is not clear to me. But it is clear to me that the "unjust annexation" clause will often be significantly less straightforward in application and adjudication than Buchanan's account suggestions. I shall, however, largely leave these issues aside for the rest of the paper.

determination, but to prevent serious wrongdoing against the population. This seems easy to justify, but again, in real life, these cases too almost always give rise to population transfers that are themselves straightforwardly unjust. (If we take Kosovo's secession from Serbia as an instance justified by a remedial rights account, then the subsequent ethnic cleansing of Serbs by Kosovars would be a clear example.) Or these population transfers may be due to unjust programs enacted against the residual population of the new state. (If, following Buchanan, and despite my misgivings, we treat the secession of, say, Estonia from the Soviet Union as a case justified by the remedial rights approach, then the subsequent unjust, but perfectly expectable, treatment of the remaining ethnic Russian population would be a clear example.)

However, even if we do not have cases of "backlash" injustice such as these, we are still left with the problem faced in the primary rights case, of a significant population of "dissenters", many of whom may be morally blameless in the events justifying the secession on remedial rights grounds, trapped in the new state. Now, per hypothesis, on a remedial rights account, there is no claim here of a primary right to live in association with others based on mutual consent, as there is on the primary rights account. So the new state, on the remedial rights account, has not harmed or wronged those trapped in the new state, at least not in the particular way postulated by the primary rights account, assuming that the new state meets all of its moral and political obligations. This would be rare if it ever actually happens in the sort of cases that give rise to secession justified by a remedial rights account, but we shall assume this qualification is met for now. Then, on the remedial rights account, the new state owes no special compensation to those "trapped" in the new state. But those so trapped may still want to leave, have good reason to want to do so, and be disadvantaged by the need to do so. The cause of this need to leave, however, is the bad acts of the parent state. So, here, it is the parent state that has the obligation to make the move easy, both by granting admission and by paying compensation for those relocating. (We may note that, in real-world cases, many parent states in this situation do not want the "trapped" population to relocated, often for nakedly political reasons. The example of Russian populations in Ukraine – all too prominent recently – and Moldova are examples of this phenomenon, even though the secessions of Ukraine and Moldova from the Soviet Union were not plausibly remedial rights cases. This, however, is itself both a mistake and an injustice on the part of the parent, so we will condemn it and move on.)

What of cases where the new state in turn engages in bad acts? This is the more common scenario in real life, it seems, so it is worth considering to a greater degree than have most theorists of self-determination. Of course, the first obligation in such cases is for the new state to stop committing the bad acts. But suppose the bad acts have already been committed, and the remaining group of dissenters can no longer feel safe in the new state. Who owes what then? We here face difficult questions of casuistry that I cannot hope to fully answer, both because of space considerations in this paper and also because there may not be any useful general answers. But, in such instances, I will contend that both states owe some degree of compensation. The original, parent state does, both for the reason noted earlier and because its original bad acts were the proximate cause of the new bad acts. But the new state also owes compensation, since it had no right to drive out or persecute the remaining population of dissenters, and so must compensate them for making life in the new state unacceptable. This may be done by helping them, if they so wish, to move to the parent state. That is, the compensation may be paid by facilitating a voluntary population transfer.

6. CONSENSUAL SECESSION

The last form of justification for secession that I will address is consensual (sometimes also called or characterized as "constitutional") secession. As noted, Allen Buchanan has done as much or more than anyone else to distinguish consensual/constitutional secession from "contested" cases, where the latter group would include secession sanctioned by both primary rights and remedial rights only accounts, so long as they were undertaken unilaterally. Consensual cases of secession, Buchanan notes, may either be negotiated or take place by means of a constitutional clause.[59] Such cases of secession are unproblematic, Buchanan contends, so long as "both parties" consent, and there are not violations of "individual or minority rights" during or after the process.[60] On its face, this seems completely plausible. In real life, again, issues are often much less clear, since it is unclear, both in morality and as a matter of international law, who the relevant "parties" are and how they must or may make this decision. In many well-known cases of supposedly "consensual" secession or disunion, such as the split between the Czech Republic and Slovakia and the dissolution of the Soviet Union, the decision to split the country was made by political elites, arguably for their own benefit, and without the input, and quite possibly without the support, of the local

[59] Buchanan, *Justice, Legitimacy, and Self-Determination*, 338.
[60] Buchanan, *Justice, Legitimacy, and Self-Determination*, 304.

population. Whether such cases can properly be called "consensual" is at least unclear, though I shall largely leave this particular issue aside.

The deeper issue with respect to even cases of consensual secession undertaken in legitimate democratic form is that it, too, allows for people who do not agree with the majority to have their citizenship changed without their consent. Just as we would not think it acceptable for a majority in a state to decide, even by democratic vote, to take away the citizenship of a minority, and this even if a new citizenship would be given to the minority by another state, we ought not be satisfied with a procedure that allows majorities to change the citizenship of dissenters against their wishes. (Imagine that Spain wanted to reacquire Florida, and that the rest of the United States, perhaps tired of paying to rebuild after hurricanes and looking to cut Medicare costs, decided to give Florida to Spain. I contend that even if everyone in Spain, and everyone in the United States outside of Florida, consented to this via a democratic vote, it would still be unjust to current Floridians to transform them into Spaniards if they, each one, did not consent to this. But this is a close parallel to what happens to dissenters, even in the case of consensual secession. In both cases the citizenship of the dissenters is unilaterally changed by a majority in a way that seems problematic, at best.) Something has gone wrong, or has been ignored, in discussions of consensual secession, it seems.

As with the general primary rights account, we could take this to show that the idea of consensual secession is incoherent, absent the agreement of every single person affected, and so must be dropped. But again, that seems too quick and extreme. The possibility of providing compensation that allows for voluntary population transfers between the two resulting states can arguably solve the most troubling issues that result from consensual secession. As with unilateral primary rights cases of secession, the purpose of providing this compensation is not to make the dissenters indifferent between the pre- and post-secession state. Certain of their losses will, again, be "merely political" – the sort of losses we expect losers in any democratic system to put up with. Rather the point and goal of this compensation is to help the dissenters avoid the particular wrong of having their citizenship changed against their will, by helping them move, if they so desire, to one of the other states. The first thing that will be required here is that each citizen, regardless of where she or he lives after the split, must have the right to retain citizenship in either country. Now, if either country does not wish to extend dual citizenship to those living in it (a situation that seems to me likely), then any person who ends up living in the "wrong" country will be owed compensation sufficient to make movement to the "correct" country relatively easy. This is not based on a right to association, as in the primary rights account, but rather on the principle that a state may not unilaterally change the citizenship of its members without their actual, individual, consent.[61]

Here, unlike unilateral primary rights cases, both sides are likely to have to provide compensation to a significant number of dissenters. (Note how this differs from unilateral cases. If Quebec unilaterally decided to withdraw from Canada, some francophone Canadians living outside of Quebec would likely want to leave the remaining part of Canada for Quebec, but I would see no reason for the remaining part of Canada to have any obligation to pay compensation in such a case, as Canada would have not changed anyone's citizenship without her or his consent.) We see here, then, that even consensual or constitutional approaches to secession must be able to deal with the problem of dissent and population transfers if they are to be complete and plausible.

7. CONCLUSION

The desire for secession is never unanimous in any territory. In any case, there will be a dissenting population. This problem is obvious, and yet has been largely ignored in the philosophical or normative literature on secession and self-determination, except for calling for the protection of minority rights. Since the protection of minority rights is an obligation every state has anyway, it is clear that no real effort has been put into dealing with the problem of dissenters. Given the real-world results of this situation – quite often major human rights violations, but essentially always significant wronging of many people – this omission is unacceptable. In this paper I have tried to take a first step towards addressing this problem, by looking at the problem of population transfers, to see how, and if, it may be transformed from a serious wrong to a means of overcoming wrongdoing, while still accepting that some cases of secession are acceptable and very likely. While, I think, unilateral primary rights approaches to secession have the most obvious and far-reaching

[61] That a state may not render citizens *stateless* is set out in the UN Convention on the Reduction of Statelessness (see https://treaties.un.org/pages/ViewDetails.aspx?src=TREATY&mtdsg_no=V-4&chapter=5&lang=en). While many important countries, including the United States, are not participants to the treaty, the principles set out therein seem to me to be impeccable. The case in question would not render former citizens stateless, but that even the involuntary denaturalization of current citizens against their will when they have access to other citizenships is incompatible with due process and the equal protection of the law has been long recognized by the U.S. Supreme Court, among others. See, e.g., *Afroyim v. Rusk*, 387 U.S. 253 (1967). For discussion of this point, see my paper, "Citizenship, in the Immigration Context," 70 *Maryland Law Review* 175, 226–29 (2010). My thanks to Larry May for pointing out the need to say more on this point.

problems to overcome here, I have tried to show that similar issues arise in any approach to secession, including remedial rights only and consensual approaches. Importantly, in all three cases, the problem arises from the internal logic of the theory of secession itself, and not because of any "outside" considerations. I do not claim to have given a comprehensive theory, and perhaps there are other ways of addressing these serious wrongs accompanying all instances of secession. But I hope that from this point it will be clear that any serious theory of secession and self-determination, if it hopes to be close to comprehensive, and if we are to judge its plausibility, will have to address the status of dissenters and the problem of population transfers.[62]

[62] My thanks to Fernando Tesón and Michael Blake for helpful discussion at the conference where this paper was first presented, to Martin J. De Nys, for insightful comments at faculty workshop on this paper at the Higher School of Economics in Moscow, Russia, and to Gerald Vildostegui and Larry May for very helpful and insightful written comments on an earlier draft.

8

Civil Disobedience, Dirty Hands, and Secession

MICHAEL BLAKE

> [T]he task which the Court is called upon to perform is to determine whether or not the declaration of independence [by Kosovo] was adopted in violation of international law. The Court is not required by the question it has been asked to take a position on whether or not international law generally conferred a positive entitlement on Kosovo unilaterally to declare its independence, or, *a fortiori*, on whether international law generally confers an entitlement on entities situated within a State unilaterally to break away from it. Indeed, it is entirely possible for a particular act – such as a unilateral declaration of independence – not to be in violation of international law without necessarily constituting the exercise of a right conferred by it.
>
> Accordance with International Law of the Unilateral Declaration of Independence in Respect of Kosovo, Advisory Opinion, I.C.J. Reports 2010, p. 403, at 425–26.

Most philosophical discussions of secession begin with the idea of a right to secede.[1] This right is understood as a sort of claim right: a group with the right to secede has the moral right to withdraw from a given political community – and that political community has the moral duty to permit this departure. If the group has no such right, in contrast, the political community in question has no obligation to let them go. We are thus asking, in many of our discussions, about when a group is possessed of this sort of claim-right against an existing political society.

These discussions are important. They are not, however, the only sorts of moral discussions we might have about secession. In particular, I want to explore cases in which the moral story we tell might be more complex.

[1] See, most famously, Alan Buchanan's distinction between primary right and remedial theories of secession; both sorts of theories represent answers to the question of when groups have a right to secede. See Buchanan, *Secession: The Morality of Political Divorce from Fort Sumner to Lithuania and Quebec* (Boulder, CO: Westview, 1991).

I believe it is possible that there can be some cases in which a secessionist group has moral permission to announce that it will no longer consider itself a part of the larger political community, and to act against the efforts of that community to maintain itself – even while that community has a moral permission to act to keep its territory and jurisdiction intact.[2] I want to examine when this set of circumstances might exist, and how we ought to react to the potential existence of such cases.

There are some advantages to extending our moral analyses to examine this sort of case. The first one is, I believe, that it reflects the true moral complexity such cases often involve. While some cases of secession involve a clear judgment that the secessionist party is (or is not) possessed of a moral claim-right to leave, others do not. Such complex cases may involve moral analyses that require more nuanced form of judgments than the conventional approaches allow. The moral complexity of these cases, moreover, may also involve the complex moral stories we may have to tell about those who *act* so as to secure that secession. If I am right about what I say here, those who act for secession sometimes engage in actions that are permitted, but morally risky – whose performance might be thought to tarnish the souls of those who perform them. If there is a place in our moral universe for the concept of dirty hands, it may be here, in the cases of those who work for the dismemberment of political societies. Those who secede may be morally akin to those who break valid moral norms, in the name of making the world a more just place: they deserve neither simple condemnation nor wholehearted approval.

The second advantage of this method is to explain, at least in part, the somewhat mystifying decision of the International Court of Justice in the case of the declaration of independence by Kosovo.[3] Rather than addressing what many felt would be the key moral question – did Kosovo have a right, under international law, to be independent? – the Court focused instead on the more narrow question of whether or not making a secessionist *declaration* was itself contrary to international law. This modesty has sometimes been thought to represent institutional cowardice. If I am right, however, it might reflect something more noble: a recognition that the question of the *right* to secede is not the only moral question we ought to ask – and that assimilating all

[2] I am here speaking only of the morality of working to dismember (or maintain) the existing political community; I am not simultaneously speaking of the morality of all the potential means one might use to achieve these aims. The question of violent means, notably, is a separate issue, which requires a separate theory to be fully addressed.

[3] See the note entitled "Recent International Advisory Opinion," 124 *Harv. L. Rev.* 1098 (2011) 1098, criticizing the Court for sidestepping the most important issue, while focusing on "technical" issues.

questions to this blunt question of rights is likely to reduce the quality of the moral and political discussions we ought to have. I do not, of course, claim that this was in fact the Court's motive. I do, however, think that the modesty of this decision is worth celebrating, rather than lamenting. By deciding that the Kosovo declaration was not itself illegal, the Court left open the possibility that the best moral story we tell about Kosovo is one that is nuanced: one in which neither side has a right that the other side abandon their efforts. There are times in which the best thing a court can say, after all, is very little; while we prize clarity and bright-line standards, we do not want that clarity to obscure the moral complexity of our social and legal world.[4]

1. SECESSIONIST DECLARATIONS AND THE RULE OF RECOGNITION

Discussions of secession often begin with an analogy between secession and divorce.[5] I think there are serious difficulties with this way of understanding the moral questions involved in secession. The notion of divorce implies that there were, and are, two parties in a relationship, and that the questions that must be asked – for marriages and for societies – is whether these two identifiable agents will continue their association. (Even the best marriages, after all, leave the two individuals involved identifiable as persons.) Secession seems to be different; the seceding entity might not even exist *as* an entity prior to the events giving rise to the secessionist movement. We can imagine, perhaps, that the secessionist entity is created out of wholesale oppression by the central government – but that the target of this oppression did not understand itself as a unified group prior to the oppressive policy. To analogize secession to divorce is to overlook a variety of complexities in the ways in which individuals and societies are distinct from one another. Even the term "self-determination" seems to be somewhat presumptuous here; self-determination tends to assume that there is a known self that exists prior to the secessionist declaration, and that the question we face is whether or not

[4] Fernando Tesón has suggested to me that this may make the Court's action akin to a suggestion that warfare is the rightful means by which the competing claims here might be adjudicated. I think this is a possible worrying outcome of a refusal to judge; it is also worth noting, though, that not all confusing moral questions need to involve the use of force. If the Court is best read as showing a genuine moral sensitivity to the multifaceted nature of the moral claims here, then it might be understood as endorsing a more complex negotiation, rather than simply violence. The use of violence, moreover, would not have been precluded even by a clear decision in favor of a single party; clarity in international law is rarely enough to prevent the use of state violence abroad. I am grateful to Téson for his comments on this point.

[5] See Alan Buchanan, *Secession*; see also Christopher Heath Wellman, *A Theory of Secession: The Case for Political Self-Determination* (Cambridge: Cambridge University Press, 2005).

that self shall be free. All of this tends to prejudge the issue of whether, or when, a distinct society within some other society might be thought to exist.

In face of these issues, I think we might start our present discussion by looking at secessionist declarations through a distinct lens: that of lawbreaking. I should note, to begin with, that this does not cover all cases of secession; a negotiated end to a federal state – such as the dissolution of Czechoslovakia – might be undertaken without any lawbreaking of any kind. But the unilateral declaration by a federal subunit that it is henceforth its own sovereign state does seem to constitute, on the account I give here, a form of lawbreaking. What it announces, in sum, is that the most basic legal norm of all – the norm identifying what shall *count* as a legal norm – will henceforth be altered within a particular territorial jurisdiction. The secessionist declaration, in other words, announces a program of disobedience toward what H. L. A. Hart calls the rule of recognition – the rule identifying norms as obligatory within the legal system of a particular jurisdiction.[6] When a secessionist agent makes a declaration of independence, it does so in a context in which the disobedience announced is one that goes to the heart of what makes something legally obligatory; the secessionist announces that, henceforth, the norms we follow shall not be the norms we have followed. Disputes will be settled, and agreements made, within an alternative set of norms and practices. If this is a declaration made against the wishes of those agents identified as authoritative under the current rule of recognition – which it will, in practice, generally be – then the declaration is a form of announcement of disobedience. It announces that disobedience shall be forthcoming, as the new legal norms are brought into place to replace the old. It might, indeed, *constitute* a form of lawbreaking, insofar as it is itself a form of perlocutionary act intended to constitute a revocation and replacement of the rule of recognition.[7] The speaking of words sometimes creates a legal reality, and it might do so here in a manner that counts as a violation of the most basic legal norm of all.

If all this is right, though, then we might begin our analysis of the morality of secessionist declarations with an analysis of the morality of principled

[6] H.L.A. Hart, *The Concept of Law* (Oxford: Clarendon Press, 1961.)

[7] On the notion of a perlocutionary act, see J.L. Austin, *How to Do Things with Words* (Oxford: Oxford University Press, 1962.) It is important to note that for my analysis here to work, the secessionist declaration must actually be susceptible of causing some effects; merely mouthing the words "I hereby secede" does not constitute lawbreaking, on this account, if they are largely ignored or simply taken as rhetorical excess. The perlocutionary account I give here begins with the analysis of those secessionist declarations that are capable of actually beginning an alternative project of legal community, and so are able and likely to attract adherents. I am grateful to Alan Patten for urging me to be more precise here.

lawbreaking.[8] We might therefore ask whether or not we can gain any critical purchase on the morality of secessionist movements by seeking to understand when it is possible for us to justify lawbreaking more generally. I am most interested here in discussing secession from those societies which have not violated human rights in a manner that might justify secession as a claim-right. I assume that secession from such societies, however legally controversial, is morally defensible; we have little reason to think that the tyrant has any legal right to continue tyrannizing. I will therefore have to focus in particular on societies that are capable of imposing a duty of obedience upon their inhabitants. A society that is not capable of imposing such a duty upon its inhabitants, after all, renders the discussion of disobedience somewhat irrelevant; lawbreaking in general is permissible, since there is no obligation to obey the law in the first place. (We might, of course, have an obligation to do what the law commanded – but this obligation would not be found in the fact *that* the law so commanded.) The question thus becomes interesting only in the context in which a society is capable of imposing binding legal norms in such a way that we have a general obligation of obedience towards these norms. John Rawls gives an analysis in his *The Law of Peoples* that argues that a variety of well-ordered societies – both liberal peoples and certain forms of illiberal societies – can be understood as capable of imposing such duties.[9] For my part, I will take no stand as to how large or small the set of such duty-imposing societies might be. (I will emphatically *not* be assuming that Serbia is a member of that set; it might well be true that Serbia exercised its authority in such a way that the inhabitants of Kosovo had no duties to obey the law to begin with.) I will, instead, assume that the question we are asking is one that is pressed against a well-ordered society, in which these legal obligations do in fact exist. If there is such an obligation, then, can we simply say that secessionist declarations – understood now as disobedience toward laws that generate such duties of obedience – are always morally impermissible?

The answer, I think, is no; there will be – or, perhaps, there *might* be – cases in which secessionist declarations are morally permissible even when pressed against well-ordered societies. This might be, at first blush, confusing; we are obligated to obey the legal norms of well-ordered societies, and the secessionist

[8] This is not a thought that is original to me. For analyses that begin with secession as closely related to civil disobedience, see Lee Seshagiri, "Democratic Disobedience: Reconceiving Self-Determination and Secession at International Law," 51 *Harv. Int'l L. J.* 553 (2010); and J. Angelo Corlett, "The Right to Civil Disobedience and the Right to Secede," *Southern Journal of Philosophy* 30(1) (1992).

[9] Rawls borrows heavily from the analysis of Philip Soper on this point. See John Rawls, *The Law of Peoples* (Cambridge, MA: Harvard University Press, 1999).

here does precisely the opposite. She attacks the most basic legal norm, and insists that she (and those for whom she speaks) will henceforth refuse to obey those commands that are grounded in that norm. What possible rationale could there be for such disobedience?

The rationale, of course, issues from the idea that different forms of lawbreaking have different moral characters; some forms of lawbreaking might, in fact, be morally defensible, if they are grounded in a due sense of what law might *become*. The history of civil disobedience is, of course, a testament to these possibilities. I am interested, here, in discussing only nonrevolutionary civil disobedience – the civil disobedience of Martin Luther King, Jr., rather than that of Mahatma Gandhi.[10] Gandhi, after all, was dealing with the colonial rule of the British Raj, and his actions could be justified with reference to the impossibility of justice emerging from that colonial relationship. His disobedience has similarities in aim to the secessionist declarations we are considering – Gandhi's disobedience was intended to bring about a change in the legal norms holding sway over India. Gandhi's argument, though, was with a government he felt (rightly) had no legitimate right to expect obedience. King, in contrast, believed fervently that the Constitution and the government it had created were worthy of allegiance, and that the laws promulgated by that government were obligatory. (Whether he was right about that, of course, is a separate question.) King's analysis thus seems a good starting point from which to examine the issue of secession from well-ordered societies. We should therefore inquire about the moral account given by King, and those who followed him, in justifying disobedience even against well-ordered societies. What stories can we tell about the moral character of such disobedient acts?

2. CIVIL DISOBEDIENCE AND SECESSIONIST DISOBEDIENCE

King's account of civil disobedience has proven to be enormously influential, both in practice and in philosophy.[11] I will here extract only a few aspects of this account, which I believe will be sufficient to motivate the idea that there

[10] Gandhi's form of civil disobedience was revolutionary in character, in that it sought to displace British authority and replace it with indigenous Indian government. See, on this, Rex Martin, "Civil Disobedience," *Ethics* 80(2) (1970), 123–39.

[11] King's account is found most explicitly in his "Letter from the Birmingham Jail," available at www.thekingcenter.org/archive/document/letter-birmingham-city-jail-0. This account influenced, among others, John Rawls, who adapts it for his discussion of civil disobedience in *A Theory of Justice*. See John Rawls, *A Theory of Justice*, rev. ed. (Cambridge, MA: Belknap Press, 1999), 319–43.

can be justifiable forms of disobedient action against the laws of well-ordered societies. I will focus on three aspects of this account in particular – the idea that justifiable disobedience must be *conscientious*, must be *open*, and must eventually be *punished*.

We can begin by looking at the idea that lawbreaking must be conscientious. King himself believed that justified disobedience must be undertaken for the right reasons, and indeed must be done with the right motivations in the heart of the agent. We might think that this is an overly demanding ideal; most of us accept that those who act in politics, even those who act rightly, do so from a variety of competing impulses. The core of the ideal, though, seems right; the justifiable disobedient acts for reasons of conscience, with the intention of bringing about some morally necessary change in the world. This means that disobedience is justifiable as a response to *injustice*.[12] The disobedient cannot simply disobey because disobedience is convenient; to disobey laws that are burdensome or annoying is to announce that there is no duty of obedience. King and those who followed him are neither skeptics nor anarchists. Disobedience is possible as a response to significant injustice, and then only when the ordinary channels of political discourse have failed.

We might, of course, wonder whether or not the existence of this sort of injustice is possible, in a society capable of imposing duties of obligation on its citizens. It might, that is, seem that where such injustice exists, we find the right to disobey generally – rather than the limited right King asserts. This view, though, is unduly dismissive of the sorts of injustice that can exist in even the most justified political communities. These communities, after all, are made up of people, and people are limited in their powers of empathy and of judgment. It is possible, then, for a community to have the most ideally justified sorts of political rule and institution, and still simply get many things wrong, perhaps horribly so. If this is a live possibility, though, then it seems possible that a community can produce many norms or rules that are unjust, without thereby losing the right to understand itself as a well-ordered society. King, at least, believes that this is a good description of the American political community in which he found himself; while the United States of 1963 was unjust in its political and social norms – sometimes grotesquely so – it did not thereby lose

[12] Fernando Tesón has suggested that a significant injustice might be enough to justify secession; I agree with him on this point, but want to hold out the possibility of an imperfectly just state whose imperfections might be alleviated through secession. States that are simply malign are states from which secession seems morally rightful, and perfect states seem to be ones from which secession is simply wrongful; I am interested in the states falling in the messy world between these extremes.

the right to have its laws obeyed. As such, disobedience must take the conscientious form King defended; we could not simply choose which laws to obey.

The second aspect of justified disobedience I want to discuss is the idea that lawbreaking must be *open*. If the goal of disobedience is to call attention to the injustice, so as to prompt a discussion about the failures of deliberation that have produced that injustice, then the disobedience cannot be hidden. King's vision entails the public presentation of disobedience, with the intention that the society in question use its legal and political institutions to respond to that disobedience. The idea, of course, is to create deliberation where deliberation has failed; as such, the disobedience itself must be presented as a move within a deliberative chain, calling attention to what has not been said in previous discussions, and creating in itself a topic for further discussion. Part of this, of course, is that the deliberation must be peaceful. This is justified, perhaps, in part because of the prudential benefits of peaceful disobedience; King's civil disobedience was likely more effective than the more radical solutions of (among others) the Nation of Islam. The justification, though, is moral as well as prudential. King's argument demands that those who disobey a law do not regard that law as a nullity. Instead, they disobey it publically and peacefully, so as to prompt new discussions with those who brought that law into being. Violence is, on this account, prohibited – not because there can never be justified violence, but because the very goal of disobedience precludes such violence. If the justification of disobedience is the creation of more egalitarian form of political deliberation, then it cannot be violent. Violence is, after all, very much like the opposite of respectful dialogue; respecting others, and the institutions and laws they have made, often begins with respecting their right to be free from physical attack.

The last aspect of civil disobedience I will discuss here is its insistence on the acceptance of punishment. This has proven to be more controversial than some other parts of King's account.[13] King does, though, have a very strong moral case to make; those who break a law attack both the law itself and the authority of the political community to make that law. They do, through their action, make the law less law-like than it would otherwise be. In accepting their punishment, they act so as to reinforce the right of the political community to be regarded as authoritative. We may look at the law as a series of

[13] Ronald Dworkin, for example, argues that King overemphasized the importance of punishment; we have reason, on Dworkin's argument, to think that those who engage in civil disobedience should not in fact be punished, whether or not they take themselves to be rightly subject to that punishment. See Dworkin, "On Not Prosecuting Civil Disobedience," *The New York Review of Books*, June 6, 1968.

conditionals, if we like: do not do this thing, or bad consequences shall follow. Ideally, the law and those who make it would like us to avoid doing those things the law prohibits. But those who do those things *and* receive punishment at least affirm the truth of the conditional. They do, in their acceptance of punishment, acknowledge that the law's demands on us are demands that persist, and that the law has the right to make. Those who both do the forbidden thing and escape without punishment undermine the law itself. King's argument here acknowledges that those who disobey the laws of a well-ordered society are obliged to do whatever they can to make that well-ordered society persist, and continue to think itself as able to make authoritative commands as before. The act of being punished, then, is morally significant; it acknowledges that the well-ordered society has a right to be protected from disobedience. Those who disobey openly and accept punishment thereby acknowledge that the laws of a well-ordered society – even the imperfect ones – emerge from a set of institutions we are morally bound to respect. Those who disobey and are not punished demonstrate, on this account, disrespect for those institutions; we cannot simultaneously respect these institutions and work against their continued existence as authoritative.

None of this is especially novel. I want, though, to apply these ideas in the somewhat novel context of a secessionist declaration. The question to be asked, now, is whether or not these ideas – or ideas similar to them – might be sufficient to generate a permission to engage in secessionist activity against a well-ordered society. If there is such a permission, I believe it would have to emerge from ideas like these; the well-ordered society, after all, has a right to have its norms and institutions regarded as authoritative, and as such any disobedience against those norms will have to be justified in the face of such rights. Can we, then, use the ideas we see here to justify secessionist declarations?

The first two of the aspects discussed earlier seem, on first blush, to be applicable to the discussion of secession. Secessionist declarations, after all, can emerge from a conscientious decision that the policies or practices of a government are significantly unjust – so much so that some alternative set of institutions ought to exist within a particular territory. If we are capable of being deceived or self-interested in our reasoning on this score, well, we are similarly capable in every context, including that of civil disobedience. The idea that the secession can be done in a peaceful and open manner seems similarly possible. It is, of course, difficult to say that secession can be done in a manner that does not create a risk of violence; the secessionist should expect that her or his declaration may be met with the possibility of force. We might think that this is, again, distinct from the context of civil disobedience, and so it is – but in degree, not in kind; both the civil disobedient and the secessionist are likely to prompt a response from political leaders, and historically speaking this response has tended to be violent. The purposes of the secessionist and of the disobedient are distinct, of course, as we will discuss shortly; their character as violent or peaceful seems to be equivalent. If the civil disobedient is able to describe her acts as peaceful, even though they may prompt the violence of others, then the secessionist is similarly empowered.

On these two scores, then, it seems as if the tests we have developed for civil disobedience might be able to be used to justify the issuance of a secessionist declaration. The final aspect of civil disobedience, though, seems to pose considerable difficulties. The civil disobedient wants to initiate a discussion, and to thereby improve the quality of democratic deliberation within her society. She thus accepts punishment, so as to demonstrate her continued allegiance to that society and its institutions. The secessionist wants to end that discussion; she wants to replace the democratic deliberations that occur within that society with an alternative set of deliberations within a more limited territorial jurisdiction.[14] She does not, in this, accept the moral necessity of punishment; the goal of her project is the elimination of the punishing agent's authority, within a particular area, to engage in actions such as punishment. If the secessionist is successful, she will have dislodged the ability of that political community's right to punish her. Her action dislodges the right of that state to punish her; if she fails, she will perhaps be punished, but that punishment is not a part of the story she tells explaining the legitimacy of her action. Far from accepting her punishment, she will try very hard to avoid it; even the most conscientious and principled secessionist is working to make the world a place within which the existing state has no right to punish people such as her.

We might, then, decide that the ideas we have developed in the context of civil disobedience are simply inappropriate for the discussion of secessionist declarations. I think this conclusion is too hasty. We might, from the three aspects discussed earlier, derive a more general moral story about when we have a permission to violate existing duties – including the duty to obey the law. This story would ground the account given of civil disobedience, but it

[14] Ronald Dworkin regards civil disobedience aimed at creating discourse as more justifiable than civil disobedience that does not do so. This distinction might be more appropriate within an ongoing political community, where simply raising the costs for those with whom one disagrees might be disrespectful, and therefore less justifiable, than disobedience intended to create debate. We should not infer, though, that this reaction entails that civil disobedience not intended to create debate is always unjustifiable – nor that secessionist declarations are similarly impermissible. See Dworkin, "On Not Punishing Civil Disobedience."

would be more general than it. Let us suppose, then, that the broader reason we have to accept some sorts of civil disobedience amounts to something like the following: *we have a limited permission to violate the commands of a government whose commands are morally binding upon us when that violation would effectively lead to more just governance.* That account, or something like it, would seem to cover the case of civil disobedience as described earlier; the disobedient has a limited permission to break the laws of a well-ordered society, and obtains this permission because her disobedience is directed toward making that society's rules more just. I think something like this principle might also undergird a practice of secessionist declarations. The secessionist declaration, on this account, is a response to an ongoing injustice within a territorial jurisdiction; it is intended to make government more just – in this case, by making some other set of governing institutions hold power within a particular jurisdiction. Not all secessionist demands will meet these tests; some secessionists, after all, do not care about making the government more just – they simply want a different government, one in which they are in charge. These sorts of secessionists will not find any comfort from what I say here. For the secessionist declaration to be morally justifiable, it has to meet the demands imposed by this sort of principle. Even if a government has a right to expect obedience to its commands, we might obtain the right to disobey when doing so is likely to make the world a more close approximation of what justice would demand.

I believe that something like this might make the making of a secessionist declaration morally permissible. There are, of course, several immediate things to note here. I want here to focus only on three. The first is that the principle is radically incomplete. We do not know the limits of the permission to seek secession from a well-ordered society; we do not have a general theory of justice sufficient to tell us when a particular secessionist action is permitted. We do, further, face the prospect of somewhat perverse incentives; malign political actors might have some incentive, on my account, to cite moral principles in the name of their secessionist adventures. I cannot here rectify these shortcomings. If the theory I offer is plausible, though, we can now identify these questions as the ones a secessionist will have to answer: the secessionist, to justify her claim, will have to show why a given ongoing practice is unjust, and how her action is likely to lead to better results. The second thing to note is that there is a strong note here of practical reasoning; secessionism is permitted when – and only when – it is in fact likely to better results. This means that there is no right to engage in disobedience that is not, in fact, likely to lead to good results – good, I mean, from the standpoint of justice itself. While this is doubtless controversial, I believe this is morally justifiable, both for civil disobedience and for secession. If the government is able to impose duties of obligation on us, we are only able to violate those duties when we can show why disobedience is in fact likely to make the world less unjust. King's disobedience was justified because the dialogue it created was in fact one that was likely to lead to substantive improvements in the social and legal rights of African Americans. If disobedience does not have an adequate likelihood of leading to such an improvement, I believe we will find it difficult to make the case that the disobedience is itself legitimate. If we believe that the state imposes valid duties of obligation on us, it seems hard to imagine that we can violate those duties simply to make a gesture, when that gesture is likely to make no practical difference.[15] Similar considerations seem to hold true in the area of secession. We are permitted to engage in action contrary to our legal duties of obligation, but only when doing so is likely to lead to a world in which justice is more closely approximated than it is in the status quo. Again, here, I am not talking about the right to secede from an abusive or malign state; secession from such states may in fact make the world more just, but the right to secede from them proceeds from the fact that their inhabitants have no duties to obey them. I am speaking of secession from well-ordered states, capable of imposing a general obligation of obedience upon their citizens. To act contrary to that obligation may sometimes be permissible, but only when the disobedience is likely to make the world itself more just.

The last thing I want to note about the principle, though, is what it does not say: it does not say that the state in question does not have a right to expect obedience, nor that the duty to obey the law should be regarded as suspended or eliminated in cases of permissible disobedience. King's disobedience, after all, insisted that the law continues to have authority over us, and we are obligated to pay our respects to that law through the practice of punishment. The pull of law continues even during the practice of lawbreaking. This seems true in the case of secessionist activity as well; while the individual secessionist might have a permission to violate the law, she does not thereby earn the right to regard the law as a nullity. The best way to describe the practice of principled lawbreaking in both cases is that a limited permission is given to the conscientious lawbreaker to violate her moral duties of obedience – but

[15] It is possible to deny that the government imposes a general duty of obligation on us at all; under this account, fruitless gestures might be legitimate, since the law that is broken in the gesture might not be one we have an obligation to obey at all. This is not implausible, but I am assuming in the present essay that the well-ordered state is capable of imposing the obligation to obey the law generally. For a contrary view, see M.B.E. Smith, "Is There a Prima Facie Duty to Obey the Law?" *Yale L. J.* 82(5) (April 1973), 950–76.

that this permission does not eliminate the rights of the state to expect and demand obedience. These rights persist, and they ground a claim on the part of the state that the agent in question has built up a moral debt toward that state. The disobedient is able to discharge this debt through punishment. The secessionist, though, is unable to do so. Her debt is her own, and – if she is successful – she will continue to have it. Even if we have a limited moral permission to disobey the law, that is, this permission necessarily involves the commission of an act contrary to moral duty. This act is not justified with reference to some other duty, as we might at first think; King is clear that the disobedience here is permitted, but that the duty to obey the law is not simply trumped by a stronger right. The disobedience builds up a genuine debt to the legitimate institutions of that society, and the disobedient ought to regard herself as morally deserving of punishment. If this is true for the disobedience of the civil disobedient, it is equally true of the secessionist, when her secession is from a state capable of imposing the duty to obey. From the fact that she will never in fact be punished we should not infer that she does not merit that punishment.

This means that there is something very strange in the attitude we should have toward the secessionist. I think we might regard the secessionist as having done something morally wrong, so much so that punishment is in principle legitimate – where that secession, of course, is from a well-ordered society. We might also simultaneously regard this secessionist as having done an action that is praiseworthy, or at the very least more morally praiseworthy than most forms of lawbreaking; the secessionist will have created a more just world, when she succeeds, and we ought to give some praise to those who have made the world more just. This combination of attitudes is confusing. It is similar to the attitudes expressed by Immanuel Kant toward the revolution in France. Kant regarded the revolution, like all revolutions, as morally impermissible; there was no right held by the people to throw off political authority. And yet he felt personal admiration for those who created the revolution, and eagerly awaited news of revolutionary successes.[16] This combination of attitudes is confusing, but we might think that there is something comprehensible here. We can regard an action as the violation of a duty, while still thinking that those who perform that action are sometimes morally praiseworthy. Our

[16] Kant's attitudes are discussed in L. W. Beck, "Kant and the Right to Revolution," *Journal of the History of Ideas* 32(3) (1972), 411–22. See also Christine Korsgaard, "Taking the Law into Our Own Hands: Kant on the Right to Revolution," in Andrews Reath et al., eds., *Reclaiming the History of Ethics: Essays for John Rawls* (Cambridge, MA: Harvard University Press, 1997), 232–62.

attitudes toward such people – those who do what is impermissible, but do so in a manner that makes the world what it ought to be – are complex. We might simply dismiss this complexity, and argue that the right response to such people is simply say that they have done something right, all things considered; the duty they violated was not, in the context of their action, obligatory. I do not want to dismiss the complexity. I believe the attitude we have toward such people is complex because they act in a manner whose ethical quality is itself complicated.

We might therefore imagine that there is, in cases of principled disobedience – both civil disobedience and secessionist disobedience – something like the phenomenon of dirty hands. As discussed by Michael Walzer, the phenomenon involves those people who do wrong actions, but do so in the name of what is morally rightful; such people might be thought to be both praiseworthy, or at least not worthy of condemnation, and yet also deeply implicated in wrongful actions, so much so that they ought to regard their souls as somewhat tarnished.[17] Walzer is clear that we should regard this tarnish as a real moral phenomenon; the taint is not erased by the good results. I do not want here to commit to this moral analysis. I am not sure we can always understand what it means to have a tarnished soul. I do believe, though, that if there is any area of public life in which the concept is likely to make sense, it is here – in the spaces in which we propose to violate our duties, in the name of justice. This sort of disobedience involves doing what is wrong in order to do what is right. If there is any place in which we might think the phenomenon of dirty hands holds sway, it is in cases like this. Both the disobedient and the secessionist are susceptible to dirty hands, if this phenomenon is both real and comprehensible. Both of these sorts of agents do what they are not permitted to do, and in so doing they put those very institutions we require for the preservation of our rights at risk. If they succeed in what they do, they have made the world a more just place, and should be praised for having done so. But the actions they do are not made morally permissible through this transformation. They remain prohibited actions. The civil disobedient can receive her punishment, and thereby expiate the taint from her soul; her punishment reasserts the supremacy of the law, and removes – in whole or in part – the wrongness of her lawbreaking. The secessionist can receive no such expiation. In her action, she taints her soul, and that taint cannot even in principle be removed. She has, if successful, removed the authority of the

[17] Michael Walzer, "Political Action: The Problem of Dirty Hands," *Philosophy and Public Affairs* 2(2) (Winter 1973), 160–80.

agent that might remove her moral guilt. She is praiseworthy, perhaps, but her moral stain persists even as that praise is offered.

3. DIRTY HANDS, SECESSION, AND THE COURTS

All of this suggests, I believe, that the moral status of the secessionist declaration is considerably more complex than we might often believe. In particular, the ideas I have described here make it at least plausible that the full moral account we ought to offer about secession includes ideas other than claim-rights; the morality of secession might require us to examine issues that are not easily reduced to issues of rights that all states are obligated to respect. In particular, the moral quality of secession against a well-ordered society is rather complex; we do, and should have, complex attitudes toward those who seek secession from such societies, when they do so in the name of justice. Such individuals will engage in actions that violate their moral duties. They may also be praiseworthy, all things considered. This combination of moral facts seems difficult to make coherent; it may also be the right way to describe our moral reactions to this case.

Three things follow from this. The first, of course, is that the one who engages in secessionist action is taking a significant moral risk. Even in the best case, in which she remakes the political world so as to make it more just, she has tarnished her soul – and, humans being what they are, she cannot always be confident that her judgments, both of the injustice she faces and her chances of overcoming them, are sound. Being a secessionist is thus a morally risky business.

The second thing I want to note follows from this. Even if the secessionist is not unreasonable in her belief that the injustice she faces justifies her activity, she cannot count on outsiders to assist her in her secession. The reason for this is simple: even if we are permitted to accept moral risk for ourselves, we cannot insist that others bear that risk with us. We can ask them, of course. They may decide to help. But they are under no obligation to do so. If the state from which we are seceding is not well-ordered, of course, this conclusion does not hold; outsiders may have an obligation to get their hands dirty, so to speak. But when the dirty hands we are speaking of involving a potential tarnishing of the soul, we cannot insist that others join us. A permission to take a risk and endanger the soul is a permission that attaches to us, not to those whose assistance would be most helpful. This is significant, I think in the international system. We often speak as if the moral analysis of international relations reduced to rights and duties – and, often, it does. But morality goes further than this. It includes notions of permission and supererogation that do not reduce to the concept of right. If the secessionist's declaration is permissible, it is nonetheless something that she is not able to insist that others assist her in making. Outside states may have a permission to assist, of course; I am not here taking a position for or against this possibility. But this permission would be, at most, a permission; there is no obligation to join the secessionist in the adventure of principled lawbreaking.

The third point to be discussed notes simply that this is true of the remainder state as well as of third parties. The state from which the secession is sought, if it is well-ordered, has the right to insist on obedience to its legal norms. Those against whom the secessionist declaration is pressed, in other words, are under no obligation to accept it. This is uncomfortable; we are rightly wary of situations in which two agents are in conflict, and neither is in the right. Here, though, the state is permitted to insist upon obedience, even while the secessionist has a limited permission to withhold that obedience. This conflict seems unavoidable; if there is any permission to disobey a well-ordered society, it includes the idea that the well-ordered society can work against that disobedience. The state, after all, need not embody perfect justice for it to have the right to enforce its commands. What we ought to conclude here is that there is nothing normatively impermissible in the actions of a well-ordered state that takes steps to ensure its preservation and integrity – and, in short, to work against the secessionist. This fact does not mean that the state is able to use any and all means in defense of its integrity, any more than the secessionist can make use of any available means; there are important constraints on the methods that can be used in pursuit of even a valid government objective. But the state's objective, in preserving itself and in punishing the secessionist, does not here seem invalid. The state may, of course, decide to allow the secessionist region to leave; this may, in some cases, represent virtue, if the state believes that the secessionist agents are in fact more likely to build a just social and legal world than the current state contains. This judgment, though, is supererogatory, rather than obligatory. The well-ordered state is not obligated to allow secession, and may work against those who seek to secede.

This may lead to somewhat odd results: a court that operated on these principles would have to, in a particular case, admit that the law could not simply decide a victor. It could not insist that the secessionist action is simply an act of lawbreaking without moral reason behind it – nor that the state in question is obligated to allow itself to be dismembered. Does this not, in the end, abdicate this particular court's responsibility to adjudicate disputes? Does it not move us further from a world in which law, rather than violence, is the mechanism by which disputes are resolved?

I believe that these worries are powerful ones – but that a response to such worries might begin by noting the role of international law in international politics. In contrast with domestic law, international law rarely solves disputes with any degree of finality; the enforcement of international law is, famously, somewhat arbitrary and imperfect, there being no standing international executive or police force. International law, in contrast, often takes the form of a rhetorical tool by which particular state policies are justified and evaluated. As such, international law does not work simply to end disputes; it often functions as a way of speaking about, and within, these disputes. International law shapes the debate, by giving one or the other party the power to begin the negotiations with a powerful rhetorical cudgel in their hands. In the case under consideration, the Court might be read as saying that it is not appropriate for either party to have sole possession of that cudgel. The circumstances under consideration are so complex that a simple determination in favor of one party would necessarily ignore morally relevant parts of the landscape. The Court's refusal to judge, in the end, is not an abandonment of international law, but a recognition of its limited role in a complex moral universe.

We can see this best by returning to the judgment of the international court of justice. Again, many observers wanted the court to here declare when there exists a right to secede – a right, that is, that is a claim validly pressed against existing states, that those states are obligated to respect. The court did not address this issue, preferring to focus on the more narrow issue of the secessionist declaration; the court's decision refused to engage with the more charged issue of whether or not a right to secede was a valid right under international law. I believe the court was right to focus on the narrow question. The reason for this is that the question of a right to secede is only part of the normative landscape against which we ought to evaluate secessionist actions. It might be thought possible, if what I say here is correct, that there can sometimes be a situation in which one party is permitted to work in favor of secession – or, at the very least, in which the agent is praiseworthy in that work – while the state from which secession is sought has the right to resist that secession. Cases like this are ill-described in a discussion that focuses only on a possible right to secede. The court's decision might here represent not institutional cowardice, but rather the settled judgment that there are some practices and institutions whose moral character cannot easily be described in simple bright-line principles of right and wrong.

I do not claim that the court itself actually took this as the motivating principle for their decision; I also do not claim that the court thought that the case of Serbia and Kosovo represented secession from a well-ordered society, as I have described it here. I make only this more limited assertion:

that courts are sometimes wise to say less, rather than more, when what it is they say is likely to inadequately describe the moral landscape. The court's decision here has left it to a complex set of institutional agents – state, of course, but also nongovernmental agents, commentators, and transnational bodies – to work out in particular cases what the right moral evaluation ought to be of a secessionist movement. It may be that this complex set is more likely to give nuanced and accurate analyses of particular secessionist acts than the court itself. If this is right – and I cannot here defend the conclusion that it is – then the court is commendable in refusing to make a simple declaration in a complex world. I have, in this essay, only sought to establish the possibility that the stories we ought to tell about secessionist declarations are complex. I have not, and cannot, fully defend the proposition that the court's decision gives us the right tools to deal with this complexity – or, rather, that a more expansive decision would have given us worse tools. All I want to say in the present context is that this conclusion seems, at the very least, plausible. What appears at first as institutional timidity might instead express a very admirable respect for moral complexity; the court may perhaps be rightly praised for its willingness to say less, when saying less opens up space for others to say more.

9

"Mars for the Martians"?

On the Obsolescence of Self-Determination

JOHN R. MORSS

My intention in this chapter is to defend the argument that the concept of self-determination has outlived its usefulness in international law. It will be proposed that self-determination was a phenomenon of the twentieth century from which we have collectively and globally moved on, normatively if not historically. The assertion that the twentieth century was characterised by self-determination aspirations, articulations, and achievements is of course a familiar one. Many of the causal connections between the developing international law of self-determination and other political and historical processes, during the twentieth century, are equally familiar: the impact of the World Wars, of Woodrow Wilson's program, of the decolonisation process, of the decline of empires and of the end of the Cold War, and so on. What needs to be defended is the claim of obsolescence. Towards the end of the chapter consideration will be given to some counterarguments the tendency of which is to moderate and to constrain, but in my view not to undermine, the strong claim. Thus the claim that self-determination is obsolete could be said to reflect the privileged position of powerful states that have long ago achieved the independence still aspired to by other populations. It might therefore be a matter of cultural and geopolitical hegemony to define that aspiration as anachronistic. In any event the hope is that the rigorous articulation of a strong claim will contribute to the larger debate.

It will thus be argued in the larger portion of this chapter that the concept of self-determination obscures our understanding and our development of policy relating to those legal and political questions which it purports to illuminate. The rights and responsibilities of various collectives of people, including states, governments, nations and local communities, are at stake in these questions. Significant violence, dislocation, and loss of both collective and private property is often involved, or at least risked, in pursuing or implementing policies guided by the notion of self-determination. The question needs always to be posed as to whether such costs are outweighed by benefits that can be attributed to the implementation of a principle of self-determination. For as Allen Buchanan observes, the recognition of self-determination 'is surely one of the most important and perilous developments in international law in the last half-century.'[1]

Buchanan defines legitimate self-determination, as substantive principle and justification for secession, as a remedial technique in circumstances of grave violation of human rights norms. Buchanan's contribution to the debate is a key resource for this chapter, but it does not seem to go far enough. Jeremy Waldron's approach, while lacking the detailed exposition of Buchanan's, is to be preferred in several respects. Waldron's approach to self-determination involves the differentiation of two broad conceptions: an orthodox, identity-based conception (a form of identity politics, as Waldron sees it), and a 'territorial' conception. Waldron rejects identity politics tout court as the driving force of self-determination. Identity politics, in this context, is the politics of national or communal identification with particular territory.[2] Instead Waldron's approach to territory is pragmatic; the world is divided into geographically distinct polities, and self-determination, to the extent it is legitimate, presupposes arrangements that are in significant ways internal to those polities or that in other ways respect state boundaries as we find them. Waldron's 'territorial' conception of self-determination comes down to the assertion that the inhabitants of a territory should be enabled to govern themselves without outside domination.

Setting aside Waldron's twofold model for the moment, three senses of self-determination should be differentiated for the purposes of the present discussion. Two are substantive and one arguably empty. An activist and a conservative form of appeal to self-determination should be especially noted. Self-determination is frequently invoked in situations where a change in political structures, having international consequences, is advocated or proclaimed. But it may also be invoked in support of the political status quo. Examples of the former include the Unilateral Declaration of Independence made in Kosovo in 2008;[3] examples of the latter include the current circumstances pertaining to

1 Allen Buchanan, *Justice, Legitimacy, and Self-Determination: Moral Foundations for International Law* (Oxford: Oxford University Press, 2004), 1–2; also see Allen Buchanan, 'The Legitimacy of International Law', in S. Besson and J. Tasioulas (eds.), *The Philosophy of International Law* (Oxford: Oxford University Press, 2010), 79–96.

2 Jeremy Waldron, 'Two Conceptions of Self-determination', in S. Besson and J. Tasioulas (eds.), *The Philosophy of International Law* (Oxford: Oxford University Press, 2010), 397–413; also see Jeremy Waldron, 'Minority Cultures and the Cosmopolitan Alternative', 25 *University of Michigan Journal of Law Reform*, 1992, 751–93.

3 *Accordance with International Law of the Unilateral Declaration of Independence in Respect of Kosovo*, Advisory Opinion, *ICJ Reports* 2010, 403.

the Islas Malvinas/Falkland Islands. Processes and aspirations in Palestine[4] exemplify both the activist and the conservative styles of appeal to self-determination. A third genre of the invocation of self-determination must also be identified. In this third genre self-determination is otiose. To state that the inhabitants of France, of Japan, or of the United States enjoy self-determination is generally speaking to say very little. If the political status quo is seriously threatened then the argument might qualify as the second, conservative form. If a subsection of the population of such a country attempts to secede then the activist form of the argument might arise. Similarly, the arguments of British Eurosceptics might take the form of assertions about 'regaining British self-determination' by leaving the EU. But to the extent that neither is the case, the statement that self-determination is a characteristic of such settled populations has little substance in a political sense and, arguably, no significance at all in terms of international law. To be sure, the counterarguments from cultural hegemony and evolutionism, to be addressed in the following, revolve around the status of self-determination in exactly such places; for the familiarity and taken-for-granted nature of self-determination in stable modern states is precisely what those counterarguments fasten on. But outside that context, the identification of self-determination as a characteristic of such countries, self-identified as advanced, contributes nothing to our understanding of the situations in which its implementation might actually make a difference.

One reason for emphasising this is the role played by such examples in scholarly debate. Many discussions of self-determination in political theory and in international relations theory focus, in effect, on such easy cases. This happens as a consequence of the assumption that the same general principles underlie easy (settled or uncontentious) cases and hard (contested or problematic) cases. The factors that make hard cases hard may well seem like a distraction from the search for general principles. For example, the question of the relationship between territory and self-determination is typically explored, by political theorists, as a matter of general principles.[5] Quite properly, critical enquiry refuses to endorse the comfortable orthodoxy by which established states complacently sequester their own territorial

4 The term 'Palestine' is used here to refer to the larger geographical region, broadly corresponding to the area of the League of Nations Mandate. See Michelle Leanne Burgis-Kasthala, 'Over-Stating Palestine's UN Membership Bid? An Ethnographic Study on the Narratives of Statehood', 25 *European Journal of International Law*, 2014, 677–701.

5 Anna Stilz, 'Why do States Have Territorial Rights?' 1 *International Theory*, 2009, 185–213; Anna Stilz, 'Nations, States and Territory', 121 *Ethics*, 2011, 572–601; Cara Nine, *Global Justice and Territory* (Oxford: Oxford University Press, 2012); Anna Moltchanova, *National Self-Determination and Justice in Multinational States* (Dordrecht: Springer, 2009).

sovereignty from scrutiny, while questioning territorial claims of 'foreign' national groups. Yet this critical levelling has the effect of obscuring the real differences between hard and easy cases.

It should be emphasised that the discipline of international law is not being singled out for praise in this regard. If in comparison to sister disciplines international law focuses more successfully on the two contested genres of self-determination claim noted earlier (the activist and the conservative), that is to say on what I am calling hard cases, this has to be attributed to professional factors rather than to greater wisdom. The contestedness of the hard cases brings them directly to the attention of the international lawyer in ways which may not arise in other disciplines. The wider scholarship of international law as represented by its textbooks includes examples of the same kind of indiscriminate generalisation from easy cases as other disciplines. It is just as difficult to find rigorous examination of self-determination as a general concept in international law as it is elsewhere.[6] In any event the present chapter will attempt to maintain a focus on hard cases and on the kinds of issues that they give rise to. What role does self-determination play in the claims, counterclaims, and presuppositions of the British and Argentinian governments over those windswept islands in the South Atlantic, or in the rhetoric of Palestinian or Israeli leaders over control of the former British Mandate?[7] What will be suggested is that everything that is legitimate and substantive about the connotation of this term, in these situations, is more adequately articulated in terms of the civil and political rights of communities.[8] In some ways that legitimate content is best expressed in negative terms rather than in the positive assertions of self-determination as the 'right' of some entity. In his history of the Balkans, Misha Glenny observes:

> Between 1711 and 1829, seven major wars were fought on the territory of Moldavia and Wallachia [modern day Romania]. The Principalities stood at the intersection of the Russian, Austrian and Turkish empires, and acted as the land bridge which Russian armies had to cross into the Balkan peninsula.... The fate of such a crucial region could not possibly be left to the people who happened to live there.[9]

6 John R. Morss, *International Law as the Law of Collectives: Toward a Law of People* (Farnham: Ashgate, 2013).

7 Shlomo Sand, *The Invention of the Land of Israel: From Holy Land to Homeland* (London: Verso, 2012); also see Anthony Carty, 'Israel's Legal Right to Exist and the Principle of the Self-determination of the Palestinian People? [sic]', 76 *The Modern Law Review*, 2013, 158–77.

8 Morss, *International Law as the Law of Collectives*, 118.

9 Misha Glenny, *The Balkans: Nationalism, War and the Great Powers 1804–2012* (London: Granta, 2012) 58.

Glenny's irony is not subtle but neither are the processes of which he writes. The argument connects with the debate over nondomination and with related issues in the literature of republicanism and neorepublicanism.[10] But the issues are even wider.

1. GUIDING IDEAS

Attention should first be given to articulations of self-determination in the contemporary literature. Theoretical contributions to our understanding of self-determination continue to be made by scholars from a range of disciplines. From legal philosophy, two major, contemporary voices are those of Allen Buchanan and Jeremy Waldron. Important contributors from other disciplines, closer to the social and political sciences and to political philosophy more narrowly, include Anna Moltchanova and Anna Stilz.

Buchanan's approach focuses on the moral dimension of international law. The international legal system should according to Buchanan be grounded in 'principles of justice, understood primarily as principles that ascribe basic and relatively uncontroversial rights to all persons as such.'[11] Legitimacy for political entities on the international plane consists for Buchanan in the institutionalised protection of those basic human rights. It is only when grave injustices, correspondingly defined in terms of these basic rights, are occurring, and on a sufficient scale, that unilateral secession arises as a possible avenue for self-help in the relevant community. Self-determination as an entitlement to secede from an existing state at will – an activist form of self-determination, in the terms used here – is 'a remedy of last resort' against such grave injustices.[12] Buchanan therefore endorses a highly conditional version of self-determination. One might draw an analogy with the contemporary status of self-defence in international law. Self-defence is in effect a remedy of last resort by a state suffering armed attack. It is a state reaction to what might be called an international emergency[13] arising from an illegal act. Its scope as well as the precipitating circumstances are severely circumscribed. Similarly, in Buchanan's view, what might be called a protostate should be thought of as

[10] Ian Shapiro, 'On Non-domination', LXII *University of Toronto Law Journal*, 2012, 293–335; Philip Pettit, 'Legitimate International Institutions: A Neo-republican Perspective', in S. Besson and J. Tasioulas (eds.), *The Philosophy of International Law* (Oxford: Oxford University Press, 2010), 139–160; Mortimer Sellers, *Republican Principles in International Law: The Fundamental Requirements of a Just World Order* (Houndmills: Palgrave Macmillan, 2006).

[11] Buchanan, *Justice, Legitimacy, and Self-Determination*, 4.

[12] Ibid., 5.

[13] On the role of emergency with respect to self-determination activism see Moltchanova, *National Self-Determination*, 175.

beneficiary of an entitlement to activist (state-breaking) self-determination as a last resort in an international emergency of a different but equally serious kind. For in Buchanan's view, human rights abuses of sufficient scale as to justify secession are precisely matters of international concern.

Of course the persuasiveness or otherwise of Buchanan's account relies in large part on his articulation of such details as the specification of basic human rights, of relevant institutional frameworks for their protection, and of grave failures in such protective systems. Leaving those matters aside, however, Buchanan's 'last resort' approach to secessionary self-determination is in any event an important candidate in the search for an adequate theory of self-determination. In many ways it is a negative formulation in the sense that self-determination is not thought of as an enduring or inherent entitlement but as a technique or form of redress. It is entirely secondary to the question of the institutional protection of basic rights; an epiphenomenon, one might say, or an emergent characteristic. In vocabulary closer to Buchanan's own, self-determination is thus an institutional feature: a characteristic of the international infrastructure of human rights protection. To be clear, self-determination is for Buchanan emphatically not a positive entitlement (or 'primary right') drawn from collective identity or from collective connections to particular territory. Thus Buchanan asserts that 'international law should unambiguously repudiate the nationalist principle that all nations (or "peoples") are entitled to their own states.'[14]

Buchanan has usefully categorised primary right theories of self-determination into 'ascriptivist' and 'plebiscitary'[15] versions, both of which of course he rejects. The former is well exemplified by Buchanan's comments on nationalism. Nations, 'peoples', or 'encompassing cultures' are taken under the 'ascriptivist' approach to be kinds of political community that in some strong sense 'deserve' independent statehood. Typically, Buchanan notes, cultural connections between members of the nation or people are asserted and relied on even if an encompassing culture is not expressly identified. In the latter, 'plebiscitary' version of the primary right approach, a democratic majority (however defined) in a given geographical region is held to retain at all times a collective liberty to withdraw from the sovereignty of the prevailing state or states. The model is somewhat along the lines of a hypothetical federal system under which component polities are constitutionally enabled to withdraw from the federal structure at any time, that is to say without such withdrawal amounting to secession. (This would of course be

[14] Buchanan, *Justice, Legitimacy, and Self-Determination*, 331. [15] Ibid., 373, 379.

a remarkably loose form of federation and real examples, such as the United States, Australia, or Germany, typically set more stringent conditions for withdrawal.) It could be thought of as a particular manifestation of a social contract to the extent that contracts may be voluntarily revised or terminated.[16]

There are practical difficulties in an open-ended, indeed kaleidoscopic liberty to reconfigure state boundaries at what might appear to be the whim of transient majorities. Moreover there are objections of a more principled nature.[17] One set of these objections relates to the rights of the wider population of the current state, for example the rights of nationals of the United Kingdom as a whole should a majority of the residents of Scotland have opted for independence in the 2014 referendum.[18] As Buchanan puts it, this form of majority rule, treated as adequate to give rise to strong self-determination, is 'the rule of the present majority within a portion of the state's territory to override the rights of the citizenry as a whole to the entire territory of the state.'[19] We will return to some aspects of this problem in the following. At this point Buchanan's emphasis on this objection to the plebiscitary model of a primary right to self-determination should be highlighted. It relies on connections between populations and territories. For Buchanan the territory as a whole is connected with the population as a whole; for 'the state's territory is more accurately described as the people's territory, the point being that it is the territory of the people as a whole, not just a collection of parcels of territory each owned by those who at a particular time happen to reside in them.'[20] Therefore, 'a plebiscitary unilateral right to secede is incompatible with the rights that are included in popular sovereignty.'[21] Most particularly Buchanan rejects the claim of the local majority to sovereign domination of the territory that it already occupies.

Buchanan's analysis here invokes territorial rights of the whole population (the population of the whole state across its whole territory) in order to defeat the claim of subpopulations to subterritories. Buchanan does not seem to have fully substantiated 'the claim on the part of the whole citizenry to the

[16] Ibid., 244, 376.

[17] The fluidity or instability problem can itself of course be treated as a matter of principle as well as a matter of the practical; democracy that is too fluid may be said to be not democracy at all. The celebration of lively debate in politics, as the essence of democracy, may need to respond to normative demands: Jurgen Habermas, 'On Law and Disagreement: Some Comments on "Interpretative Pluralism"', 16 *Ratio Juris*, 2003, 187–94.

[18] Stephen Tierney, 'Legal Issues Surrounding the Referendum on Independence for Scotland', 9 *European Constitutional Law Review*, 2013, 359–90.

[19] Buchanan, *Justice, Legitimacy, and Self-Determination*, 374. [20] Ibid. [21] Ibid.

state's whole territory', although he indicates that he has done so.[22] His argument relies on the legitimacy of territorial connections between a people or nation and a defined territory, and this legitimacy seems to be intuitive, or to be perhaps better thought of as a default condition, absent facts on usurpation. Territoriality seems to play an explanatory role in Buchanan's argument that it does not play in Waldron's, as will be discussed in the following. Before examining this, it is valuable to refer to Moltchanova's position because Moltchanova deals directly with matters of nationhood and she defines nations in terms of the centrality of 'a political culture of self-determination with which its members self-identify.'[23] For example, Moltchanova considers the Kosovars to be a national group in this sense.[24] Like Buchanan, Moltchanova focuses attention on moral rights. According to her analysis, primary moral rights do indeed arise for certain types of group agent, of which nations are the best example. Self-determination 'is an important good' for such agents.[25] Thus 'a nation can be considered to be a group agent constructed through the engagement of a set of individuals with a political culture of self-determination.'[26] Moltchanova agrees with Buchanan that an open season on secession is not desirable. The legitimate moral aspiration to self-determination can be satisfied at the substate level in most cases. Moltchanova thus converges with Buchanan so far as practical policy is concerned. But she disagrees with Buchanan's analysis of the rights of minorities below the threshold of severe violation of human rights. For Moltchanova, Buchanan is, in that sense, too respectful of existing state boundaries.[27]

Moltchanova's approach might be categorised by Buchanan as a version of the ascriptivist primary right approach. Buchanan's analysis will not be pursued any further here. But its general orientation to self-determination is a key marker in the debate. Self-determination as remedy is an important model. It is a robust alternative to the primary right theories, according to which self-determination is an expression, not a reaction. It is important next to discuss Waldron's contribution since, like Buchanan, Waldron rejects the quasi-nationalistic notion of self-determination as identitarian entitlement or expression, and similarly downplays the explanatory or foundational role of territorial correspondences. As noted earlier, Waldron calls his preferred approach the

[22] Ibid. As Waldron notes, 'There is a dearth of theorizing about the boundaries of political communities in the liberal tradition: writers in the social contract tradition proceed as though the group whose members contract together to solve the problem of conflict were predetermined': Waldron, 'Two Conceptions', 409.

[23] Moltchanova, *National Self-Determination*, 71. [24] Ibid., 169. [25] Ibid., 131.

[26] Ibid. [27] Ibid., 146.

'territorial' conception because it takes territorial populations as given ('anyone who lives permanently within the country in question'[28]). On this approach, this is the set of persons who 'have the right to work out their own constitutional and political arrangements without interference from the outside.'[29]

'The people of a country' thus defined, say, by denizenship, may of course be more or less homogeneous in terms of cultural or ethnic composition and so on. The diversity may be increasing or decreasing, relationships may be harmonious or tense. These matters are irrelevant to self-determination in Waldron's preferred sense. Waldron contrasts this virtuous sense of self-determination with the identity-based conception that precisely values and centres on these cultural or ethnic distinctions. The identity-based conception of self-determination asserts that the entitlement arises in communities that regard themselves as distinct from other communities in cultural or ethnic terms. This position, rejected by Waldron, is of course closely related to the position similarly rejected by Buchanan under the term 'ascriptivist' primary right. But Waldron's objections are stronger. The identity-based conception is for Waldron not only misconceived, it is also dangerous. It is 'inapposite to a world of mingling and migration, a world of fluid and compromised identities.'[30]

To be sure, as Waldron notes, the identity-based approach comes in a variety of forms, some less troublesome than others. It does not always involve gross discrimination, ethnic cleansing, or worse. It may be benign, in the sense of well-intentioned: wishing 'that each people with a culture were in charge of its own affairs' and looking 'for an acceptable moderate version of that.'[31] But the identity-based approach gives hostages to fortune. It 'has to constantly battle [the] tendency' to pursue outcomes 'that might only be achieved by unacceptable methods.'[32] In contrast, Waldron's preferred approach treats cultural or ethnic differences as matters that may on occasion give rise to disputes within the polity (although often they will not) but that are in any case not the grounds for the constitution of the polity. One might say that however much some individuals self-identify as male and others as female, and however much discrimination, violence, or other collective social injustice bears the marks of the gender distinction, it is no answer to send all the men home to Mars and all the women home to Venus. Instead,

28 Waldron, 'Two Conceptions', 397. 29 Ibid.

30 Ibid., 398; also see Sergei Prozorov, 'Generic Universalism in World Politics: Beyond International Anarchy and the World State', 1 *International Theory*, 2009, 215–47.

31 Waldron, 'Two Conceptions', 412. 32 Ibid., 413.

> [t]he juxtaposition, confrontation, intermingling, and *mélange* of cultures that characterizes modern multicultural societies is a good thing: its raggedness, its infiltrations, and the indistinctness of cultural boundaries to which it gives rise are all healthy.[33]

As noted earlier, Waldron's account of the two conceptions (identity-based and territorial) is a fairly brief one. One aspect that might deserve more detailed consideration relates to nationalism, which is designed, sometimes quite deliberately, to achieve what Waldron seems to desire: good enough coexistence among diverse communities with disputes and frictions managed, defused, or contained. Yugoslavia as a postwar socialist republic was designed to manage differences among Serb, Croat, and Muslim inhabitants of the one overall geographical territory. So, in many ways, was its predecessor the Kingdom of Serbs, Croats, and Slovenes, set up after the fall of the Ottoman Empire, which itself shared such aims.[34] Of course Waldron rejects the view that one of the functions of political community is 'the preservation and nourishing of a particular culture or way of life.'[35] Nationalism in many ways encapsulates the view that Waldron rejects. But a more detailed discussion would elucidate these matters.

2. KOSOVO AND OTHER QUESTIONS

Scholars of international law have dissected the Advisory Opinion on the Kosovo UDI.[36] Many commentators have expressed disappointment over the position taken by the International Court of Justice (ICJ) with respect to the scope of the question posed to it. The ICJ focused its attention on the question of the authorship of Kosovo's declaration of independence, that is to say on the status or standing of its authors in the context of international law. Briefly put, once it had determined that the particular circumstances of authorship had not amounted to an impediment, there were no grounds on which to impugn the legality of the Declaration. Without entering that debate at any length, it can be observed that the decision of the ICJ to circumscribe its task so as to focus exclusively on the Declaration itself, and not on the larger aspirations with which it was connected, reflects limitations of the international law

33 Ibid., 402–03. 34 Glenny, *The Balkans*. 35 Waldron, 'Two Conceptions', 401.

36 Helmut Philipp Aust, 'The Kosovo Opinion and Issues of International Responsibility', in P. Hilpold (ed.), *Kosovo and International Law: The ICJ Advisory Opinion of 22 July 2010* (Leiden: Brill, 2012) 209–32; Zoran Oklopcic, '*Populus Interruptus*: Self-determination, the Independence of Kosovo, and the Vocabulary of Peoplehood', 22 *Leiden Journal of International Law*, 2009, 677–702.

of self-determination just as much as it reflects timidity or conservative obduracy on behalf of the bench. It also seems appropriate to recognise that the question of the authorship of the Declaration was indeed of the essence so far as the Advisory Opinion was concerned. There was already a provisional governance structure in place in Kosovo, under the aegis of the United Nations, namely a suite of 'Provisional Institutions of Self-Government of Kosovo', one of which was the Assembly of Kosovo (para. 102). It would have been *ultra vires* for the leaders or representatives of that structure, acting in that capacity, to have legitimately issued such a Declaration.

The authors of the Declaration on the facts included the President of Kosovo, not a member of the Assembly (para. 76). For this reason, and others, the Declaration was not issued by or on behalf of the Assembly. Yet this argument seems to cut both ways when seen in the larger context of self-determination. The Assembly was established as a body representative of the inhabitants of Kosovo. It included members representing minority communities in Kosovo, in particular, ten members representing 'the Kosovo Serb community'. These individuals declined to attend the meeting at which the vote was taken on the Declaration. While the make-up of the meeting that approved the Declaration patently differed from the make-up of the Assembly, thereby avoiding one constitutional snare, the nature of the difference raises its own questions of legitimacy. This is a reminder, if nothing more, that we simply do not know whether the collection of individuals who met on the day and expressed their views by a vote should be thought of internationally (or indeed within Serbia) as expressing 'the will of our people'[37] of Kosovo. According to the ICJ, the authors were 'representatives of the people of Kosovo' (para. 109). Numerically, the affirmative vote of 109 of the 120-member Assembly (para. 76) would certainly have sufficed to meet the requirements of the Assembly's approval of a new Constitution as envisaged by the Special Envoy of the Secretary-General (para. 70). The Special Envoy proposed that a two-thirds majority would suffice. But the vote on the Declaration was of course not an act of the Assembly and was not governed in any respect by the Special Envoy's proposals. By placing such weight on the matter of authorship, and therefore on the disjunction of the Assembly from the collectivity of the authors of the declaration, the ICJ abandons the possibility of applying any constitutional characteristics of the former to the latter. It may seem patent that the authors of the Declaration validly represented the majority community within Kosovo, but the legitimacy of their claim to

[37] *Accordance with International Law of the Unilateral Declaration of Independence in Respect of Kosovo*, Advisory Opinion, *ICJ Reports* 2010, 403, Para 75.

represent 'the people of Kosovo' is a different matter. This question of the plebiscite and its numerical criteria (what numbers or fractions are required for what functions and what effects) of course runs through the whole debate on self-determination.

Elsewhere in Europe, the U.K. government implemented an independence referendum in Scotland in September 2014. Residents of Scotland (aged 16 and above) were entitled to vote on the single question of whether Scotland should become an independent country.[38] The U.K. government was committed to respecting the outcome. It is to be presumed that membership of the EU would have had to be renegotiated by Scotland were this process to have given rise to independence. Indeed the probable difficulty or ease of future reentry to Europe was a matter of contestation as between the two camps in the referendum. Independence for Catalonia, an aspiration of its current provincial government, would also give rise to questions about EU membership.[39] As would have been anticipated, advocates for an affirmative vote in the Scotland referendum made reference to self-determination among other matters. Buchanan's caveat in this connection is to look at the bigger picture: the legitimate expectations of the entire 'people' or population of the United Kingdom as currently constituted. How would they feel about losing territory, population, resources, perhaps identity, as a result of Caledonian independence? The U.K. government rejected the suggestion that the views of the inhabitants of England and Wales with respect to Scots independence should be sought, in a comparably direct manner.[40] In effect the U.K. government had taken it upon itself to represent those interests, under the general democratic mandate of parliamentary elections. It has been under such executive authority, after all, that permission has been granted to the already devolved Scottish Parliament (Pàrlamaid na h-Alba), physically located in Edinburgh, to hold the referendum. That Parliament was established by the U.K. government. The executives of democratically elected governments enjoy considerable powers over constitutional and territorial changes, although written

38 There was thus no franchise for people of Scots birthplace or descent living elsewhere (including elsewhere in the United Kingdom) at the time of the referendum: as one might say, no 'diasporran' franchise. In Waldronian fashion the franchise was residence-based.

39 Montserrat Guibernau, Francois Rocher, and Elisenda Casanas Adam, 'Introduction: A Special Section on Self-Determination and the Use of Referendums: Catalonia, Quebec and Scotland', 27 *International Journal of Political and Cultural Sociology*, 2014, 1–3.

40 However, these questions of the attitudes of the inhabitants of England and Wales residents were enlivened by assurances made by Westminster politicians in the lead-up to the Scotland referendum. These assurances or 'vows' related to the further devolution of powers to the Scottish Parliament if independence was rejected.

constitutions may expressly constrain such powers. Buchanan's concerns seem to be addressed by this democratic framework especially when it is recalled that in the case of Scotland (unlike Catalonia) it is not a unilateral secession that is at issue but rather an agreed political development, in some respects more comparable to the process of decolonisation. It is clear that Buchanan would not countenance self-determination for the inhabitants of Scotland if by that is meant a primary right.[41]

More generally, however, the example of Scotland makes the point that in practice, aspirations either of whole populations or of provincial (i.e. substate) populations are expressed in mundane, institutionalised ways, not in the form of a Rousseauian collective will. Connections between populations, whether whole or partial, and territories, correspondingly whole or partial, are overwhelmingly connections of administration and of governance rather than connections of affect.[42] In other words it is important to be sceptical about affect-laden rhetoric on 'homeland' whether emanating from Israeli, Palestinian, Irish, or Serbian voices. When state-level geopolitical reorganisation takes place, such as German or Vietnamese reunification or the sundering of Czechoslovakia, self-determination cannot be attributed any role beyond the symbolic. Nothing is explained by reference to that concept. Indeed mischief can be caused by focusing in claim and counterclaim on the status of the population of a given territory. The U.K. government in effect treats the population of the Falklands as a 'people' (thereby entitled to self-determination); the Argentine government has rejected that characterisation of the inhabitants of the Malvinas.[43] According to the latter view the dominant, majority population is descended from a plantation or settler community, and is thus still in effect a foreign population.[44] Of course this argument could equally be applied to Israel, to Australia or New Zealand, to the United States, or indeed to Argentina itself; all owe their dominant populations to incomers over the centuries. This applies to any state that cannot plausibly claim indigenous supremacy.[45] The cause of the

41 Buchanan in any event dismisses Scots Nationalism: Buchanan, *Justice, Legitimacy, and Self-Determination*, 381.

42 But see Alex Schwartz, 'Patriotism or Integrity? Constitutional Community in Divided Societies', 31 *Oxford Journal of Legal Studies*, 2011, 503–26.

43 James Crawford, *The Creation of States in International Law*, 2nd edition (Oxford: Oxford University Press, 2006) 125.

44 Argentina's territorial claim has been expressed since the beginning of the contemporary (UN) era; ibid., 608.

45 To describe the United Kingdom as characterised by indigenous supremacy would in my view be absurd, just as the ascription of achieved self-determination to its population would be otiose. Indigenous supremacy is also of course a problematic notion as exemplified by the political history of Fiji.

differential status and political history of Northern Ireland ('the Six Counties') with respect to the Republic of Ireland, and hence of 'the Troubles', is in large part the plantation policies under the first Queen Elizabeth.[46]

Such historical patterns of the movement of populations, including voluntary and involuntary, sporadic and systematic, 'push' and 'pull',[47] economic and ideological, are of the essence of world history and of global human geography. If these are hard cases, in the context of the relationships between territories and populations, then they are hard cases that must be faced up to. The present-day population of the Falklands/Malvinas, a population that voted overwhelmingly for a British rather than an Argentinian political identity when invited to choose in 2013, has no inherent entitlement to self-determination such as might be read into such an expression.[48] Nor does it have an absolute entitlement to occupation of those particular islands. Nor, however, are they (the change of grammar seems appropriate) mere 'blow-ins'.[49] To coercively displace them or dominate them would be to violate legitimate international expectations of decent treatment, just as was inflicted on Palestinians by Israeli settlements in Occupied Palestine.[50] From a United Nations perspective, the status of the Falkland Islands is still that of a 'non-self-governing territory'[51] along with Gibraltar, Tokelau, Pitcairn, St. Helena, the Western Sahara, and another ten territories. As of 2005 it was the third smallest by population among that group. By definition these territories are unresolved problems for the UN system, without necessarily being pressing problems.[52] There are of course independent states with smaller geographical area or population than the

46 Anthony Carty, *Was Ireland Conquered? International Law and the Irish Question* (London: Pluto Press, 1996).

47 Terms used in Australian discussion of the motivation of asylum-seeking populations, referring respectively to forces causing people to leave places of risk and forces encouraging people to direct their journey to particular locations perceived as desirable.

48 David Keeling, 'A Geopolitical Perspective on Argentina's Malvinas/Falkland Claims', 3 *Global Discourse: An Interdisciplinary Journal of Current Affairs and Applied Contemporary Thought*, 2013, 158–65.

49 An Australian term that seems apt; a 'blow-in' is a recent and ephemeral arrival.

50 The International Court of Justice referred to Palestinian self-determination in its Advisory Opinion on the legality of the security wall being constructed by the Israeli Government: *Legal Consequences of the Construction of a Wall in the Occupied Palestinian Territory*, Advisory Opinion, *ICJ Reports*, 2004, 136. This was a right that was violated by the Israeli Government's actions. But this reference can be taken as a collective term for a range of rights both individual and collective, including rights of association, free movement, and so on.

51 Crawford, *The Creation of States*, 634.

52 Ibid., 637; note that the Falkland Islands and Gibraltar 'arguably fall into [the] category' of 'colonial enclave', ibid., 348.

sixteen non-self-governing territories.[53] The Falkland Islands/Malvinas could become independent. Its current population could unilaterally declare independence, somewhat along the lines of Southern Rhodesia. Self-determination still seems an empty phrase in this connection: a smokescreen.

3. CONCLUSIONS AND COUNTERARGUMENTS

There are a number of objections to the argument presented here. One of the more serious revolves around cultural hegemony. Self-determination, it may be said, has been achieved and consolidated among the leading industrialised powers, and for the intelligentsia drawn from those elite states to talk of self-determination as an obsolete aspiration or objective smacks of colonialism or of evolutionism. Just as earlier forms of any activist political program, such as feminism or gay rights, are sloughed off in the global North as each new wave advances, with the older waves considered passé, so self-determination in the global South may be erased from the agenda because of geopolitics or intellectual fashion. To take another equally apposite example, legal scholars in privileged places – London for example – find it easy to be superior about, and in some respects dismissive about, the continuing relevance of human rights advocacy and struggle in other parts of the world.[54] Sophisticated scepticism can be a two-edged sword. As Waldron has observed, 'of course it is a little unfair to wait until *minorities* invoke identity-based self-determination rights before criticizing the idea.'[55]

In relation to self-determination, there are clearly interests for geopolitical 'winners' in the ongoing stability of territorial boundaries. The territorial integrity of states is robustly defended in the Charter of the United Nations and elsewhere, and the costs and benefits of this status quo are unequally distributed. It need hardly be pointed out that the victorious postwar Allies (who were using the term 'United Nations' about themselves well before the war had ended[56]), under whose aegis this regime was devised and installed, would not have agreed to an arrangement by which their hegemonic status was seriously threatened. The make-up of the United Nations Security Council of course exemplifies this. To proclaim the obsolescence of self-

[53] Such as Monaco or the quasi-state of Vatican City/Holy See: see John R. Morss, 'Riddle of the Sands: Time, Power and Legitimacy in International Law', in P. Singh and B. Mayer (eds.), *Critical International Law: Postrealism, Postcolonialism and Transnationalism* (Oxford: Oxford University Press, 2014), 53–73, 67.

[54] See John R. Morss, 'Saving Human Rights from Its Friends: A Critique of the Imaginary Justice of Costas Douzinas', 27 *Melbourne University Law Review*, 2003, 889–904.

[55] Waldron, 'Two Conceptions', 400; emphasis in original.

[56] Rick Atkinson, *The Day of Battle: The War in Sicily and Italy, 1943–1944* (New York: Holt, 2007), 13.

determination might be to reassure the government of the People's Republic of China in relation to Tibet and other places under its control, and to reassure the government of the Russian Federation over Chechnya, just as much as it is to undermine the complacency of the British Government over the Malvinas or indeed to challenge the Russian Federation over Ukraine.

The appropriate response to this legitimate concern is, I think, to bring to centre stage the question of the legitimate demands of the populations concerned. Broadly speaking, these legitimate demands are the same across levels of administration: villages, boroughs, cities, provinces, federated states, sovereign states, regions. There is nothing about the concept of a 'country' as usually understood that endows the population defined by that level of political governance with rights that differ in kind from the rights attached to the populations of smaller, larger, or intersecting polities. To assert that the populations of 'countries' possess such rights – and self-determination would be the paradigm of such rights – is to understand 'countries' as 'nations.' In many ways it is the particular contribution of international law as a discipline in these debates, in contrast with political science, for example, to bracket nationhood and to treat it quite differently from nationality. From the point of view of international law, *nationhood* confers no rights nor does it convey any obligations. It is merely polemical. To be sure, states owe duties to other states and in turn possess rights in relation to other states.[57] But these are not the rights or obligations of their populations as such. Just as the City of Melbourne or the State of Victoria may enter into contracts or other agreements with various entities, public or private, so the Commonwealth of Australia (the federated state) may enter into various kinds of reciprocal arrangements with other states around the world or indeed with private entities. A Free Trade Agreement between Australia and the United States expresses no substantive legal relationship between the inhabitants of those two geographical territories as such. Similarly, the City of Melbourne might enter a contract to purchase French-made rolling stock for its rail system without thus binding the inhabitants of Melbourne. To put it another way, it adds no more to the fact of a Free Trade Agreement to say that the agreement represents or manifests the self-determination powers of the nations of Australia and of the United States than it would add to the fact of the rolling stock deal to say that it expresses the self-determination of the people of Melbourne.

To return to the contrast between nationality and nationhood: the former establishes various legal relations between the citizen and various states, including a state or states of citizenship as such as well as states in which

[57] Helmut Philipp Aust, *Complicity and the Law of State Responsibility* (Cambridge: Cambridge University Press, 2011).

the citizen may be working, temporarily resident, and so on.[58] The latter does not establish legal relations.[59] Self-determination is of the same nonlegal register as nationhood. The legal situation of the population of the United Kingdom, for example, is not well articulated by the terminology of self-determination.[60] The advanced, privileged, comfortable, or otherwise favourable situation of residents of the United Kingdom is not captured by this vocabulary. It is too imprecise. One telling point is that the notion of self-determination is entirely inadequate for describing any residual patterns of injustice, discrimination, and so on in stable states. Without wishing to downplay the overall differences of quality of life and opportunity between a typical resident of the English home counties and a typical resident of a rural Third World setting, injustice and inequitable distribution of opportunities in housing, education, or employment are hardly eradicated from the former. The vocabulary of self-determination obscures such matters, in both cases. It is not simply a matter of Northern hegemony, with the dominant thinking of elite states repudiating a Third World aspiration to self-determination simply because those powerful states have already achieved that to which the weaker states still aspire. Setting aside the vocabulary of self-determination has a number of beneficial effects. It clears the ground for a more precise and potentially more efficacious analysis of injustice, whether in the First or Third Worlds. It reduces the salience of territorial claims and therefore reduces the likelihood that the displacement of populations will be entertained. It defuses nationalism. In Amartya Sen's terminology, it displaces transcendental frameworks for articulating injustice in favour of a comparative approach.[61] It is internationalist. Self-determination may be a strategic, rhetorical means: but it is not an end.

58 Sonia Morano-Foadi and Stelios Andreadakis, 'The Convergence of the European Legal System in the Treatment of Third Country Nationals in Europe: The ECJ and ECtHR Jurisprudence', 22 *European Journal of International Law*, 2011, 1071–1088.

59 Tellingly, self-determination looks no better as a candidate for international legal status when international law is widened to include informal international lawmaking, see Joost Pauwelyn, Ramses Wessel, and Jan Wouters, 'When Structures Become Shackles: Stagnation and Dynamics in International Lawmaking', 25 *European Journal of International Law*, 2014, 733–763.

60 It should be noted, however, that self-determination has been appealed to by the German Federal Constitutional Court in the context of the implementation of the Lisbon Treaty on European integration: Helmut Philipp Aust, 'Fundamental Rights of States: Constitutional Law in Disguise?' forthcoming in *Cambridge Journal of International and Comparative Law*, 2015.

61 Amartya Sen, *The Idea of Justice* (London: Penguin, 2009) 15; Amartya Sen, 'Thirteenth Annual Grotius Lecture Series: The Global Status of Human Rights', 27 *American University International Law Review*, 2012, 1–15.

10

The Evolution of Self-Determination of Peoples in International Law

ELIZABETH RODRÍGUEZ-SANTIAGO

1. INTRODUCTION

"All peoples have the right of self-determination. By virtue of that right they freely determine their political status and freely pursue their economic, social and cultural development."[1]

That formula reappears repeated[2] in different international instruments, from an extensive record of UN resolutions to the Human Rights Covenants of 1966 to agreements at both multilateral and regional levels. The right it proclaims – *self-determination* – has been qualified by the International Court of Justice (ICJ) as an *essential principle of international of law*. In the political arena it has become a sort of maxim that is slipped, every time it seems appropriate, in the discourses of separatist and pro-independence movements all over the world. They claim that they have the right to self-determination because it is a *right* that they have as a *people* under international law.

Do they? The answer is not easy. The clarity and certainty of some political doctrines, convictions, and demands are usually a step ahead of the developments in positive law. If it is clear, under international law, that all peoples have the right to self-determination, it is not yet so clear who these peoples are. *All* peoples are not necessarily all the *peoples* for whom the right really exists. And even when there is a certain consensus about whether or not a certain group of people is in fact a *people* with the right to self-determination, the consensus disappears over what is really the scope of this right. For instance, the ICJ has confirmed that the right of self-determination entitles the colonial peoples to independence; but it has not answered the question of whether noncolonial peoples, by virtue of that same right, would be entitled to secede.

1 Article 1 of the International Covenant on Civil and Political Rights, 16 December 1966.
2 With sometimes only slight grammatical variations among them.

The international law of self-determination is in fact full of gaps, contradictions, and incongruences; and the truth is that is has always been. The contemporary right of self-determination is the result of its evolution during the past centuries, but along that process the contradictions and the gaps have never disappeared; they have only been replaced with new ones.

This work follows a historical approach, assessing the past evolution of the right of self-determination, its present state, and its future possibilities. This approach seeks to show that self-determination, under international law, is an ever-evolving standard; that is has not yet settled because it still needs to evolve; and that, even if the international law on the matter has not always been in harmony with the political demands, it has eventually evolved in order to satisfy them.

I will argue that in order to merit a jus cogens status, self-determination of peoples, as a legal standard, needs to evolve even further. It must be recognized as a legitimate entitlement for remedial secession and should also be flexibilized in cases of secession. The ethnicity criteria to identify the *people*, historically justified during the nineteenth and twentieth centuries, should be replaced because it is no longer in accordance with the democratic exigencies of the principle itself.

2. SELF-DETERMINATION BEFORE THE TWENTIETH CENTURY

When the legal concept of self-determination of peoples is usually defined, many authors make the distinction between the Wilsonian and the Leninist conceptions of this right. The first one refers to the internal exercise of the right, while the second one refers to its external exercise.[3] Yet both ideas had been the object of claims long before Wilson's and Lenin's proposals.

However, when we refer to self-determination before the twentieth century, we can only identify some forms of what we call *self-determination* today, because the term had not yet been coined in the vocabulary of international law. In fact, we can only use the actual classifications as a reference in order to appreciate what forms or modalities of that right were recognized or advocated at different periods.

2.1 *The Rights of Indigenous Peoples under Natural Law*

One of the oldest modern claims for self-determination can be traced back to the period of the European colonization of America. A defense of the

[3] For a precise resume on both doctrines, see A. Cassese, *Self-Determination of Peoples*, Cambridge University Press, Cambridge, 1995, pp. 14–23.

sovereignty of the indigenous peoples was then advocated by some European authors and by the Catholic Church. Authors and priests, such as Domingo de Soto, Balthasar de Ayala, Bartolomoe de Las Casas, Francisco de Vitoria, Francisco Suárez, Gentilli, and Grotius, among others, defended the sovereignty of indigenous peoples and denounced the European conquest.

Bartolomeo de Las Casas (1474–1566), for instance, argued that the indigenous peoples were capable of governing themselves and he pleaded for the restitution of the possessions acquired by conquest, since they had been acquired illegally by an unjust war.[4] He also argued that their allegiance to the Kingdom of Spain should be established on a voluntary basis; and, even then, their autonomy should be respected.[5] Francisco de Vitoria (1480–1546) argued that the indigenous peoples were masters of their lands and that they were self-governed before the arrival of the Spaniards.[6] Francisco Suárez (1548–1617) considered that they were sovereign nations under the Law of Nations and argued that there was no justification for the use of force against them, except in the cases of human sacrifices and cannibalism.[7]

Among other European jurists and philosophers, Erasme de Rotterdam (1466–1536) denounced the conquests, arguing that any authority over a people should rely on their consent.[8] Grotius (1583–1645), in his work *Mare Liberum*, defended the sovereignty of the native peoples of America and Orient.[9] Pufendorf (1632–1694) claimed that the native peoples of America were independent peoples with their own sovereignty; therefore, they had the right to forbid foreigners to enter their territory and the right to self-defense against the European conquerors.[10] During the sixteenth and seventeenth centuries, many Catholic priests also defended the idea that indigenous

[4] See M. Morin, *L'usurpation de la souveraineté autochtone*, Montréal, Boréal, 1997, p. 37. For a description of Las Casas works defending the indigenous peoples, such as "Breve Relación de las destrucción de las Indias," among others, see *The Encyclopaedia Britannica*, 11th edition, Vol. 16, The Encyclopaedia Britannica Company, New York, 1911, p. 232.

[5] Morin, *L'usurpation*, p. 32.

[6] About Vitoria's doctrines, and about their influence on the doctrines of other authors, see Morin, *L'usurpation*, pp. 32–40.

[7] Morin, *L'usurpation*, pp. 37–38.

[8] See. S. Calogeropoulos-Stratis, *Le droit des peuples à disposer d'eux-mêmes*, Bruylant, Bruxelles, 1973, pp. 16, 182.

[9] See *ibid.*, pp. 40–44. Also, in the *Law of War and Peace* (1625), Grotius made a severe critique of the entitlements of Roman Emperors to conquer far away peoples; and, quoting Vitoria, he argued that it was illegitimate to claim, as a discovery, the property that belonged to other peoples, as well as it was illegitimate to submit them by force. See H. Grotius, *Le droit de la guerre et de la paix*, trans. P. Pradier-Fodéré, P.U.F., Paris, 2005, pp. 534–535.

[10] See Morin, *L'usurpation*, pp. 52–55.

peoples had, under natural law, the natural rights to liberty and property;[11] the Catholic Church explicitly recognized those rights in the papal bulls of 1537 and 1639.[12]

The doctrines defending the rights of the autochthonous peoples in America or Orient were, however, mostly based on interpretations of natural law, and the practice of the states did not follow them.

While since the Peace of Westphalia in 1648 the sovereignty of the nations became a principle accepted by most European states as being part of the Law of Nations, this law drew a fundamental distinction between the *civilized nations* and the *peuples sauvages*. Only the first ones had any legal personality. They were entitled to enjoy the respect of their sovereignty without external interference, which is something we consider today as external self-determination. Since the *peuples sauvages* were not recognized as part of the international community of civilized nations, these nations considered themselves entitled to conquer them.

This distinction between the civilized nations and the *peuples sauvages* will be essential to understand the evolution of the right to self-determination during the past four centuries.

2.2 *The Rights of Peoples Living inside the* Civilized Nations

Before the French Revolution the international community of civilized nations was in fact composed by the European states. The people or the minorities inside these states did not have any recognized right to choose their sovereign. There were, however, some doctrines arguing that in some circumstances they should have the right to be consulted or even to separate from the state.

Among others, Erasme de Rotterdam claimed that the sovereign should not make any cession of territory without the consent of the people living on it.[13] This position was also defended by Grotius, who argued that, in order to alienate a part of the territory, it was necessary to have the consent of the population living on it.[14]

[11] For the arguments and the actions of the Dominican priests in favor of the indigenous peoples, see F. Picó, *Historia general de Puerto Rico*, Ediciones Huracán, San Juan, 2004, pp. 50–51; F. A. Scarano, *Puerto Rico cinco siglos de historia*, McGraw-Hill, México, 2000, pp. 210–212.

[12] See Morin, *L'usurpation*, p. 37.

[13] See. J. F. Guilhaudis, *Le droit des peuples à disposer d'eux-mêmes*, Presse Universitaire de Grenoble, Grenoble, 1976, p. 17.

[14] Grotius affirms this doctrine by referring to the work of Gailius, *De pace publicâ*. See Grotius, *Le droit de la guerre*, p. 251.

Even if Grotius did not recognize a general right to separation for the people living inside the state, he defended the natural right of a population to self-preservation. His doctrine on this matter was very similar to what we call today *remedial secession*. He argued that a part of the state could not separate from the rest, except in the cases where the separation was necessary to ensure the conservation of that part, in which case the right to self-preservation of the people living on that territorial space superseded the rights of the sovereign over them.[15] It was, however, a very restricted idea of self-preservation because it was limited to what Grotius called the extreme necessity (*extrême nécessité*). According to him, this extreme necessity only existed if there were an imminent threat of death for the people[16] and, even then, the people had the right to resist their sovereign, but not to use violence against him.[17]

This remedial solution to ensure the safety and survival of the population is also present in Emerich de Vattel's doctrine. Vattel (1714–1767) argued that the people could separate from the state if they had been abandoned by the sovereign. This *abandon* existed if the sovereign refused or neglected to provide security or protection to the people.[18] Vattel also defended an idea of external self-determination. On grounds of natural law, he advocated for the sovereign equality of the states as free and independent entities,[19] and he argued that conquest by force was a vicious motive to make war.[20]

Remedial secession on Grotius's and Vattel's doctrines was grounded on a natural right to preservation and not on a recognition of any legal personality to the *people*. However, Vattel's doctrines, along with others, inspired the American and the French revolutions, leading to the birth of that personality.

2.3 *The French Revolution as an Exercise of Self-Determination*

Arguably, the French Revolution of 1789 set the origins of the modern principle of internal self-determination by recognizing the people as the

15 See Grotius, *Le droit de la guerre*, p. 252.

16 H. Grotius, Le droit de la guerre et de la paix, *trans. Jean Barbeyrac*, Pierre de Coup, Amsterdam, 1724, pp. 181–182. (Bibliothèque nationale de France, Gallica: image mode, PDF format.)

17 See Grotius, *Le droit de la guerre* (1724), p. 185.

18 See E. de Vattel, *La droit des gens ou principes de la loi naturelle*, . . . Vol. I, J. P. Aillaud, Paris, 1835, p. 264 (book I, chapter XVII, § 202).

19 See E. de Vattel, *Le droit des gens*, pp. 93–97 (front matter; §11-§ 20), 364 (book II, chapter III, § 36). This is, however, a doctrine that is present in Vattel's discussions all over his book.

20 See E. de Vattel, *Le droit des gens ou principes de la loi naturelle*, . . . Vol. II, J. P. Aillaud, Paris, 1835, p. 95 (book III, chapter III, § 30).

holders of sovereignty, as government derived its powers from the consent of the governed.[21] The recognition of external self-determination was also part of the political values of the revolution. For instance, a decree project of the Constitutional Assembly of May 1790 recognized the equal rights of all nations and declared that no nation had the right to invade another one;[22] in the project of the constitution of 1791 (although it never entered into force), France renounced any conquest over other peoples.[23] The next constitution of 1793, although assuming a more conservative position, proclaimed that France would not interfere in the affairs of other countries.[24]

These doctrines and values of the French Revolution had been influenced by the American Declaration of Independence and the American Revolution.

2.4 *The American and Latin American Independences as Exercises of Remedial Secession*

The American Declaration of Independence of 1776 was a proclamation of self-determination, both internal (the government deriving its just powers from the consent of the governed) and external. But American independence was, above all, an act of remedial secession, in the sense that this term has today. Even if, until the twentieth century, the term "secession" was mainly used to mean the withdrawal of a state from a confederacy or a composite state,[25] and the colonies were not confederated entities, their separation from the parent state was an act analogous to our present concept of secession.

21 See Cassese, *Self-Determination*, pp. 11–13; Calogeropoulos-Stratis, *Le droit des peuples à disposer d'eux-mêmes*, pp. 18–20.

22 See the decree project quoted in G. Scelle, *Précis du Droit des gens, 2ème partie*, Recueil Sirey, Paris, 1934, pp. 263–264.

23 See decree project quoted in Scelle, *Précis du Droit des gens*, p. 264.

24 Article 119 of the Constitution provided that the French nation "ne s'immisce point dans le gouvernement des autres nations; il ne souffre pas que les autres nations s'immiscent dans le sien."

25 See, for instance, C. Calvo, *Dictionnaire de Droit international public et privé*, Vol. 2, Puttkammer & Mühlbrecht, Berlin, Guillaumin & Cie, G. Pedone-Lauriel, A. Rousseau, Paris, 1885, p. 205; C. Calvo, *Dictionnaire manuel de Diplomatie et de Droit international public et privé*, Puttkammer & Mühlbrecht, Berlin, Guillaumin & Cie, G. Pedone-Lauriel, A. Rousseau, Paris, 1885, p. 384; *The Encyclopaedia Britannica*, 11th edition, Vol. 24, The Encyclopaedia Britannica Company, New York, 1911, p. 568; W. E. Baldwin (editor), *Bouvier's Law Dictionary Students Edition*, Banks Law Publishing, New York, 1928, p. 1096. For the historical evolution of the semantics of the term since the seventeenth century, see *Oxford English Dictionary*, 2nd edition, Vol. XIV, Clarendon Press, Oxford, 1989, p. 823.

Our contemporary definition of secession denotes the separation of a part of the population from the state.[26] Until the beginning of the twentieth century, under international law, the colonies were indeed simply a part of the state's territory.[27] The unilateral independence of the British colonies in North America during the eighteenth century was then, in practical terms, a separation of a part of the territory from the state; in other words, a secession. And, as this separation was carried out as a remedial solution against the abuses of the British Crown, it is then fair to equate it to the contemporary figure of remedial secession.

The language of the declaration demonstrates that the remedial separation was at the heart of it, as the independence was made necessary because of the actions of the British Crown:

> When in the course of human events it becomes necessary for one people to dissolve the political bands which have connected them with another ... a decent respect to the opinions of mankind requires that they should declare the causes which impel them to the separation....
>
> [W]henever any form of government becomes destructive of these ends, it is the right of the people to alter or to abolish it and to institute new government ...
>
> Prudence, indeed, will dictate that governments long established should not be changed for light and transient causes ... but when a long train of abuses and usurpations, pursuing invariably the same object, evinces a design to reduce them under absolute despotism, it is their right, it is their duty, to throw off such government, and to provide new guards for their future security. Such has been the patient sufferance of these colonies; and such is now the necessity which constrains them to alter their former systems of government.

[26] See J. Salomon, *Dictionnaire de Droit international public*, Bruylant, Bruxelles, 2001, pp. 1021–1022.

[27] For the nineteenth century, see C. Calvo, *Le Droit international théorique et pratique*, A. Durand et Pedone-Lauriel, Guillaumin et Cie, Paris, 1870, p. 119; C. Calvo, *Manuel de Droit international public et privé*, Arthur Rousseau, Paris, 1892, p. 86 (replica edition, Elibron Classics, Adamant Media Corporation, 2006).

The independence of a colony was not considered, at that moment, an act of decolonization, because the legal concept of *decolonization* did not emerge until the second half of the twentieth century and after a long evolution of the *colonial* concept itself. For the definition of colony until the nineteenth century, see M. Diderot, *Encyclopédie ou Dictionnaire raisonné des sciences, des arts et des métiers*, Vol. VIII, Chez Jean-Leonard Pellet, Genève, 1778, pp. 518–522; A. Ott, *Dictionnaire des Sciences Politiques et Sociales, Tome I*, J.-P. Migne, Paris, 1854, p. 1182 (Bibliothèque nationale de France, Gallica – mode image, format PDF); J. Bouvier, *Law Dictionary*, Vol. 1, George W. Childs, Philadelphia, 1862, p. 242 (replica edition, Classic Reprint Series, Forgotten Books, 2012); Calvo, *Dictionnaire manuel de Diplomatie*, p. 79.

The declaration continued with a detailed description of the oppressions from the crown and concluded:

> In every stage of these oppressions we have petitioned for redress in the most humble terms: our repeated petitions have been answered only by repeated injury.

So the thirteen colonies did not decide to separate because they capriciously preferred to have their own government or because they felt that they were a nation ethnically different than the British one. They separated because they believed that it was their last remedy solution against the injustices of their sovereign. Had the British government provided them with a just and fair treatment, they would not have had to resort to the extreme act of unilateral separation. In other terms, as in the actual doctrine of remedial secession, their separation was the last resort remedial solution to guarantee their self-preservation.

The American independence also influenced the independence movements in the Spanish colonies in America, these also motivated by the abuses of the Spanish crown against them. Inspired by the American Declaration of Independence, the texts of some declarations of independence of Latin American countries were very similar to it,[28] proclaiming that their unilateral separation was the last resort against the abuses of the Spanish crown. Their unilateral independence can therefore be also equated to an act of remedial secession.

2.5 *The Reinforcement of the Westphalian System after the Independences in America*

The American and Latin American revolutions, as exercises of self-determination, carried out with them the independence of colonial entities. However, none of them led to the birth of a right to self-determination for the colonial peoples, or a right to decolonization, or even less to a general prohibition of colonial conquests.

On the contrary, as the independence of the colonies in America led to a multiplication of states, the result was to strengthen the sovereign state in accordance with the Westphalian system. The distinction between civilized nations and *peuples sauvages* remained, and the former colonies simply

[28] For the declarations of independance of Venezuela, Bogotá, Chili, Uruguay, and Paraguay, see S. García Samudio, *La independencia de Hispanoamércia*, Fondo de Cultura Económica, México, 1945, pp. 104–113.

became new members of the international community of civilized nations. Under international law, the colonies continued to be considered just a part of the state's territory[29] and, even if their independence was a possibility (as history had shown), they had no right to it or any specific status under positive law. The right of preservation of the sovereign state continued to be one of the main principles of international law[30] and it superseded any interests of the inhabitants of the colonies. Even if other states could recognize the independence of a colony *post facto*,[31] during an insurrection they should either remain neutral[32] or assist only the government, as any assistance to the rebels was considered as an act of aggression and a violation of the state's sovereignty.[33]

Any recognition of the principle of national self-determination was then predicated in the principle of the state's sovereignty, both internal and external; the former referring to the ideal of the government deriving its just powers from the consent of the governed, the latter referring to the notion of independence vis-à-vis other nations.[34] As a corollary of this sovereignty, the state had the right to preservation and to the respect of the integrity of its territory. It also had the right to expand and enlarge its territory and to increase its population, its resources, and its power via the conquest and colonization of other countries.[35]

29 See C. Calvo, *Le Droit international théorique et pratique*, p. 119; Calvo, *Manuel de Droit international*, p. 86.

30 See J. B. Davis, *Outlines of International Law*, Harper & Brothers, New York, 1887, p. 71; T. Woolsey, *Introduction to the study of International Law*, Scribner, Armstrong & Co., New York, 1875, p. 56.

31 See Calvo, *Le Droit international théorique et pratique*, p. 179; Calvo, *Manuel de Droit international*, pp. 93–94; H. Wheaton, Elements du Droit international, Vol. I, Brockhaus & Avenarius, Leipzig, 1848, pp. 36–37.

32 Calvo, *Manuel de Droit international*, pp. 93–94.

33 See Davis, *Outlines of International Law*, p. 75; Woolsey, *Introduction to the Study of International Law*, p. 56.

34 See Wheaton, *Elements du Droit international*, p. 31.

35 See ibid., p. 77; Calvo, *Dictionnaire manuel de Diplomatie*, p. 79; L. Levi, *International Law with materials for a Code of International Law*, Kegan Paul, Trench & Co., London, 1887, p. 103; Woolsey, *Introduction to the Study of International Law*, p. 37.

Calvo, however, while defending the right of the "civilized Nations" to conquer and colonize other lands, argued that if the land to be colonized was already occupied by indigenous peoples having their own government, then – as a matter of equity – the conqueror should not steal by force the land and the property but should instead recognize their government and negotiate with it the buying of the land that was going to be occupied. It was, however, only a formality based on equity concerns and not a defense of any rights for these indigenous peoples.

Woolsey, on the other side, was against the conquest and colonization, but considered that it was part of the positive international law.

The state's right to preservation and to the integrity of its territory implied, however, the denial for minorities, or other social communities, of any right to separate from it and to form an independent political entity. Concomitantly, the state's right to expansion implied the denial of any recognition of sovereignty or territorial integrity right to the noncivilized nations or *peuples sauvages.*

2.6 *The Progressive Doctrines of the Nineteenth Century*

In spite of this reality, there were some doctrines that anticipated ideas of self-determination similar to those that were going to emerge and develop in the twentieth century.

For instance, Von Martens (1756–1821) in Germany opposed the conquests and proposed in his doctrine that the state's right to expansion should only be restrained to unoccupied lands.[36] In France, Fustel de Coulanges (1830–1889) argued that the people should be part of a state only if it is by their free will, and he suggested even the possibility of secession just by the will of the population.[37] In Italy, Mancini (1817–1888) proposed the *principle of nationalities* according to which every nation that had its own ethnical, linguistic, cultural, religious, and historical characteristics had the natural right to become an independent state.[38] This principle was defended in America by William B. Lawrence (1800–1881) who, opposing and criticizing the majoritarian doctrine, argued that the principle was already part of the conventional European Law.[39]

The Italian jurist Pasquale Fiore (1837–1914) also defended the principle of nationalities, but on grounds different than those of Mancini. He called it the *right of nationality*[40] and argued that it arose from the natural *right of sociability*. He made a clear distinction between the *state*, the *nation*, and the *people*, arguing that, by virtue of the right of sociability, every nation had

[36] See J. F. de Martens, *Précis du droit des gens modernes de l'Europe*, Vol. I, Guillaumain et Cie, Paris, 1858, p. 308 (Bibliothèque nationale de France, Gallica – mode image, format PDF).

[37] He proposed this doctrine in his defense of the right to choose of the peoples of Alsace and Strasbourg. See his notorious correspondence with professor Mommsen of Berlin in F. de Coulanges, *Questions contemporaines*, Hachette, Paris, 1919, pp. 89–102 (Bibliothèque nationale de France, Gallica – mode image, format PDF).

[38] See Calogeropoulos-Stratis, *Le droit des peuples*, pp. 26–28.

[39] See W. B. Lawrence, *Commentaire sur les Eléments du Droit international et sur l'Histoire des progrès du Droit des gens de Henry Wheaton*, F. A. Brockhaus, Liepzig, 1868, pp. 155–160.

[40] P. Fiore, *Nouveau Droit international public, Vol. 1, trans. P. Pradier-Fodéré,* Auguste Durand et Pédone-Lauriel, Paris, 1868, pp. 95.

the right to become an independent state and that the people had the natural right to independence and secession. However, in contrast with Mancini's principle of nationalities, Fiore argued that people forming a nation was not the result of natural and physical circumstances, but the result of their natural right of sociability. Therefore, if people from different races would like to associate under the same nation, they then had the right to form a state or to secede from another only by their will.[41] Fiore's doctrines proposed a progressive idea of self-determination that not even today has been recognized by the international law.

None of these progressive doctrines was followed by the practice in the nineteenth century. The principle of nationalities, for instance, did not become a general principle of positive law, regardless of the importance it played in the reunification of Italy. No improvements were made either in the view that the population's allegiances to a sovereign should rely on its consent. Even if some treaties of cession and of peace established warranties for the citizens of a ceded or defeated territory,[42] those were provisions for their protection only, and international law did not require for them to be consulted before the cessions.

In the arena of international relations and international law, the distinction between the civilized nations and the *peuples sauvages* prevailed during the nineteenth century and the beginning of the twentieth. The Berlin Conference of 1884–1885 and the Scramble for Africa are the best examples. The partition of Africa, as an exercise of the *right to conquer*, according to the sole economic interests of the European colonial powers and not to those of the African peoples concerned, was in fact blessed by international law at a moment when this law was fundamentally created by these powers.

International law did not recognize any rights to the colonial peoples, as for this to happen the state's right to conquer needed to be challenged first. That right to conquer began to be contested by the great powers (although not

[41] See ibid., pp. 95–131.

[42] That was the case, for instance, of the United States practice regarding the acquisition of territory. The treaty for the acquisition of Louisiana in 1803 provided that the inhabitants of the ceded territory shall be incorporated in the Union of the United States to become citizens and protected in the free enjoyment of their liberty, property, and religion; and similar provisions were incorporated in the treaty of 1819 with Spain for the cession of Florida, the treaty of 1867 with Russia for the cession of Alaska, the treaty of Guadalupe–Hidalgo in 1848 ending the Mexican-American war, and the treaty of Gadsden in 1853 for the cession of a part of New-Mexico and Arizona. See J. Trías Monge, *Historia Constitucional de Puerto Rico*, Vol. 1, Editorial de la Universidad de Puerto Rico, San Juan, 1980, pp. 153–154; C. W. Elliot, *American Historical Documents – The Harvard Classics*, Grolier Enterprises Corp., Danbury, 1990, pp. 250–254.

forbidden) for the first time during World War I, and around that same period national self-determination was advocated by authors as a political principle.

3. SELF-DETERMINATION BETWEEN THE TWO WORLD WARS

3.1 *Wilson's Doctrine during the First World War*

President Woodrow Wilson's famous fourteen points speech before the American Congress on January 8, 1918, contained what many authors consider to be the starting point in the evolution of self-determination during the twentieth century. In the fifth point he advocated for:

> a free, open-minded, and absolutely impartial adjustment of all colonial claims, based upon a strict observance of the principle that in determining all such questions of sovereignty the interests of the populations concerned must have equal weight with the equitable claims of the government whose title is to be determined.[43]

This fifth point has been interpreted by some authors as the start of a recognition by the great powers of a right to self-determination for colonial peoples.[44] However, this was not its intent. Had it been a claim for self-determination for all the colonial peoples, then it would have also meant an American intention to relinquish its own colonial power over its own colonies and that was not the case. Neither the United States nor the Allies intended to recognize self-determination to the peoples of their own colonies.[45] In fact, Wilson later even made declarations regretting the misinterpretation of his fifth point[46] and clarifying that "it was not within the privilege of the conference of peace to act upon the right of self determination of any peoples except those which had been included in the territories of defeated empires."[47]

Regarding the colonial cause, the significant contribution of Wilson's speech was not in the fifth point but in its introductory statement – sometimes neglected by the historians – that "the day of conquest and aggrandizement is

[43] See transcription of the full speech in *Messages and Papers of the Presidents*, Vol. XVII, Government Printing Office, Washington, pp. 8421–8426.

[44] See A. Cobban, *National Self Determination*, The University of Chicago Press, Chicago, 1944, pp. 19–22; Cassese, *Self-Determination*, pp. 19–23. Regarding other messages delivered by President Wilson between 1915 and 1918 and referring to this right, see G. Scelle, *Précis du Droit des gens, 2ème partie*, Recueil Sirey, Paris, 1934, pp. 267–268.

[45] See Cassese, *Self-Determination*, pp. 22–23.

[46] See Cobban, *National Self Determination*, p. 21, quoting H. W. V. Temperley in A *History of the Peace Conference 1920–1924*, Vol. IV, p. 429.

[47] Part of speech given on September 17, 1919, quoted in ibid., p. 22.

gone by."[48] In fact, the birth of a right to self-determination for colonial peoples needed to be concomitant with a renunciation, from the Great Powers, to their right to aggrandizement via conquest, which had precisely led to the establishments of their colonial empires. Indeed, after the new postwar world order, the states could no longer undertake conquering adventures without facing at least the disapproval of the international community; and the right to aggrandizement could not any longer be legitimately invoked as a state prerogative. This was one of the lessons of the war.

3.2 *The League of Nations and the Mandates System*

Although the Covenant of the League of Nations made no explicit mention of the concept of self-determination, its Article 10 encompassed the principle of external self-determination under the political independence and territorial integrity of the members. According to this article the members of the league undertook "to respect and preserve as against external aggression the territorial integrity and existing political independence of all Members of the League." This article concerned, however, only the members of the organization and did not comprise the states outside it or the non-independent territories. This provision even excluded the possibility of recognizing any self-determination right to minorities or other groups, as it protected the territorial integrity of the state.

An embryo of a self-determination right for colonial peoples – as it will later evolve after the creation of the United Nations – can be found in the mandates system of Article 22 of the Covenant. This system placed the former colonies and territories of the defeated countries under the administration of members of the League and under the supervision of the organization.[49]

However, the mandate system had no intention of extending a right to self-determination to those peoples. Indeed, when in their war speeches the Allies had defended the self-determination of the occupied countries, what they meant was the right of already independent nations not to be invaded. It had nothing to do with a recognition of self-determination for the colonies or territories who were not independent states. And when the winners forced the defeated countries to relinquish their colonies, they did not proclaim their

[48] See the introduction of the speech in *Messages and Papers of the Presidents*, Vol. XVII, Government Printing Office, Washington, p. 8423.

[49] For a resume with comments on the different kind of mandates, see A. Rougier, "La première Assemblée de la Société des Nations," *Revue Générale de Droit International Public*, Vol. 28, 1921, pp. 333–340 (Bibliothèque nationale de France, Gallica – mode image, format PDF).

liberation in accordance with the same self-determination right that they had recognized to the occupied – yet *civilized* – European countries.[50] The Covenant did not legitimate the mandates with a rhetoric of liberation for the peoples of the colonies. The system was justified as a *trust of civilization* over peoples who had no capacity of governing themselves. With the mandates system, the classical distinction between civilized nations and *peuples sauvages* was just replaced with a new dichotomy between "advanced nations" and peoples "not yet able to stand by themselves," the former having this time not the right but the responsibility to civilize the latter.

Nevertheless, as the Covenant stipulated that "the well being and development of such peoples form a sacred trust of civilization," the system was supposed to aim at their protection. The mandates were indeed executed under specific parameters on behalf of the League, and it was the first time that the administration of nonindependent territories was carried out with external surveillance. This was certainly a historical innovation. Before World War I the practice was that the colonies of the defeated countries became spoils of war for the victors. But this time the colonies were placed under a particular regime and, even if the tutelage was justified because they were considered not able yet to stand by themselves, the colonies became recipients of specific rights. It would then be fair to say that the mandated territories acquired a sort of legal personality under international law, something they did not have under the colonial regimes. In fact, half a century later, in the Namibia opinion,[51] the ICJ interpreted the mandate system in retrospect and concluded that the "sacred trust of civilization" enshrined in it was meant to aim, in the long run, the independence for these territories.[52] The birth of a right to self-determination for the mandated territories can hence be traced back to Article 22 of the League's Covenant, even if it was not at the time the intention of its drafters.

This is not, however, the case with regard to all colonial people. The colonies of the League's members were not mentioned in the Covenant and these members had no intention of questioning their own power over them. Nevertheless, the principle of self-determination was gaining more acceptance in practice. For instance, after the war, some bilateral peace treaties did

[50] For the preliminary works of the Treaty of Peace and the different points of view of the Allies, see Cobban, *National Self Determination*, pp. 16–34.

[51] See *Legal Consequences for the States of the Continued Presence of South Africa in Namibia*, Advisory Opinion, I.C.J. Reports 1971, p. 16.

[52] See ibid., p. 31, para. 53.

recognize a principle of self-determination, designating it with that name. The League was even called to take a position on some of them.

3.3 *The League of Nations and the Aaland Islands case*

The Aaland Islands case is frequently interpreted in contradictory ways. Sometimes it is referenced to demonstrate that self-determination was not a legal standard at the time of the League, while in other cases it is used to show the recognition by the League's Council of the existence of the right to self-determination.

In this case Sweden was asking Finland to hold a plebiscite in the Aaland Islands for the population to decide if they wanted to be part of Finland or Sweden. Sweden argued that by virtue of the right to self-determination, the people of the islands had the right to decide to which country they wanted to belong. Finland, on the other side, argued that according to international law this was an internal issue over which only Finland had competence. The case was referred to the League's Council.

The first committee appointed by the League's Council to decide on preliminary questions concluded in a first phase that, even if the principle had been invoked during the war, was part of the modern political thought, and had been included in some international treaties, it was not part of positive international law, as it had not been incorporated in the League's Covenant.[53] In a second phase of the case, regarding the merits of the question, the Council adopted a commission's report concluding that Finland had sovereignty over the Aaland Islands. However, it required Finland to guarantee certain internal autonomy and cultural rights to the population.[54]

The Commission of Jurists held that the principle of self-determination had the same object than the principle of protection of minorities,[55] which was "to assure to some national Group the maintenance and free development of its social, ethnical or religious characteristics."[56] In this case there was no oppression from Finland over the Aalanders that could justify a separation. Therefore a compromising solution was to respect Finland's sovereignty over the islands while warranting to the population the protection of minorities.[57] The remarks of the Commission are worth quoting:

[53] See Cassese, *Self-Determination*, p. 28.

[54] See *Minutes of the Fourteenth Meeting of the Council, June 24th 1921*, League of Nations Official Journal, September 1921, p. 697.

[55] See Cassese, *Self-Determination*, p. 30. [56] Quoted in ibid., p. 30. [57] Ibid., pp. 30–31.

> The separation of a minority from the State of which it forms a part and its incorporation in another State can only be considered as an altogether exceptional solution, a last resort when the State lacks either the will or the power to enact and apply just and effective guarantees.... The Aalanders have neither been persecuted nor oppressed by Finland.[58]

We can see here an argument for remedial secession, although for the Commission this secession would not have been enabled by a right to self-determination, but by the principle of protection of minorities, this second one being indeed part of the positive international law.[59]

The legacy of the case is that the Council of the League recognized the existence of self-determination as a political principle, as well as the right of the protection of minorities with a right to remedial secession on grounds of this protection.

3.4 *The League of Nations and the Eastern Carelia Case*

In 1920 the Council of the League of Nations asked the Permanent Court of International Justice to give an advisory opinion regarding the obligatory character of the provisions of two instruments, both of which recognized the right of self-determination of the people of Eastern Carelia.[60] The first instrument was the 1920 Treaty of Peace between Finland and Russia signed at Dopart. It stipulated:

> Finland shall ... withdraw its troops from the Communes of Repola and Porajärvi. These Communes shall be re-incorporated in the State of Russia and shall be attached to the autonomous territory of Eastern Carelia, which is to include the Carelian population of the Governments of Archangel and Olonetz, and which shall enjoy the national right of self-determination.[61]

The second instrument was the declaration of the Russian Delegation with regard to the autonomy of Eastern Carelia. Among other things, it stated: "The Carelian population of the Governments of Archangel and Olonetz (Aunus) shall enjoy the right of self-determination."[62] The Court declared itself unable to give the opinion due to the lack of consent on jurisdiction of both parties. However, the case remains important in that it provides an example of bilateral treaties recognizing the right to self-determination, which shows an

58 Quoted in ibid., pp. 31–32, note 58.

59 For a transcription of the Commission's report see ibid., pp. 30–32, notes 56 and 58.

60 See *Status of Eastern Carelia*, Advisory Opinion, 1923 P.C.I.J. (ser. B) No. 5 at 7 (July 23).

61 See ibid., p. 18. 62 See ibid., p. 21.

increasing acceptance of the principle. At least in the case of these two parties, Russia and Finland, the clear reference in the treaties to the right of self-determination evidences their unequivocal *opinio juris*.[63]

4. SELF-DETERMINATION AFTER THE CREATION OF THE UNITED NATIONS

4.1 *Article 1 of the UN Charter*

According to Article 1, Paragraph 2, of the Charter of the United Nations (UN), one of the purposes of the organization is "To develop friendly relations among nations based on the respect for the principle of equal rights and self-determination of peoples." This was the first time that the principle of self-determination was explicitly recognized in a multilateral legal instrument.[64] But what did it mean by then and for whom was it recognized? This article of the Charter has too often being misinterpreted as recognizing the self-determination right for *all* peoples. This was not, however, the intent of its drafters.

Article 1, Paragraph 2, was only intended to express a recognition of the external self-determination for the members of the UN, which was simply a reference to the respect of the principle of the state sovereignty, something that already existed at the customary and conventional levels. As such, it was only conceived in the Charter to apply to the member states of the organization.

Some authors support this interpretation by simply calling for a literal reading of the provisions of the article. Professor Guilhaudis, for instance, points out that Article 1, Paragraph 2, only concerns the relations between the UN members.[65] It is worth recalling that the Charter uses the term "peoples" to name the states because "nation" and "state" had been used until then as synonyms in international law.[66] He also points out that in the preamble of the Charter the contracting parties refer to themselves as "We the peoples of the

63 Regardless of the double standard used by Finland, which took the opposite position in the Aaland Islands case.

64 Article 55 of the Charter also refers to the principle of self-determination but in the context of the economic cooperation of the members of the UN.

65 Guilhaudis, *Le droit des peuples*, p. 169.

66 Regarding the definition of *people*, as synonym of state on international law, see J. Bouvier, *Law Dictionary*, Vol. 2, J. B. Lippincott & Co., Philadelphia, 1880, p. 321 (replica edition, Classic Reprint Series, Forgotten Books, 2012); J. Basdesvant, *Dictionnaire de la terminologie du Droit international*, Sirey, Paris, 1960, p. 450.

United Nations"[67] and there is no doubt that here the term "peoples" refers only to the member states of the UN and not to other territories who were not members of the organization at the time.

Now, a reading of the French version of the Charter can better clarify the confusions that might have arisen from the English or the Spanish versions of it. The French version of article 1, Paragraph 2, states: "Développer entre les nations des relations amicales fondées sur le respect du principe de l'égalité de droits des peuples et de *leur* droit à disposer d'eux-mêmes." In this, the phrase "leur droit à disposer d'eux-mêmes" translates to English as "their right to self-determination." The possessive adjective "their" designates the same peoples for which the first part of the sentence had proclaimed the principle of equal rights. In the French text it is clear that the two parts of the sentence refer to the same subject, the peoples, and not to two different subjects, the states and the peoples. In other words, the sentence refers to the equal rights among the member states and the right of those members to self-determination.

The preparatory works of the Charter are of even more help here. Professor Cassese's analysis of these works shows that the right to self-determination in Article 1, Paragraph 2, was only intended for the member states of the UN.[68] Indeed, during the San Francisco conference the drafting of this article generated strong debates given the difficulty of defining self-determination and the fear of some states that the wording could be misunderstood as legitimating secessions.[69]

The past seven decades have proven these concerns justified. Not only has the article been misinterpreted and invoked as a legitimation for secession – the Russian actions and words on Ukraine being the most recent example – but it has also been interpreted as a recognition of the self-determination right for all the peoples that were not originally encompassed by it.

In fact the evolution of self-determination since then has been precisely shaped by the misinterpretation of this article by both the General Assembly (GA) and the ICJ.

67 Guilhaudis, *Le droit des peuples*, p. 195, note 35.

68 See Cassese, *Self-Determination*, pp. 37–43. The author here resumes and analyses the discussions during the preparatory works, and specially the report of the Syrian reporter, to arrive at the conclusion that the drafters of the Charter did not wanted the non-self-governing territories to be inside the scope of Article 1. See also Guilhaudis, *Le droit des peuples*, pp. 172–173.

69 Ibid.

4.2 *The Colonial Peoples and the UN Charter*

Chapter XI of the UN Charter, entitled "Declaration Regarding Non-Self-Governing Territories," created certain obligations for the members of the organization who administered these kind of territories. Chapter XII, entitled "International Trusteeship System," created a regime for the administration of the territories that had been under the mandates system of the League of Nations. The trusteeship system was similar to the mandates, but with further provisions leading to the self-government or the independence of the territories.

In the case of the non-self-governing territories, Article 73 under Chapter XI specifically declared:

> Members of the United Nations which have or assume responsibility for the administration of territories whose peoples have not yet attained a full measure of self-government recognize the principle that the interest of the inhabitants of these territories are paramount and accept as a sacred trust the obligation to promote to the utmost . . . the well being of the inhabitants of these territories. . . .

To that end the article also created specific obligations for the administering powers over the territories, including the obligation to ensure their political, economic, social, and educational advancement, to develop their self-government, and to transmit (according to Article 73 (e)) regularly to the Secretary General some information regarding the territories.

It has frequently been argued that Article 73 had the effect of extending to the colonial peoples the right of self-determination recognized in Article 1, Paragraph 2, of the Charter. Professor Calogeropoulos-Stratis, among others, argues that the provisions of this article would have stripped the colonial powers of their sovereignty over these territories. From then on the peoples of the territories would be the owners of their own sovereignty. But being incapable of exercising it yet, the administering powers assumed the responsibility of a provisional administration until they could become fully capable of doing it on their own; a provisional administration that was controlled by the UN via the mechanism of transmission of information to the Secretary General.[70]

This interpretation is not, however, accurate. Chapter XI was never intended to recognize the self-determination right to the peoples of the non-self-governing territories, as the *peoples* of this chapter were not the same kind of *peoples* of Article 1, Paragraph 2.

Here again, a comparison with the French version of the Charter can better clarify the spirit of the text. The English version of the text refers to the "territories

[70] See Calogeropoulos-Stratis, *Le droit des peuples*, pp. 113–114.

whose *peoples* have not yet attained a full measure of self-government," while the French version refers to the "territoires dont les *populations* ne s'administrent pas encore complètement elles-mêmes." The English term *peoples* is here translated in French as *populations*, which designates the populations who inhabit the territories and not the *peoples* in the sense of Article 1. As we have seen, in Article 1, Paragraph 2, the English term "peoples" was translated in French as *peuple*, but in the French version of Chapter XI the term "*peuple*" does not even appear. The French text only mentions the *populations* (populations) and the *habitants* (inhabitants) of the non-self-governing territories.

Also, Chapter XI did not create any special decolonization right for these territories. It is true that one of the obligations for the administering powers under Article 73 is "to develop self-government," but self-government only meant a certain autonomy and not external self-determination. The reference to "independence" does not appear in Chapter XI as it appears in Chapter XII for some of the trusteeship territories. We can also point out that Article 73 does not suggest any condemnation of the relationship of subordination between the administering power and the territory. It actually refers to the members who "have or assume *responsibilities* for the administration of territories." These responsibilities signified a legitimation, rather than a condemnation, of the subordination of those territories to the administering Powers.

In any case, there is no reference in the Charter to any "subjection to alien domination" or "colonial domination." For these concepts to appear, the GA resolutions and the ICJ opinions had to interpret Chapter XI retroactively, and they interpreted that it was intended to apply to colonial territories. The GA resolutions and the ICJ opinions will transform the "responsibility for the administration of territories" into an illegal "colonial domination."

4.3 *The General Assembly Resolutions and the Development of Customary Law*

Though Article 73 required the administering members to transmit some information about the administered non-self-governing territories, it did not define what was a non-self-governing territory, nor did it provide a mechanism for the surveillance of the obligations under Chapter XI.[71] The administering powers were the ones that initially decided which territories they wanted to

[71] See United Nations, *Non-Self-Governing Territories: Summaries and Analyses of Information Transmitted to the Secretary-General during 1946*, United Nations Publications, New York, 1947, pp. 131–139. See also United Nations, *Year Book of the United Nations 1946–47*, United Nations Publications, New York, 1947, p. 571.

send the information about.[72] In other words, they were the ones who unilaterally diagnosed the territorial condition. In fact, since the beginning of the organization, they advocated that they were the only ones who could decide which territories were non-self-governing territories. They even argued that the GA had no authority to discuss Chapter XI because their relationship with their territories was a matter within their domestic jurisdiction falling under the provisions of Article 2, Paragraph 7, of the Charter.[73] The GA had to impose its jurisdiction, against the administering powers, to control the implementation of Chapter XI.

A first stage can be located between 1946 and 1952 when the GA started to adopt resolutions that would progressively strengthen its role in the light of Chapter XI. During this period it adopted resolutions creating a guide for the members for the preparation of the information due under Article 73.[74] The GA indicated that the UN should be informed of any changes in the status of the territories and declared itself competent to discuss the matter.[75] To this aim, it created special committees to study the information sent by the administering powers and to study the factors to identify the Chapter XI territories,[76] encouraged the participation of the non-self-governing territories on the works of these committees,[77] and adopted lists of factors to identify the non-self-governing territories.[78] This gave the GA a certain surveillance role and it succeeded in imposing its competence to control the execution of Chapter XI and to determine which territories fell under the scope of this chapter.

A second phase took place between 1952 and 1958, when the GA adopted several resolutions establishing a link between the right of self-determination and human rights[79] and recognizing this right to the non-self-governing and trust territories.

[72] See G.A. resolution 66 (I) of 1946, enumerating the non-self-governing territories according to the information sent by the administrating states.

[73] See United Nations, *Non-Self-Governing Territories: Summaries and analyses of information transmitted to the Secretary-General during* 1949, United Nations Publications, New York, 1950, pp. 3–4.

[74] See G.A. resolutions 142 (II) and 143 (II) of 1947.

[75] See G.A. resolutions 222 (III) of 1948 and 334 (IV) of 1949.

[76] See G.A. resolutions 146 (II) of 1947, 219 (III) of 1948, 332 (IV) of 1949, 445 (V) of 1950 and 565 (VI) of 1952.

[77] See G.A. resolutions 566 (VI) of 1952, 647 (VII) of 1952 and 744 (VIII) of 1953.

[78] See G.A. resolutions 567 (VI) of 1952, 648 (VII) of 1952, 742 (VIII) of 1953.

[79] See G.A. resolutions 545 (VI) of 1952 (incorporating the right to self-determination in the texts of the Human Rights Covenants), 637 (VII) of 1952, 738 (VIII) of 1953, 837 (IX) of 1954 and 1188 (XII) of 1957.

In 1952, the GA resolution 637 (VII) – entitled "The right of peoples and nations to self-determination" – recognized the right of self-determination for these territories for the first time. It demanded that the members recognize and promote the realization of the right of self-determination of the peoples of non-self-governing and trust territories under their administration and to facilitate the exercise of this right according to the "principles and spirit of the Charter" and the wishes of the peoples concerned. The preamble of the resolution established a link between human rights and the right of "peoples and nations" to self-determination and for this referenced to the principles of Articles 1 and 55 of the Charter. In other words, in the spirit of the resolution, self-determination for the non-self-governing territories did not arise from the provisions of Chapter XI, but from human rights and Article 1 of the Charter. At the same time, other resolutions adopted during the same period regarding the application of Article 73 did not make any reference to the right of self-determination for these territories.[80]

In the following years, further resolutions were adopted by the GA recalling resolution 637 (VII).[81] As a result, in the GA resolutions, the recognition of self-determination for the territories of Chapters XI and XII was detached from the provision of the chapters themselves and linked to the principles of Article 1 of the Charter. In favor of these territories, and by virtue of human rights, the *self-determination of peoples* consecrated at the Article 1, Paragraph 2, of the Charter was reinterpreted as the right of *peoples and nations to self-determination* and extended to those that had never been considered in its original wording.

A third phase started in 1960 with the birth of a right to decolonization. Until then, Chapters XI and XII had framed the relationships of subordinations between the administering powers and the non-self-governing and trusteeship territories, and had legitimized them as a necessary transitional situation. For a true recognition of self-determination for these territories to take place, it was necessary to question the relationships framed by those chapters. The changes in the GA composition, that were taking place with the access to the United Nations of the recently independent Third World countries, set the conditions for that.[82] Influenced by the results of the Bandung Conference,[83] in 1960 the GA adopted resolutions 1514 (XV) and 1541 (XV).

[80] See G.A. resolutions 567 (VI) of 1952, 648 (VII) of 1952 and 742 (VIII) of 1953.

[81] See G.A. resolutions 637 (VII) of 1952, 738 (VIII) of 1953, 837 (IX) of 1954 and 1188 (XII) de 1957.

[82] For a study on the representation distribution of countries at the principal UN organs during the 1950 and 1960 decades, see P. Buirette-Maurau, *La participation du Tiers monde à l'élaboration du Droit international*, L.G.D.J., Paris, 1983, pp. 42–57.

[83] The text of the resolution 1514 is in fact very similar to the text of the Bandung Declaration. For the text of the Declaration, see C. P. Romulo, *The Meaning of Bandung*, The University of North Carolina Press, North Carolina, 1956, pp. 92–102.

Resolution 1514 (XV), entitled "Declaration on the granting of independence to colonial countries and peoples," condemned for the first time colonial relationships. The *colonial* reference was indeed an innovation, as the term was not present in the text of the Charter and, in the language of international law, the illegitimate connotation it has today had not yet been consolidated.[84] According to the resolution, "All peoples have the right to self-determination; by virtue of this right they freely determine their political status and freely pursue their economic, social and cultural development." The resolution also condemned all subjection of peoples to alien subjugation, domination, and exploitation and urged that immediate steps be taken to advance the independence of the non-self-governing territories, the trust territories, and all other territories that had not yet attained independence, in order to transfer all powers to the peoples of these territories. Resolution 1541 (XV) complemented resolution 1514 (XV) by establishing the factors to determine when it was necessary to send the information required by Article 73 (e) of the Charter, which served then as way to identify the colonial territories. There were two *prima facie* factors to identify them. First, the territory had to be geographically separated and ethnically or culturally distinct from the country administering it. Second, once this was established, the colonial condition was then confirmed if the relationship between the metropolitan state and the territory placed the latter in a position or status of subordination.

In the following decades the principles contained in these two resolutions consolidated into new customary law. An abundant record of resolutions adopted every year, since 1960 until now, reiterating[85] or supplementing[86]

[84] For the evolution of the term *colony* in the past centuries, see M. Diderot, Encyclopedie ou Dictionnaire raisonné des sciences, des arts et des métiers, Vol. III, Briasson, David, Le Breton & Durand, Paris, 1753, pp. 648–650; Ott, *Dictionnaire des Sciences Politiques*, p. 1182 ; Bouvier, *Law*, Vol. 1, p. 242; Calvo, *Dictionnaire manuel de Diplomatie*, p. 79; J. Basdevant, *Dictionnaire de la terminologie du Droit international*, Sirey, Paris, 1960, p. 124; B. A. Garner (editor), *Black's Law Dictionary*, 8th edition, Maine, West, 2004, p. 281.

[85] See G.A. resolutions 1810 (XVII), 1956 (XVIII), 2105 (XX), 2189 (XXI), 2326 (XXII), 2465 (XXIII), 2548 (XXIV), 2708 (XXV), 2878 (XXVI), 2908 (XXVII), 3163 (XXVIII), 3328 (XXIX), 3481 (XXX), 31/143, 32/42, 33/44, 34/94, 35/119, 36/68, 37/35, 38/54, 39/91, 40/57, 41/41, 42/71, 43/45, 44/101, 45/34, 46/71, 47/23, 48/52, 49/89, 50/39, 52/78, 53/68, 54/91, 55/147, 56/74, 57/140, 58/111, 59/136 and 60/119.

[86] See G.A. resolutions 2288 (XXII), 2425 (XXIII), 2554 (XXIV), 2703 (XXV), 2873 (XXVI), 2979 (XXVII), 3117 (XXVIII), 3299 (XXIX), 3398 (XXX), 31/7, 32/35, 33/40, 34/41, 35/28, 36/51, 37/31, 38/50, 39/42, 40/52, 41/14, 42/74, 43/29, 44/84, 45/17, 46/64, 47/15, 48/46, 49/40, 50/33 ; 52/72, 53/61, 54/84, 55/138, 56/66, 57/132, 58/103, 59/128 & 60/111 ; 2649 (XXV), 2787 (XXVI), 2955 (XXVII), 3070 (XXVIII), 3246 (XXIX), 31/34, 32/14, 33/24, 34/44, 35/35, 36/9, 37/43, 38/17, 39/17, 40/25, 41/101, 42/95, 44/79, 46/87, 47/82, & 49/151 ; 36/10, 37/42, 38/16, 39/18, 40/24, 41/100, 42/94, 44/80, 46/88, 47/83, 48/93, 49/148, 50/139, 52/113, 54/155, 55/85, 56/141, 57/197, 58/161, 59/180 and 60/145.

the principles of resolution 1514 (XV) established an unequivocal *opinio juris*. The creation of a committee of decolonization in charge of the surveillance of the application of the resolution[87] and even the steps taken by the trusteeship committee to apply it to the trust territories[88] led to a modification of the regimes of Chapters XI and XII of the Charter in favor of the birth of a customary right of self-determination for the colonial peoples.

In 1970 the GA adopted resolution 2625 (XXV), entitled "Declaration on Principles of International Law concerning Friendly Relations and Cooperation among States." This resolution reiterated the rights already established in favor of colonial peoples by resolution 1514. Its main object was not, however, the colonial question, but the relations among states. In this spirit it made a broader approach of the self-determination, recognizing it for *all* peoples by "virtue of the principle of equal rights and self-determination of peoples enshrined in the Charter of the United Nations."

In contrast with resolution 1514 (XV), resolution 2625 (XXV) established a balance between the self-determination right of the peoples and the territorial integrity of the states. According to its provisions:

> Nothing in the foregoing paragraphs shall be construed as authorizing or encouraging any action which would dismember or impair, totally or in part, the territorial integrity or political unity of sovereign and independent States ... conducting themselves in compliance with the principle of equal right and self-determination of peoples as described above and thus possessed of a government representing the whole people belonging to the territory without distinction as to race, creed and colour.

The reiteration of the principle of the territorial integrity of the state was nothing new; it had been at the base of international law since the Westphalian system and it is an essential principle of the UN Charter. But the requirement for democracy in order to protect it was something novel in the UN doctrine. The clause can fairly be interpreted as recognizing the possibility of remedial secession when a state does not respect the internal self-determination of its people.

[87] See G.A. resolutions 1654 (XVI) of 1961 and 1810 (XVII) of 1962.

[88] See G.A. resolution 1607 (XV) of 1961. About this and other actions of the General Assembly during its 15th session regarding the trusteeship territories, see United Nations, *Year Book of the United Nations 1960*, United Nations Publications, New York, 1961, pp. 447–449; *Year Book of the United Nations 1961*, United Nations Publications, New York, 1963, pp. 476–477, 480; *Year Book of the United Nations 1962*, United Nations Publications, New York, 1964, pp. 453–454.

4.4 *The Right of Self-Determination in Treaty Law*

In the decades following the establishment of customary law from the GA resolutions, the right of self-determination of peoples – as it had been developed and defined by the GA – was incorporated in different international and regional instruments.

It was incorporated in the first article of each one of the two Human Rights Covenants of 1966.[89] The covenants actually start, in the first paragraph of this article, with the recognition of the right of self-determination for all peoples. Then, replicating the clause of the GA resolution 1514 (XV), they state that "by virtue of that right they freely determine their political status and freely pursue their economic, social and cultural development." The third paragraph of the article requires the states party to the treaty, including those administering non-self-governing and trust territories, to promote the realization of that right.

At the regional level, the African Charter of Human Rights of 1981 also incorporated the principle of self-determination in its Article 20.[90] Its provisions are quite similar to the first article of the Human Rights Covenants and to the principles of the GA resolution 1514 (XV). But it also contains the addition that "colonized or *oppressed* peoples shall have the right to free themselves from the bonds of domination by resorting to any means recognized by the international community." The addition of the right of oppressed peoples to free themselves can be interpreted as a validation for the possibility of remedial secession.

Also at the regional level, in the Helsinki Final Act of 1975, the states participating in this diplomatic agreement pledged to respect the equal rights of peoples and their right to self-determination, by virtue of which they "have the right, in full freedom, to determine, when and as they wish, their internal and external political status, without external interference, and to pursue as they wish their political, economic, social and cultural development."[91]

5. SELF-DETERMINATION IN THE ICJ JURISPRUDENCE

The ICJ has been paramount in recognizing the customary value of the self-determination right emerging from the GA resolutions 1514 (XV) of 1960 and 2625 (XXV) of 1970.

89 See International Covenant on Civil and Political Rights, 16 December 1966, and International Covenant on Economic, Social and Cultural Rights, 16 December 1966.

90 See African Charter on Human and People's Rights, 27 June 1981.

91 See Conference on Security and Cooperation in Europe Final Act, Helsinki, 1 August 1975.

5.1 *The Namibia Opinion and the Retroactive Interpretation of the Mandates System*

In the Namibia advisory opinion, rendered in 1970, the ICJ was called to pronounce itself about the legality of the continued South African presence in Namibia.[92] South Africa had been exercising a mandate over the territory of Namibia since the League of Nations, but in 1970 the Security Council had ordered it to retreat from the territory, an order it refused to comply with.

The Court understood that the South African presence was violating the right to self-determination of the Namibian people, a right it localized in both the spirit of Article 22 of the Covenant of the League of Nations – under which the mandates system had been established – and the evolution of self-determination after the creation of the UN. The Court made a retrospective interpretation of Article 22 of the Covenant to conclude that the ultimate objective of the mandates system had been the self-determination and independence of the peoples concerned.[93] It also resolved that the right of self-determination had evolved, since the Charter, in favor of the non-self-governing territories and of the mandated territories, especially in the light of the GA resolution 1514 (XV) of 1960, applicable to all colonial peoples.

With this opinion the ICJ recognized the right to self-determination for all peoples, including the colonial ones, as well as the normative value of the principles contained in GA resolution 1514 (XV).

5.2 *The Western Sahara Case and the Normative Value of GA Resolution 1514 (XV)*

A second stage in the evolution of the ICJ jurisprudence regarding self-determination was the Western Sahara advisory opinion rendered in 1975.[94] The Court was asked if Western Sahara was *terra nullius* at the time of colonization by Spain and, if not, what were the legal ties between this territory and Morocco and Mauritania. After examining the historical context, the Court concluded that it could not find any legal ties between the territory and Morocco and Mauritania that "might affect the application of resolution 1514 (XV) in the decolonization of Western Sahara and, in particular, of the

92 See *Legal Consequences for the States of the Continued Presence of South Africa in Namibia.*

93 When the system of mandates had been created, however, the self-determination of the mandated peoples was not in the spirit of the drafters of the Convenant.

94 See *Western Sahara*, Advisory Opinion, I.C.J. Reports 1975, p. 12.

principle of self-determination through the free and genuine expression of the will of the peoples of the Territory."[95]

In this case the Court did not discuss, as it had done in the Namibia case, the preliminary question of the legal value of the resolution 1514 (XV). It simply directly applied it to the case, which suggests that, at that point, the right to self-determination for the peoples of the non-self-governing territories was, in the eyes of the Court, something already consolidated in the positive law.

5.3 *The East Timor Case and the* erga omnes *Character of the Right to Self-Determination*

A third stage in the ICJ jurisprudence is the East Timor case.[96] After the conclusion of a treaty between Australia and Indonesia delimitating a part of the continental shelf located between Australia and East Timor, Portugal referred the matter to the ICJ, arguing that Australia was violating, among other obligations, the right of the people of Timor to self-determination. The Court declared that it had no jurisdiction for procedural reasons, but it made in the process some relevant observations regarding the right to self-determination of the East Timor people:

> In the Court's view, Portugal's assertion that the right of peoples to self-determination, as it evolved from the Charter and from United Nations practice, has an erga omnes character, is irreproachable. The principle of self-determination of peoples has been recognized by the United Nations Charter and in the jurisprudence of the Court (see Legal Consequences for States of the Continued Presence of South Africa in Namibia . . . Western Sahara . . .); it is one of the essential principles of contemporary international law.[97]

The Court's assertion that the right to self-determination – in this case for the colonial peoples – has an *erga omnes* character, and that it is one of the essential principles of contemporary international law, brought this right to a new level. As the Court referred to its previous opinions in the cases of Namibia and Western Sahara, it confirmed what it had already stated in them: that the non-self-governing territories are recipients of the right to self-determination and that this right for them emerges from the Charter of the

[95] Ibid., p. 68, para. 162.
[96] *East Timor (Portugal* v. *Australia)*, Judgment, I.C.J. Reports 1995, p. 90.
[97] Ibid., p. 102, para. 29.

United Nations and from the customary law developed from the GA resolution 1514 (XV) of 1960. Now, since 1960 until then, all GA resolutions that had explicitly reaffirmed resolution 1514 (XV) had repeatedly said that the right of self-determination of colonial peoples is an *inalienable right* and that it is part of the *fundamental human rights*. In the Timor opinion, the Court adds a new description: it is an *essential principle of contemporary international law* that has an *erga omnes* character. Can this new equation – *inalienable* plus *fundamental human right* plus erga omnes *character* plus *essential principle of international law* – be interpreted as an intention of the Court to rank self-determination as a jus cogens norm?

The fourth stage in the Court's jurisprudence, the Palestinian Wall opinion, rendered in 2004, seemed at the moment to bring an answer.

5.4 *The Palestinian Wall Case and the* jus cogens *Status of Self-Determination*

In 2003 the GA requested from the ICJ an advisory opinion about the legal consequences of the construction of a wall in the occupied Palestinian territory, "considering the rules and principles of international law."[98] In its opinion[99] the Court stated the violation of different rights of the Palestinian people, including the right to self-determination. In this case the Court located the existence of the right to self-determination of the Palestinian people in multiple sources, as the UN Charter, the two Human Right Covenants of 1966, the customary law emerging from the GA resolutions, especially from resolution 2625 (XXV) of 1970; and it affirmed again the *erga omnes* character of this right.[100]

The novelty of this case, compared with the previous Court's jurisprudence, lies in the way the Court approaches the *erga omnes* character of the right. In the Court's terms:

> the Court has already observed . . . that in the East Timor case, it described as "irreproachable" the assertion that "the right of peoples to self-determination, as it evolved from the Charter and from the United Nations practice, has an erga omnes character." The Court would also recall that under the terms of General Assembly resolution 2625 (XXV), already mentioned above . . .

[98] See G.A. resolution ES/10–14 .

[99] *Legal Consequences of the Construction of a Wall in the Occupied Palestinian Territory*, Advisory Opinion, I.C.J. Reports 2004, p. 136.

[100] See ibid., pp. 171–172, paras. 86–89.

> "Every State has the duty to promote, through joint and separate action, realization of the principle of equal rights and self-determination of peoples, in accordance with the provisions of the Charter, and to render assistance to the United Nations in carrying out the responsibilities entrusted to it by the Charter regarding the implementation of the principle."[101]

The Court then proceeded to describe the consequences of the wall building for both Israel and the international community of states. The Court stated that, given the character and the importance of the rights and obligations involved, all states were under an obligation "to see to it that any impediment ... to the exercise by the Palestinian people of its right to self-determination is brought to an end."[102] Regardless of the practical possibilities of the Court's pretention, by drawing consequences for the international community from a violation of a right committed from only one state, the Court took to a further level the *erga omnes* classification of this right.

After the Timor opinion, questions had been raised about whether or not the Court's qualification of the right to self-determination as *erga omnes* implied an intention to rank it at the *jus cogens* level. The same questions appeared after the Wall's opinion.

It should first be clarified that *erga omnes* and *jus cogens* are two different legal concepts. According to Article 53 of the Vienna Convention on the Law of Treaties, a *jus cogens* norm is a peremptory norm accepted and recognized by the international community of states as a whole as a norm from which no derogation is permitted. *Erga omnes* obligations, on the other side, have been defined by the ICJ as those that, in view of the importance of the rights involved, all states can be held to have a legal interest in protecting.[103] The concept of *jus cogens* refers then to a quality of a norm, while *erga omnes* refers to a quality of rights and obligations that arise from specific norms. However, a confusion between both is common. Some authors claim that this confusion stems from the fact that the primary rules belonging to both categories are the same,[104] or that both notions belong to the category of

[101] See ibid., p. 199, para. 156. [102] Ibid., p. 200, para. 159.

[103] See, for instance, *Barcelona Traction, Light and Power Company, Limited*, Judgement, I.C.J. Reports 1970, p. 32, para. 33. For a complete list of all cases in which the Court returns over the definitions of *erga omnes*, see the separate opinion of Judge Dugard in *Armed Activities on the Territory of the Congo (New Application: 2002) (Democratic Republic of the Congo* v. *Rwanda), Jurisdiction and Admissibility*, Separate Opinion, I.C.J. Reports 2006, p. 87, para. 4. For a definition with comments, see also S. Kadelbach, "*Jus cogens*, Obligations *Erga omnes* and other Rules: The identification of Fundamental Norms," in *The Fundamental Rules of the International Legal Order: Jus cogens and Obligations Erga omnes*, Martinus Nijoff Publishers, Leiden, 2006, pp. 35–39.

[104] Kadelbach, "*Jus cogens*, Obligations *Erga omnes*," p. 27.

fundamental norms,[105] or that jus *cogens* norms, given the importance of the values they promote, always create obligations *erga omnes*[106] (although the opposite is not necessarily true[107]), or even that the ICJ in some cases has confused the two concepts.[108] The International Law Commission has also contributed to this confusion. In its report about the draft of articles about the responsibility of states for internationally wrongful acts, the Commission opined that the examples of *erga omnes* obligations given by the ICJ in its jurisprudence concerned obligations arising from peremptory norms.[109] Can we draw the same conclusions from the Court's proposals in the Wall opinion?

Some authors have interpreted that in the cases of East Timor and the Palestinian Wall, the *jus cogens* was implied in the Court's reference to the *erga omnes* right.[110] I would argue that it is not only the *erga omnes* reference, but the whole approach by the Court, and the severity with which it addressed the consequences of the violation of the self-determination right in the Palestinian wall case, that suggests that the Court was under the understanding that it was dealing with a *jus cogens* norm. However, the Court's position will become again unclear six years later in the Kosovo case.

[105] P. Tavernier, "L'identification des Règles fondamentales – un problème résolu?," in *The Fundamental Rules of the International Legal Order: Jus cogens and Obligations Erga omnes*, Martinus Nijoff Publishers, Leiden, 2006, p. 1.

[106] B. D. Lepard, *Customary International Law: A New Theory with Practical Applications*, Cambridge University Press, New York, 2010, p. 268. See also R. Kolb (referring to Gaja who says that "le *ius cogens* a nécessairement trait aux intérêts fondamentaux de la société internationale et son irrespect représente par conséquent toujours la violation d'une obligation *erga omnes*") in R. Kolb, *Théorie du uis cogens international, Essai de relecture du concept*, Presse Universitaire de France, Paris, 2001, p. 136. For other references of authors who argue that all *jus cogens* norms automatically create *erga omnes* obligations, see Kolb, *Théorie du uis cogens*, p. 75, note 226.

[107] See Lepard, *Customary International Law*, p. 268.

[108] For a commentary regarding the *Barcelona Traction* case in both *jus cogens* and *erga omnes* cases, see Kadelbach, "*Jus cogens*, Obligations *Erga omnes*," p. 27. See also Lepard, *Customary International Law*, p. 268 (quoting Sinclair and Hoogh). For a commentary regarding the confusion made by the Court in the Congo case and in the Palestinian Wall case, see D. Carreau, *Droit international*, 10th edition, Pedone, Paris, 2009, p. 95. Carreau argues that in the Congo case, when the Court made the reference to *jus cogens*, it was also meaning *erga omens*, while in the Wall case, when it refered to *erga omnes*, it was also meaning *jus cogens*.

[109] See "Projet d'articles sur la responsabilité de l'Etat," pp. 119–120.

[110] For the Wall case, see Carreau, *Droit international*, p. 95. Regarding the East Timor case, see Lepard, *Customary International Law*, pp. 38–39, note 52; Judge Dugard's separate opinion in *Armed Activities on the Territory of the Congo*, p. 90. Also, the International Law Commission, in its report about the draft articles on the responsibility of States, refers to self-determination as a *jus cogens* norm, while referring to the East Timor case of the ICJ. See *Annuaire de la Commission de droit international* 2001, Vol. II, 2nd part, Publication des Nations Unies, New York, 2007, p. 121.

6. THE KOSOVO CASE AND A LEGACY OF CONFUSION

The most recent stage in the ICJ jurisprudence regarding self-determination is the advisory opinion on Kosovo's declaration of independence of 2010.[111] In contrast with the previous cases, this one concerned a case of unilateral secession.

The Court was asked by the GA if the unilateral declaration of independence of Kosovo was in accordance with international law.[112] Given the nature of the question, one would have expected the Court to respond to it by examining if the people of Kosovo had, under international law, the right to make a unilateral secession, and to make that assessment by evaluating if the right of self-determination of peoples entitled the people of Kosovo to secede unilaterally. Indeed some of the arguments presented before the Court defending the right of the people of Kosovo[113] to create an independent state were based on the allegations that it had this right, either as a manifestation of the right to self-determination or as a right to remedial secession.[114]

6.1 *The Court's Refusal to Apply Self-Determination*

Unfortunately, the Court refused to address the self-determination allegations, arguing that it was not the issue in the case. The Court stated that it was not necessary to resolve the questions of whether – outside of the context of non-self-governing territories and peoples subject to alien subjugation, domination, and exploitation – "the international law of self-determination" conferred upon a part of the population of a state a right to separate from it, or whether international law provided for a right to remedial secession, and, if so, in what circumstances.[115] The Court understood that it was not required to take position on whether international law conferred a positive entitlement to

[111] *Accordance with International Law of the Unilateral Declaration of Independence in Respect of Kosovo*, Advisory Opinion, I.C.J. Reports 2010, p. 403.

[112] The question asked by the Assembly was formulated in the following terms: "Is the unilateral declaration of independence by the Provisional Institutions of Self-Government of Kosovo in accordance with international law?" See ibid., para. 1.
The question of the implications of the UNMIK in the process and its possible effect on the legality of the declaration was also examined by the Court. However, it will not be discussed here as it is not relevant for the object of discussion.

[113] It is worth mentioning that the Court, all along its opinion, did not refer to the Kosovars as the *people* of Kosovo. Instead the Court referred to them as the "population of Kosovo" or simply "Kosovo."

[114] See *Accordance with International Law of the Unilateral Declaration*, para. 82.

[115] See ibid., paras. 82–83.

Kosovo to achieve its independence unilaterally. According to the Court, the only question to address was whether or not the declaration of independence was in accordance with international law; while, on the other hand, the debate regarding the extent of the right to self-determination and of the existence of any right to remedial secession concerned a "right to separate from a State," which was an issue beyond the scope of the question (the question being limited to the declaration of independence).[116]

It is worth clarifying that however absurd the Court's reasoning might seem, there was no contradiction in it. The Court indeed stated that it is entirely possible for a particular act (in this case a unilateral *declaration* of independence) not to be in violation of international law without necessarily constituting the *exercise* of a right conferred by it.[117] In other words, as if the declaration of independence was a notion existing in an abstract level with no consequences attached to it, the *declaration* and the *separation* from a state that it is intended to carry on are issues so different that the lawfulness of the first one is not connected to the right to exercise the second one.

Therefore the Court decided that the question of Kosovo's declaration of independence should be considered only against the lawfulness of declarations of independence under general international law, and not against the right of Kosovo to self-determination or its right to remedial secession. The Court then limited its study to determine, in the first place, if there was any prohibition of the declarations of independence under the general international law. In order to assess their lawfulness it made a historical appraisal and found that during the eighteenth, nineteenth, and early twentieth centuries the practice of the states does not suggest that "the act of promulgating" a declaration of independence was regarded as contrary to international law. Regarding the second half of the twentieth century, the Court found that "the international law of self-determination" developed as to create a "right to independence" for the peoples of non-self-governing territories and peoples subject to alien subjugation, domination, and exploitation, which led to the creation of new states; but in the instances of declarations of independence outside these two contexts, the practice of the states does not point out to any rule prohibiting the "making of a declaration of independence."[118]

Then the Court concluded that, as general international law contains no applicable prohibition of declarations of independence, the declaration of independence of Kosovo did not violate general international law.[119]

[116] See ibid., paras. 82–83, 51–56. [117] See ibid., para. 56.
[118] See ibid., para. 79. [119] See ibid., para. 84.

The nonapplication of self-determination to Kosovo is not, however, without impact on the self-determination theory. The Court's approach to the Kosovo case, restricted only to the declarations of independence, has been criticized for its many inconsistencies. The first criticisms came from separated opinions and declarations of some of its own judges. Some of them regretted that the Court decided not to assess the existence of a right to self-determination of Kosovo and/or to remedial secession, considering that these were relevant issues that the Court should have treated in order to properly address the question before it,[120] and feared that the narrow reading of the question made by the Court could be misguiding[121] and misinterpreted as legitimizing independence claims by all kinds of separatist groups.[122] Justice Yusuf also criticized the distinction made by the Court between the *declaration* of independence and the *exercise* of it, since the declaration of independence of Kosovo was part of the process to create a new state, and regretted that by not addressing the question correctly, the Court lost an opportunity to bring "clarity to the scope and legal content of the right of self-determination, in its post-colonial conception, and its applicability to the case of Kosovo."[123] Here lies, indeed, the legacy of the Kosovo opinion: in its possibilities of confusion and misuse.

6.2 *The Apparent Permissibility of All Unilateral Separations*

The Court's reasoning can be dangerous. The legacy of the Court's jurisprudence will not be found in the clarifications made by the separated opinions or by any analyst trying to explain the Court's unclear intentions, but in what the prose of the opinion really said. And in this case the Court said what it said: that Kosovo's unilateral declaration of independence did not violate general international law because general international law contains no prohibition of declarations of independence.

Contrary to the Court's attempt to separate the *declaration* from the *exercise*, a declaration of independence is never an isolated act that can be assessed on its own without consequences. It is always meant to carry on a separation from a state (or at least an intent to do so). Thus, by asserting that international law contains no prohibition of declarations of independence, the Court ended up validating not only these declarations but also the claims for unilateral

[120] See ibid., Separate Opinion of Judge Sepúlveda-Amor, para. 35; Declaration of Judge Simma, para. 6; Separate Opinion of Judge Yusuf, paras. 2, 13, 17.

[121] See ibid., Separate Opinion of Judge Yusuf, para. 2; Declaration of Judge Simma, para. 1.

[122] See ibid., Yusuf, para. 5, 6, 17. [123] See ibid., para. 2, 5, 17.

separation that are always at the heart of them and – ultimately – the intents to achieve that independence.

Even more dangerous is the fact that the Court did not specify if the nonprohibition of unilateral declarations of independence was limited to groups composing a *people* (a concept that it has also never clarified). In fact, all along its opinion, when the Court referred to the Kosovars it never named them as the *people of Kosovo*. The only few times when the Court used the term *people of Kosovo* was when it quoted a Kosovar legal instrument or declaration, but when the Court itself referred to them, it did it as simply *Kosovo*.[124] Taking the risk of misinterpretation to the extreme, no intention to limit the legality of the declarations of independence to the existence of a *people* can be inferred from the Court's opinion. This can lead to the deduction that these declarations are never prohibited, no matter who makes them. Having set no boundaries into who would be allowed to make these declarations, the Court opened a Pandora's box.

6.3 *The Disregard for the Principle of Territorial Integrity*

Another regrettable aspect of the Kosovo opinion is that the Court deliberately refused to engage in any discussion about the territorial integrity of Serbia arguing that "the principle of territorial integrity is confined to the sphere of relations between States."[125] The silence of the Court on that matter can be misused to claim that not even the principle of territorial integrity can impede a group from declaring independence because that principle does not apply to the relations between these groups and the state, and that there is no prohibition, under general international law, for them to declare independence.

In fact, if international law recognizes a priori the right to self-determination to *all* peoples, the principle of territorial integrity operates as a counterbalance that impedes just any group from claiming secession indiscriminately and guarantees the continuity of the state. The self-determination of peoples and the territorial integrity of the state are then principles that operate as mutual counterpoises. By legitimizing the declarations of independence in general, while refusing to scrutinize them against the principles of self-determination and of territorial integrity of the state, the Court ended up flouting both.

That the Court also refused to address the questions of self-determination and remedial secession in the Kosovo's specific situation was even more incongruent. Kosovo's declaration of independence was definitely a secession

[124] See *Accordance with International Law of the Unilateral Declaration*, paras. 89, 105, 109.
[125] Ibid., para. 80.

exercise grounded on remedial secession claims. It was then nothing other than a self-determination issue. The Court's refusal to examine the Kosovo situation in the light of self-determination does not make it any less true. I would even argue that, given the evolution of the law of self-determination and the prime status of the principle of territorial integrity, secession situations today are always a matter of self-determination and should always be scrutinized in the light of this right. Any issue of unilateral secession, as well as any modification or alteration of any political status, should always be examined against the right of self-determination of the peoples involved.

7. THE POST-KOSOVO ERA AND SELF-DETERMINATION AS AN ENTITLEMENT FOR SECESSION

7.1 *Self-Determination and Remedial Secession*

When advocates of Kosovo's independence argued before the ICJ that Kosovo had the right to create an independent state either as a manifestation of the right to self-determination or as a right to remedial secession, they treated self-determination and remedial secession as two separated figures. The Court followed the same logic when it refused to examine any of them. The question was not made, nor answered, as to whether self-determination, to which all peoples have a right, can be an entitlement for remedial secession. Yet, it would have been of great help if the case of Kosovo had been approached by the Court from that angle.

It is actually incongruent to try to appraise remedial secession without linking it to self-determination. As we have seen, remedial secession is indeed one of the oldest manifestations of self-determination. We found it in Grotius's doctrine, as an *extreme necessity* resource; in Vattel's doctrine, as a remedy of last resort when the sovereign had abandoned its people; in the American independence, where remedial secession – inspired by Vattel's doctrine – rested engraved in the Declaration of Independence; and in the movements inspiring the independences of the Latin American colonies from Spain. During the existence of the League of Nations it was suggested by the Commission in the Aaland Islands case, and since the evolution of international law after the creation of the United Nations, a recognition of it can be gleaned from the GA resolution 2625 (XXV) and, at a regional level, from the text of the African Charter on Human Rights.

It is then fair to argue that, given the evolution of self-determination and human rights during the past centuries, a refusal to recognize self-determination as an entitlement for remedial secession would be inconsistent with the democratic principle at the heart of it. If internal self-determination – as an exercise of democracy – cannot be enjoyed by a people inside a state, then the conditions should be created for them to exercise it, even if those conditions mean a separation from the state in order to have their own democratic one. In the cases where secession is the only remedy against gross violations of human rights, this entitlement is the only solution to allow the people concerned to enjoy self-determination, both internal and external. As the oppressive situation compelling them to separate does not allow them to enjoy internal self-determination, the only way to acquire it is to separate and self-provide it from the interior of a new independent entity. The exercise of external self-determination will follow as a consequence of the first one. Not allowing them to separate from the state, which is depriving them of internal self-determination, would mean to deprive them of the right to self-determination that all peoples are entitled to enjoy. Remedial secession becomes here the ultimate exercise of self-determination.

Entitling remedial secession as an exercise of self-determination would not only serve the justice of human rights for the seceding people, but would ultimately also benefit the international community. A state that does not respect human rights becomes a weak actor in the international arena. The exercise of remedial secession by a part of its population, and the separation of it in order to establish a new democratic state, will add a new democratic member to the international community.

7.2 *Self-Determination and Secession in General*

Even if, as we have seen, the Kosovo opinion risks being misinterpreted as a general recognition of unilateral secessions with no particular restriction, in good faith we know that this is not currently the state of positive international law. Nevertheless, the necessity for flexibility of the right to secession is likely to arise in the near future.

The post-colonial era of self-determination will be one of multiplication of claims, intents, and exercises of secession, not necessarily linked to remedial cases. These claims for secession will be argued – as they already are – in virtue of the right of peoples to self-determination. And, in the same way that during the twentieth century the state had to renounce its right to aggrandizement for self-determination to evolve and to give rise to the right to decolonization, during the twenty-first century the state will be forced to soften its attachment to the territorial integrity in favor of a secession right.

It can be argued that a right to remedial secession already provides a balance between human rights for the people and the territorial integrity for the state. But to restrict the lawfulness of a secession only to remedial cases can bring up two concerns.

The first one is linked to the democratic spirit of the self-determination right. The desire of secession will always arise from dissatisfaction, but it should not be up to the law to evaluate whether a population is sufficiently dissatisfied – or has suffered enough to be dissatisfied – in order to be entitled to separate from the state. The possibility of unilateral separation should exist as a manifestation of the democratic principle at the heart of the self-determination right; this democratic standard requiring, of course, that the separation responds to the desire of a clear majority.

The second concern is one of peace and security. Restricting secession only to remedial cases can drown us in the endless and unfair dilemma of having to decide – and to prove – when a population has suffered enough in order deserve the separation; and this is something that, as history has shown, can bring long and unnecessary suffering and misery. As a mater of democracy, its will of separation should suffice without having to require it to be exposed to extreme abuses. And even if the population that wants to secede is not being abused or oppressed by the state, keeping it attached against its will can indeed lead to violence and armed conflict. If a population has clearly, and in majority, expressed its desire to separate from the state, then the territorial integrity principle should surrender before the right to secession in order to maintain peace.

This flexible arrangement can ultimately be beneficial for the people, the state, and the international community. The *abandoned* state will not have to deal anymore with an unhappy population and the violent conflicts that can arise. And, if from the fragmentation of it can emerge two or more new democratic states – able to conduct between them diplomatic and economic relations and to relate in cooperation by joining international organizations – that is more desirable than the quest to preserve territorial integrity in order to keep an unwilling population trapped, with the instability and violence that this can bring. A fragmentation of a state carried out in peaceful terms is always preferable to war.

This equation, flexibility–fragmentation–multiplication, instead of jeopardizing the state, can serve to protect its existence in this postmodern era, as this fragmentation will lead to the creation of more states in the international scenario.

This proposal does not, however, respond yet to the persistent question of what kind of population should be entitled to exercise the separation in virtue of the right of self-determination.

8. THE RIGHT TO SOCIABILITY AND THE FUTURE OF SELF-DETERMINATION

8.1 *The End of the Ethnicity Criteria*

Historically, ethnicity bonding has been the criteria to identify the peoples having the right to self-determination.[126] This ethnicity criteria is indeed the one that prevails in the contemporary claims of secession from separatist movements all around the globe. Cases such as Quebec, Cataluña, Scotland, Ireland, the Basque regions, and the Russian communities in Ukraine, for instance, provide only a few contemporary examples of groups claiming to be a *people* with the right to separation by virtue of the right to self-determination. But the ethnicity condition is also potentially dangerous. If the exercise of this right is only limited to ethnic groups – who have to be different from the rest of the population of the state – then a very dangerous thing can occur: they will try to prove that they are indeed *different*. In order to do that they will construct a national hallucination. And as history has already shown, ethnic nationalism, and the consequent obsession over the differences, can lead humanity into violence, war, and even genocide.

In the nineteenth century Pasquale Fiore's doctrine on the right of sociability did not have a large acceptance among legal scholars, nor did it influence the evolution of international law in this particular matter. Almost two centuries later, his proposal can serve to solve this impasse if a population is able to decide to separate, not because they are ethnically different, but in order to exercise their right to sociability.

Human sociability is as old as time and humans associate according to their affinities. What has changed during the centuries is the kind of affinities, their prioritization, and the political forms these associations have taken. The ethnic affinity – giving birth to the nation – is just another form of sociability, but it should not be the only one. In the twentieth century the ethnicity criterion was justified in the case of the colonial peoples in order to identify them for the purposes of applying GA resolutions 1514 (XV) and 1541 (XV) and correcting a historical injustice. It was even justified during the eighteenth and nineteenth centuries for the principle of nationalities to facilitate the unification of some European nations. But it will not be justified in face of the new challenges that humanity will have to confront.

[126] However, the concept of *people* has not been positively defined by the ICJ jurisprudence and, in the case of the GA resolutions, only the colonial peoples have been defined in the resolution 1541 (XV) of 1960.

A flexibility of self-determination by recognizing the right of sociability can even serve to prolong the existence of the state as a political territorial entity against the new challenges it will have to face in a global digital era.

8.2 *Collective Identity in the Postmodern Era*

What if tomorrow a group of people living in the same physical space wanted to form their own political unit different from the state? Another form of political organization? One, for instance, with no participation in any international organization of states? Or a large group of persons, not living in the same physical territory, whose only connection takes place through social networks, wanted to be politically organized in a form detached from the states where they physically live?

We can imagine, but we cannot for sure know, what the social organization of societies will be in the future. Human creativity is endless and in a globalized digital era the survival of the modern state as a territorial political entity can be challenged by the new ways in which people find affinities.

In an era of social networks, the human desire for sociability is more dynamic than ever and people exercise it without territorial boundaries. Their affinities (and therefore their desire to relate and socialize via those networks) do not derive from similarities in race, ethnic origins, culture, religion, language, and common history. In a virtual space, people can find more affinities with persons living in other countries than they have with their geographical cohabitants in a territorial space. The things they have in common might be far more pedestrian (at least in the eyes of our modern values) but no less powerful in the sense of providing a potential for further, unimaginable, vindications that could lead to new forms of political organizations outside the states or even in a virtual space.

8.3 *The Right of Sociability outside the Frontiers of the State*

A realistic present example of this *threat* to the state's dominance can be found in a recent initiative called the Seasteading Project launched by the Seasteading Institute.[127] This project is being crafted by entrepreneurs from all sorts of disciplines and proposes the establishment of communities on floating cities in the high seas in order to create new forms of political organization different from the state. Their discourse is not at all naive and their possibilities are real.

[127] See the project's website at www.seasteading.org, last accessed December 2013.

Arguing that "land-based rules" are preventing humanity from real advances and from justice, they want to create what they call "start-up countries" with "start-up governments"; and because all land is claimed they can only do that by migrating to the ocean. The Seasteading Project is one of the first, but it will not be the only one. Humanity can indeed expect a proliferation of them in the next centuries.

The occupation of the ocean is not per se a challenge for international law. The challenge will come when these floating communities attempt to become politically autonomous entities and claim the right to self-determination as an entitlement for that. This is where the right of sociability can provide the best legitimation. The people living in the ocean cities will not be bound by the same national/ethnic affinities than the peoples in the states. They will come from all parts of the world and there will be no requirements linked to nationality, previous residence, or any other criteria. The only requirement – as their current numerous advertisings promote[128] – is just wanting to be there.

[128] Ibid.

Index

Abkhazia, 145
Africa, 2–3, 51, 97–9, 101, 104, 211, 214, 226–7
African Charter of Human Rights, 108, 225, 235
Algeria, 3
American Revolution, 9, 206
American Society of International Law, 32, 82–3
Anderson, Benedict, 56, 73, 76
Angola, 104
annexation, 1, 7, 104, 160
Asia, 2, 99, 101
Australia, x, 105, 190, 196, 199, 227
Austria-Hungary, 97
autonomy, 9, 15, 34, 36, 38, 45, 51, 53, 60–1, 63–7, 71, 86, 88, 90, 93, 97–8, 108–10, 114, 120, 124–6, 133, 141, 143–4, 146, 148, 160, 203, 215–16, 220
  group, 9

Badinter Commission, 51
Baltic States, 3, 157, 160
Bangladesh, 53
Berlin Conference, 211
Berlin Wall, 3
Bietz, Charles, 153
Blake, Michael, ix, 12, 165–6
Bowman, Isaiah, 98
Buchanan, Allen, 5, 46, 55, 95, 112, 125–6, 128, 146, 150, 152, 154–6, 159–62, 166, 168, 185, 188–92, 195–6
Bulgaria, 97

Calogeropoulos-Stratis, S., 203, 206, 210, 219
Cambodia, 10
Cameroon, 3
Cassese, Antonio, 72, 95, 104, 106–7, 109–10, 125, 142, 144, 202, 206, 212, 215, 218
Catalonia, 8, 11, 195
Cataluña, 34, 238
Chechnya, 53, 199
citizenship, 28–9, 31, 57, 76, 155, 163–4, 199
civil disobedience, 170–80
Cold War, 3, 184
colonialism, 51, 95, 97, 99, 101, 111, 118, 198
communism, 144
comprehensive cultures, 4
confederalism, 108
consent, 12, 26–7, 29–31, 39–40, 43, 158, 160–2, 164, 203–4, 206, 209, 211, 216
Copp, David, 135, 151–7
Crawford, James, 72, 75, 95, 111, 114, 196
Crimea, 1, 6–7, 10
cultural hegemony, 186, 198
Czechoslovakia, 97, 169, 196

De Coulanges, Fustel, 210
De Las Casas, Bartolomeo, 203
De Rotterdam, Erasme, 203–4
De Vattel, Emmerich, 82, 205, 235
De Vitoria, Francisco, 203
Declaration of the Rights and Duties of Nations, 82
decolonization, 11, 49, 51, 66, 95, 100–1, 104, 128, 184, 207–8, 220, 222, 224, 226, 236
Dehousse, Fernand, 94
devolution, 110, 124, 133–4, 136–8, 195
dissent, 154–9
Donetsk, 1
droit naturel, 82

E.U. *See* European Union
East Timor, 104, 227–8, 230
effectivité, 7–8
Emerson, Rupert, 100
encompassing groups, 34–5, 37
England, 137, 195
Eritrea, 53
essentialism, 130–1, 134
Estonia, 3, 8, 97, 157, 160–1
ethnic cleansing, 44, 66, 146, 157, 161, 192
Europe, 48, 50, 97–9, 109, 140, 145, 195, 200, 210, 225
evolutionism, 186, 198
exclusivity of rule, 40

Falkland Islands, 186, 197
Fanon, Frantz, 66
federalism, 108, 124, 134, 136
Finland, 97, 215–17
Fiore, Pasquale, 210–11, 238
France, 51, 97, 178, 186, 205–7, 210, 213, 230
freedom
  from genocide, 86
  of religion, 22, *See* religious freedom
French Revolution, 204–6

Gandhi, Mahatma, 171
Gellner, Ernest, 33, 56, 73, 75–6, 122
General Will, 21
genocide, 8, 65, 71–2, 74, 77–9, 81, 83–6, 92, 111, 160, 238
Genocide Convention, 74–5, 83
Georgia, 4, 145
Germany, 97–8, 151, 190, 210
Gilbert, Margaret, 20, 25, 27–9
Glenny, Misha, 187, 193
Gourevitch, Philip, 77
Greece, 145
Grotius, Hugonis, 83, 200, 203, 205, 235
group agency, 11, 17, 20
group identity, 51, 76, 79
  other-perception, 78–9
  self-perception, 78–9
group norms
  emergent, 21–2, 24–5, 28
Guilhaudis, J.F., 204, 217–18

Hannum, Hurst, 7, 112, 126, 144
Hart, H. L. A., 169
Hegel, George Wilhelm Friedrich, xi, 16, 39, 84
Henkin, Louis, 101
Herman, Barbara, 91
Hobbes, 41
human rights, x, 2, 6, 11, 50, 54, 59, 66, 69, 78, 84, 95, 100–1, 103, 105–10, 119, 122, 138, 143, 160, 164, 170, 185, 188–9, 191, 198, 221–2, 228, 235–7
Human Rights Covenants, 201, 221, 225

I.C.J., 53, 73, 107, 185, 193–4, 197, 201, 214, 218, 220, 225–30, 235, 238, *See* International Court of Justice
  East Timor Case, 227–8
  Kosovo Case, 216–35
  Namibia Opinion, 226
  Palestinian Wall Case, 216–28
  Western Sahara Case, 226–7
I.C.T.R., 73–6, 78
immigration, ix, 14, 26
India, 3, 97, 145, 171
indigenous peoples, 126–9
Indonesia, 104–5, 227
injustice
  territorial, 11
International Court of Justice, 2–3, 5, 7, 104–5, 167, 193, 214
International Covenant on Civil and Political Rights, 49, 94, 96, 106–7, 201, 225
  Optional Protocol, 107
International Covenant on Economic, Social and Cultural Rights, 49, 94, 96, 106, 225
international law, ix–xi, 1–2, 6–9, 12–13, 45–50, 52–3, 55–6, 59–60, 65–8, 70–2, 81–2, 84–6, 88, 92, 95–6, 98–9, 101–2, 104–9, 111, 113–19, 123, 126–7, 129, 136, 140–4, 146, 162, 166–8, 182, 184–9, 193, 199–202, 207, 209, 211, 214–17, 223–4, 227–8, 231–6, 238, 240
intervention, 120, 122, 139
Iraq, 88
Ireland, 197, 238
Islas Malvinas, 104, 186, 196–9
Israel, 44–5, 76, 105, 145, 187, 196, 229
Italy, 198, 210–11

Jefferson, Thomas, 32
Jerusalem, 105
judgment aggregation, 17
jus ad bellum, 68, 81
jus cogens, 202, 228–30

Kant, Immanuel, 71, 178
Kedourie, Elie, 33, 73
Khmer Rouge, 10
King Jr., Martin Luther, 171–8
Kirgis Jr., Frederic, 112
Kosovo, 5, 7–8, 12, 53, 73, 107, 145, 157, 161, 166–7, 170, 182, 185, 193–4, 230–2, 234–6
  Unilateral Declaration of Independence, 185
Kuwait, 88

Lansing, Robert, 49, 124
Latvia, 97, 160
law of decolonization, 3
Law of Nations, 82, 203–4
lawbreaking, 169, 171–3, 177–9, 181
Lawrence, William B., 210
League Council, 98
League of Nations, 97–8, 104, 109, 186, 213, 215–16, 219, 226, 235
  Aaland Islands Case, 213–15
  Covenant, 98
  Eastern Carelia Case, 215–17
legitimacy
  state, x, 30
liberal neutrality, 138
Lieber, Francis, 92
List, Christian, 9, 17, 19, 92
Lister, Matt, 12
Lithuania, 97, 160, 166
Luhansk, 1

majoritarian rule, 18
Margalit, Avishai, 4, 34–8, 42, 44, 80, 132, 135
Mecklem, Patrick, 12
Mégret, Frédéric, x, 12, 45, 86, 105
Mexico, 1, 3, 211
Miller, David, 4, 13–14, 34, 39, 44, 56, 58, 132
Miner, David, 55
Moldova, 157, 161
Moltchanova, Anna, 186, 188, 191
Montevideo Convention, 70, 115
moral code, 17–21, 23, 25, 29
moral individualism, 15, 17
moral variation, 13–31
Morris, Christopher, 11
Morss, John, 12
Moyn, Samuel, 94, 99
Mozambique, 104

Nagorno-Karabakh dispute, 145
Namibia, 3, 104, 214, 226–7
Nation of Islam, 173
national identity, 4, 38, 43, 123, 132, 134–7, 141
national minorities, 129–32
nationalism, x, 5, 33–4, 44, 56, 58, 68, 80, 122, 128, 151, 154, 189, 193, 200, 238
nationhood, 49, 56, 58, 75–6, 79, 191, 199
Nigeria, 3
Nine, Cara, 5, 80, 186
non-interference, 14, 81, 86, 120, 122
non-intervention, 121
Nouvelle-Caledonie, 128

Ohlin, Jens, 12
Orentlicher, Diane, 96, 104, 156
Ottoman Empire, 98, 193

Pakistan, 145
Palestine, 105, 186, 197
Patten, Allan, 12
Permanent Mandates Commission, 98
Pettit, Philip, 17, 19, 92, 188
peuples sauvages, 204, 208, 210–11, 214
Philippines, 49
pluralism, 109–10
Poland, 49, 97
popular vote, 6
population transfers, 12, 145–65
principle of mutual benefit, 2

Quebec, 8, 10–11, 52, 57, 70, 72–3, 86, 113, 115, 146, 150, 164, 166, 195, 238

Rawls, John, 13, 37, 85, 121, 170–1, 178
  decent consultation hierarchy, 121
Raz, Joseph, 4, 34–8, 41–2, 44, 132, 135
religious freedom, 22
Renan, Ernest, 39, 56
Republika Srpska, 53
right
  to association, 160, 163
  to autonomy, 53, 127
  of collective self-determination, 1
  to disobey, 172, 176
  to exist, 40, 42, 71, 81–3, 85–6, 92
  to resist, 71, 81, 86–92, 182, 205
  to rule, 41–2
  to secede, 1, 3, 5, 51, 54, 143, 152, 157, 166–7, 177, 182, 190
Rodríguez-Santiago, Elizabeth, xi, 12, 201
Rome Statute, 83

Root, Elihu, 82
Rouget de Lisle, Claude Joseph, 32
Rousseau, 21, 206
rule of recognition, 168–9
Russia, 1, 6–7, 10, 145, 165, 211, 216–17
Rwanda, 74–5, 77, 229

Scotland, 2, 7, 137, 190, 195–6, 238
Seasteading Institute, 239
  Seasteading Project, 239
secession, 2–3, 5, 7, 12, 30, 34, 45, 50–4, 60, 63–5, 67–8, 73, 78, 85–6, 108–10, 112–13, 125, 128, 137–8, 141, 143–4, 146–51, 153–7, 159–60, 162–4, 166, 168–72, 174, 176, 178, 180–2, 185, 188–9, 191, 196, 205–8, 210–11, 216, 218, 224–5, 231–6, 238
  consensual, 162–4
  primary, 146, 151–9
  remedial, 5, 10, 53, 79, 128, 146, 159–62, 202, 207, 216, 231–2, 235–6
  Secession Reference, 113
self-defense, 12, 71, 78, 81–4, 86–7, 89–92, 203
  futile, 91, 93
  Success Condition, 87–90
self-determination
  democratic conception, 121–3, 127–9, 139–40, 142
  external, 50, 54, 72, 79, 86, 106, 108, 111–14, 117–18, 125, 141, 143, 204–6, 213, 217, 220, 236
  hard-voluntarism, 27
  internal, 73, 95, 108–14, 117–18, 122, 125, 128, 141–4, 205, 224, 236
  nationalist conception, 3–5, 11–12, 122–9, 132, 137–8, 140–4
  soft-voluntarism, 27
  state, 14, 25, 30
  statist conception, 72, 120, 122, 140
self-government, 4, 34–7, 42, 50, 100, 108, 110, 114, 125–7, 129, 132–6, 138, 140–1, 152, 219
Sen, Amartya, 200
separatists, 3, 154, 238
Serbia, 4, 146, 161, 170, 182, 194, 234
South Ossetia, 145
South Sudan, 53
sovereignty, ix, 7, 36, 50, 97, 106, 115, 144
  salt water thesis, 50, 86, 107
  territorial, 11, 187
Soviet Union, 3, 8, 129, 151, 157, 160–2
Srebrenica, 44
statehood, 34, 37–44, 49, 79–80, 99, 102–3, 106, 111, 115–16, 119, 141, 143, 189
Statman, Daniel, 87
Stiltz, Anna, 188
Suárez, Francisco, 203
suffrage, 6
Sweden, 215

Tamir
  Yaelle, 33–4, 44, 55–6, 132
territorial integrity, 7–8, 52, 86–7, 97, 102–4, 108–9, 111, 113, 115, 141, 143, 198, 210, 213, 224, 234, 236–7
Tibet, 53, 199
Tomuschat, Christian, 110–11
trust territories, 97, 99–100, 221, 223–5
Turkey, 97, 145

Uganda, 2, 6, 128
Ukraine, 1, 3, 7, 161, 199, 218, 238
unitarianism, 108
United Kingdom, 2, 8, 190, 195, 200
United Nations, 2, 6, 49–51, 70, 73–4, 82–3, 86, 94, 96, 99–102, 104, 106, 112–13, 115, 119, 126–7, 164, 186, 194, 196–8, 201, 213, 217, 219–22, 224, 226–9, 235
  Charter, 49–50, 70, 82, 96, 99–100, 102, 106, 198, 217–25, 227–8
  Declaration on Friendly Relations, 102–3, 111–14
  Declaration on the Granting of Independence to Colonial Territories, 100, 102–3, 106
  Declaration on the Rights of Indigenous Peoples, 119, 127–8
  General Assembly, 50–1, 99, 104, 115, 126–7
  Human Rights Committee, 107
  Security Council, 3, 6, 74, 82, 104–5, 198, 226
United States of America, 2, 5, 8, 11, 92, 164, 172, 184, 211–12
  Declaration of Independence, 206
Universal Declaration on Human Rights, 94
uti possidetis principle, 50

Van der Vossen. Bas, xi, 11, 13, 26

Waldron, Jeremy, 79, 134, 185, 188, 191–3, 198
Wales, 195
Walzer, Michael, 13–15, 44, 120, 122–4, 133, 179
  communal integrity, 120, 133, 135

war, x, 8, 47, 49, 68, 75, 92, 99, 109, 120, 126, 145, 198, 203, 205, 211, 213–15, 237–8
Wellman, Christopher, 5, 15, 151
Westphalia, 81, 204
Wilson, Woodrow, 48–9, 55, 98–9, 124, 184, 202, 212
World War
  First, 45, 97, 129, 212
  Second, 49, 95

Young, Crawford, 101
Young, Iris Marion, 60
Yugoslavia, 51, 97, 158, 193

For EU product safety concerns, contact us at Calle de José Abascal, 56–1°, 28003 Madrid, Spain or eugpsr@cambridge.org.

www.ingramcontent.com/pod-product-compliance
Lightning Source LLC
LaVergne TN
LVHW102008210926
848483LV00010B/183

9781107119130